the NARROW ROAD

Stories of Those Who Walk THIS ROAD Together

BROTHER ANDREW with **JOHN & ELIZABETH SHERRILL**

FEATURING

jars of clay

Fleming H. Revell

A Division of Baker Book House Co
Grand Rapids, Michigan 49516

Published by Fleming H. Revell
a division of Baker Book House Company
P.O. Box 6287, Grand Rapids, MI 49516-6287

Printed in the United States of America

Library of Congress Cataloging-in-Publication Data is on file at the Library of Congress, Washington D.C.

ISBN 0-8007-5793-9

The main text of *The Narrow Road* is taken from *God's Smuggler* by Brother Andrew with John and Elizabeth Sherrill (Chosen, 1967, 2001)

Published in association with Yates & Yates, LLP, Literary Agents, Orange, Calif.

Statistics and facts for the country profiles in this book were gathered from *Please Pray for Us* by Johan Companjen (Bethany House, 2000). Used by permission.

Scripture is taken from the HOLY BIBLE, NEW INTERNATIONAL VERSION®. NIV®. Copyright © 1973, 1978, 1984 by International Bible Society. Used by permission of Zondervan Publishing House. All rights reserved.

For current information about all releases from Baker Book House, visit our web site:
http://www.bakerbooks.com

interior design by Brian Brunsting

A portion of proceeds
from the sale of this book
will be donated to
Prayer for the Persecuted Church

Foreword

How Big Is God's Kingdom?

How big is God's Kingdom?

That's a dangerous question to answer absolutely. An absolute answer establishes not only the boundaries we are comfortable living in, but also, and more importantly, the strength and reach of the King who reigns.

In storybooks we find pictures of brilliant kingdoms and towers that seem to climb miles into the sky, with drawbridges stretching across dark, infested moats. But maybe we have been ill served by the storybooks of our childhood. Because their pictures of kingdoms were most often just pictures of castles. I know my own dreams of roaming a great kingdom only ever extended to the edge of the castle ground. It was easy to forget that great battles were fought in foreign lands so the kingdom could reach from sea to distant sea.

Churches and castles have a great deal in common. These are places where the soul brushes up against a piece of the infinite and makes us feel smaller, ultimately human. They allow us to see the great chasm that stands between us and the Almighty. And in both cases they might have been erected as comforting reminders that someone greater than ourselves is reigning supreme.

Whatever their original design, we seem to have lost our ability to comprehend the vast foreign landscape beyond their walls. We have given ourselves over to the familiar incense of tradition. We have grown accustomed to the perception of a King with few dimensions. We have wrapped ourselves in the robe of safety and settled into our cozy surroundings. We have fallen asleep, while a warming fire rages just out of reach. Because it has always been far less dangerous to believe in a small Kingdom ruled by a King void of surprise, mystery, or wild abandon, than to contend with the tension and confusion of the kingdom as it actually exists.

As a church kid, I was privy to the gruesome tales of Christian martyrdom common to late-night bonfires during summer camp. But those stories had little consequence for me. In fact, I was only faintly aware that they were true.

I was awakened from my slumber in November of 1998. It was Thanksgiving Day. One of our guests was a pastor who brought with him a Rwandan refugee seeking political asylum in the United States. The man's country was in the midst of a civil war between the Hutu and the Tutsi tribes. It was a deadly struggle that had been going on for generations. God had mercifully given him the gift of seeing reconciliation modeled in his own home— his father and mother were from opposite tribes. And he grew up to be a prominent magazine editor, an outspoken preacher, and an advocate of reconciliation between the warring tribes. During the Rwandan genocide of 1994, this man's entire extended family was murdered when their village was raided. He was later informed that his name was on a government list for assassinations, so he fled the country, leaving his wife and five children behind. It had been nearly a year since he had seen his family.

While my family ate turkey and did our best to conjure up thankful sentiments that day, this man across the table exploded with deep thanksgiving. He had experienced the provision of God so powerfully that he believed God would provide even if he never saw his family again. He told me that if I were to ask him about computers, he could not give an educated response. But he went on to point out that if we, the Church in the United States, were asked about the true provision of God, we could not do adequate justice to such a concept. In his opinion, our culture has been blinded from a true vision of the way God works in suffering. There is a world beyond the safety of our insular church culture. There are miracles and tragedies, passion and suffering, great joy and indescribable injustice, none of which fit into our narrow worldview.

It was time my world grew a new hemisphere.

In the spring of 2000 I read an article about religious persecution in the Sudan. Many more articles followed, along with some television reports, research, and a divinely appointed meeting with an activist named Steve Haas, the U.S. director of the International Day of Prayer for the Persecuted Church.

It became very clear to me that sleeping behind church walls would not satisfy a God who hates injustice. I had seen the pictures of torture victims. I had read the reports of Christian women and children sold into slavery. I had been confronted with the tales of murder, rape, and starvation. But all I knew were stories that seemed to fill that morbid curiosity that draws us to car wrecks and real-life TV shows. These people were not real to me. They were not brothers and sisters.

I needed to know these people. I needed to hear them tell their stories. I wanted to see how God met them. It was this need that drove me and Jars of Clay to China and Vietnam to meet and pray with leaders of the underground churches.

We were never the same.

We cried with these people. We rejoiced with them. We laughed with them. They laughed a lot—more than we thought possible, given their lives of suffering. But it was in their struggles that they found great joy. They are truly a suffering people, blessed by God.

At one time, joy in suffering did not fit into my Kingdom. My vision could not reach beyond the castle walls. My God was not big enough to speak into tragedy with laughter. At the same time my view of the Body of Christ was very small and the Kingdom of God very confining. I still marvel at the thought that the Kingdom of God has no end. And because of that, the reach of the

King is infinite. He can reach past government agendas, beyond poverty, and through injustice, into the jail cells and the prison walls to bring laughter. He can reach into the pain and suffering of torture to bring peace, into the valley of the shadow of death to bring joy!

Brother Andrew has given us the gift of testimony. He has allowed us a chance to have our Kingdom expanded. He has challenged us to know more about the Body of Christ, in all its glorious weakness and brokenness. He has called us to examine our hearts to see if we have room to know and be transformed by the knowledge of Jesus Christ, through the stories of our brothers and sisters. And he has posed two questions.

How big is your Kingdom? How big is your God?

—Daniel Haseltine
for Jars of Clay

THE SONG

A Benediction for the World

"If you're really interested in helping the Church on a broader scale . . . rather than reading about the suffering that's going on . . . why don't you go and sit across the table from these people and listen to their stories?"

So came the challenge to Dan Haseltine and his fellow Jars of Clay band members.

And so came their response. A trip to Vietnam and China.

Traveling in coordination with several ministries, band members met with indigenous underground churches and church leaders, including Pastor Li Dexian, who has been arrested repeatedly for his ministry in China.

Although not intending to perform while they were there, Jars of Clay members were prompted to sing by their guest hosts at several house churches in both countries. Though they felt at a loss to choose a song that would touch people that had been through so much and had taught them so much, the band decided to honor the requests with an a cappella rendition of "This Road." Originally written as a benediction to the church in the United States, the song took on new meaning for the band as they performed it for their brothers and sisters on the other side of the world. "This was the first time that we understood that this song was written for the world; it's a benediction for the world," they explain.

Since returning from the trip, the band has repeatedly dedicated the song to the persecuted church. When sharing about their experiences with the Vietnamese and Chinese Christians, band members challenge believers in the United States to join together in prayer for and ministry to persecuted brothers and sisters around the world. And they remind us that we are *all* called to travel this road together.

This Road

All heavy laden
Acquainted with sorrow
May Christ in our marrow
Carry us home
From alabaster
Come blessings of laughter
A fragrance of passion
Joy from the truth

Grant the unbroken
Tears ever flowing
From hearts of contrition
Only for you
May sin never hold true
That love never broke thru
For God's mercy holds us
And we are His own

This road that we travel
May it be the straight and narrow
God give us peace and grace from you
All the day
Shelter with fire
Our voices we raise still higher
God gave us peace and grace from you
All the day thru

THE STORIES

Introduction

By Johan Companjen
President of Open Doors International

I remember very clearly the first time my girlfriend, Anneke (now my wife), and I met Brother Andrew. He had spoken about the Great Commission, and Anneke and I approached him after the service. Having recently studied the Book of Acts, we were full of questions, and we hungered for more of God's Spirit. After talking for a while, Brother Andrew said to Anneke and me, "If you want to be filled with the Holy Spirit, you have to first make sure that you are empty." That afternoon, Anneke and I knelt down and committed our lives to God completely. From that time on, God would be in control. We would serve Him wherever He would lead; we would boldly walk down the road He had paved for us.

Less than half a year later, we found ourselves in Brother Andrew's living room. In an Open Doors newsletter, I had read about one of his recent trips to Vietnam. He shared about the need for someone with my technical skills to go to Vietnam to help the missionaries with their work. I felt confirmed that this was God's next step for me. So in 1968, at the height of the Vietnam War, I bid farewell to my fiancée, my family, and my friends. It was a very difficult year, but one that laid a foundation for my future ministry. And it marked the beginning of my friendship with Brother Andrew.

Several years later, at the age of twenty-nine, after Anneke and I were married and serving together as missionaries in Vietnam, our family was evacuated. After our sudden return home, Andrew asked me to join the staff at Open Doors, and a short time later I took the first of what would be hundreds of international trips, developing solid relationships with our staff worldwide and deepening my friendship with Andrew. We talked for hours at a time, praying together and studying the Scripture. He shared with me his vision for the suffering Church, his love for the Lord and His Word, and he trusted me to be a support, his "right arm." In 1995, nearly twenty-five years later, when the board began to consider our succession plan, I was named President of Open Doors International, with Andrew being given the title President Emeritus. What an honor it has been to walk in His path, serving alongside Brother Andrew and the people at Open Doors! And what a remarkable privilege to share in the suffering of our Christian family throughout the world!

As you begin your own journey down the Narrow Road through the pages of this book, I'd like to explain several features you'll be reading, so you can better understand how to support, pray for, and encourage your brothers and sisters in the persecuted Church.

A Traveler's Story: Bringing you personal testimonies of members of the persecuted Church from around the world, these sections will show you the reality of what it means to live out one's faith in Christ in places where being a Christian is not acceptable. Names of people in these stories have been changed to protect their identities so as not to increase the risks to their personal safety.

Diary of a Smuggler: These personal accounts from people who have taken trips with Open Doors to the persecuted Church demonstrate the power behind serving and encouraging those who are suffering because they follow Christ. Each story was taken from an actual post-trip report submitted to Open Doors.

Around the Globe: Read brief summaries of the conditions facing the persecuted Church in specific countries around the world. These summaries are taken from the book *Please Pray for Us*, written by mission researcher, Justin Long, and edited by me.

Imagine This: Posed at the end of each chapter are scenario questions or dilemmas meant to challenge you to think and pray through what it means to be persecuted for your personal faith in Jesus.

"This Road" CD-ROM: In the back of this book, you will find a copy of the CD-ROM, "This Road", by Jars of Clay, featuring moving photographs of the persecuted Church.

one

Smoke and Bread Crusts

"For I know the plans I have for you,"
declares the LORD, "plans to prosper you
and not to harm you, plans to give you
hope and a future."

Jeremiah 29:11

From the time I first put on wooden shoes—*klompen* we call them in Holland—I dreamed of derring-do. I was a spy behind the lines, I was a lone scout in enemy territory, I crept beneath barbed wire while tracer bullets scorched the air about me.

Of course we didn't have any real enemies in my hometown of Witte—not when I was very small—so we made enemies out of each other. We kids used our *klompen* to fight with: any boy who got himself hit with a wooden shoe just hadn't reached his own fast enough. I remember the day I broke a shoe over by enemy-friend Kees's head. What horrified us both wasn't the enormous bump on his forehead but the ruined shoe. Kees and I forgot our war long enough to try repairing it. But this is a skill gained only with time, and that night my hard-working black-smith father had to turn cobbler as well. Already that day Papa had got up at five to water and weed the garden that helped to feed his six children. Then he had pedaled four miles on his bicycle to his smithing job in Alkmaar. And now he had to spend the evening gouging a little trough across the top of the wooden shoe, pulling a wire through the trough, nailing the wire down on both sides, and repeating the process at the heel so that I could have some shoes to wear to school.

"ANDREW, YOU MUST BE MORE CAREFUL!" said my father in his loud voice. Papa was deaf and shouted rather than spoke. I understood him perfectly: he didn't mean careful of bones and blood, but of hard-earned possessions.

There was one family in particular that acted as the enemy in many of my boyish fantasies. This was the Family Whetstra.

Why I should have picked on the Whetstras I do not know, except that they were the first in our village to begin talking about war with Germany—and this was not a popular subject in Witte. Also they were strongly evangelical Christians. Their God-bless-you's and Lord-willing's seemed sickeningly tame to a secret agent of my stature. So in my mind they were the enemy.

I remember once passing Mrs. Whetstra's kitchen window just as she was putting cookies into the oven of her woodburning stove. Leaning against the front of the house was a new pane of window glass, and it gave me an idea. Here would be my chance to see if the ever-smiling Whetstras could get as mad as other Dutchmen. I picked up the piece of glass and moved ever so stealthily through the lines to the back of enemy headquarters. The Whetstras, like everyone in the village, had a ladder leading to their thatched roof. Off came my *klompen,* and up I went. Silently I placed the pane of glass on the chimney. Then I crept back down the ladder and across the street to post myself out of sight behind a fish-peddler's cart.

Sure enough the smoke backed down the chimney. It filled the kitchen and began to curl out the open window. Mrs. Whetstra ran into her kitchen with a scream, jerked open the oven door and fanned the smoke with her apron. Mr. Whetstra raced outside and looked up at his chimney. If I had expected a stream of rich Dutch prose I was disappointed, but the expression on his face as he climbed the ladder was entirely of-this-earth, and I chalked up for myself a tremendous victory against overwhelming odds.

Bangladesh   A Traveler's Story

BOLD PERSISTENCE IMPACTS OTHERS

Tofael is a young student of the Bangladesh Institute of Christian Theology. He came to know the Lord as a young person and heard His call to full-time Christian service. For one year he underwent extensive studies and training at the Institute. His training ended last year.

While he was evangelizing in a marketplace together with fellow students, a group of unbelievers who did not like to hear the truth got annoyed and tried to silence Tofael by mauling him. He was totally unconscious with bruises all over his head and body when his attackers left him, his body sprawled in the street. His fellow students were so shocked that at first they could not do anything. His teachers at the Institute were concerned that Tofael and his fellow students wouldn't evangelize anymore because they were afraid.

But the students had been studying the life of the early Church. They had learned that persecution helped spread the Gospel and that God brought great results from the believers' suffering. They were emboldened by their learning and by Tofael's persistence in sharing the Good News, despite what happened to him.

Tofael's testimony made a profound impact on his fellow students. As a result, fervor instead of fear filled their hearts. They kept on honoring God in their conduct and their words, though many people rejected them and their message.

After his graduation, Tofael returned to his home village and is now a worker in their church.

Another favorite enemy was my older brother Ben. Typical of older brothers, Ben was a master swapper. His corner of our common loft-bedroom above the main floor of our house was splendid with things that had once belonged to me or the other children; somehow we could never recall what we had received in exchange. His chief treasure was a piggy bank that had once been our sister Maartje's. In it Ben kept the pennies that he earned doing errands for the burgomaster or tending garden for Miss Meekle, our schoolmistress. Events in Germany were now in the news more than ever, and in my fantasies Ben became an enormously wealthy German munitions maker. One day while he was out earning more pennies, I took his bank down from its shelf, slid a knife into the opening, and turned the pig upside down. After about fifteen minutes of narrow escapes from the brown-shirted guards patrolling his estate, I had collected nearly a guilder from the enemy.

That part was easy. Much harder was the question of what to do with my spoils. A guilder was worth twenty-five cents—a fortune for a child in our little town. To have arrived in the sweetshop with that much money would certainly have caused questions.

I had it! What if I said I had found it! The next day, at school, I went up to the teacher and held out my hand. "Look what I found, Miss Meekle."

Miss Meekle blew her breath out slowly. "My, Andrew! What a lot of money for a little boy!"

"Can I keep it?"

"You don't know who it belongs to?"

Even under torture, they would never wring the truth from me. "No, ma'am. I found it in the street."

"Then you must take it to the police, Andy. They will tell you what to do."

The police! Here was something I hadn't counted on. That afternoon in fear and trembling I took the money into the very bastion of law and rectitude. If our little town hall had really been Gestapo headquarters, I couldn't have been more terrified. It seemed to me that stolen money must give off a telltale gleam. But apparently my story was believed, because the police chief wrote my name on an envelope, put the money inside, and told me that if no one claimed it within a year, it was mine.

And so, a year later, I made that trip to the sweetshop. Ben had never missed the pennies. That spoiled the game; instead of the flavor of sabotage behind the lines, the candy had the flat taste of common theft.

As much as anything, I think my dreams of thrilling action, my endless fantasies, were a means of escaping from my mother's radio. Mama was a semi-invalid. A bad heart forced her to spend a large part of each day sitting in a chair, where her consolation was the radio. But she kept the dial at one spot only: the gospel

Colombia   A Traveler's Story

GOD'S WORD STILL STOPS LIONS

I don't know what we would do without the Word of God. We see it being fulfilled in our lives. Just as Paul speaks about being freed from the mouth of lions, the Lord Jesus Christ has also freed us.

One night five people came to our door and took me away. After walking for about two hours, they turned to me and said, "We brought you out here to kill you because you support our enemies. If you want to live you have to tell us to which group you belong."

The commander was well known for having killed several dozen people. He put his gun to my head. I looked him in the eyes and said, "I can't fabricate a lie, because if you kill me and I go into the presence of my God, He is going to judge me for this lie. . . . So I would prefer you to kill me for telling the truth, which is that Jesus Christ loves you."

I was forced to walk farther into the jungle for him to kill me, and I asked if he would do so near my home, where my family could find my body. I told him,

"You know something? Jesus Christ loves you. I don't have anything against you. You can kill me, and I will pray to God that one day you will repent and that we will see each other in heaven." When I knelt down to pray, the man became uneasy, ordering me to get up. I said, "I'm sorry, sir. I was just kneeling down to pray before the God of my life so that He would receive my soul."

The man just stood, rooted in front of me, with the gun still pointed at my head. He said nothing for several minutes. I was still sure I would die, so the only thing I actually said was, "Lord, into Your hands I commend my spirit." There were some other men from this group mocking the commander, who held the gun pointed at my head. They were laughing and saying, "What's the matter? Why don't you kill this guy? Hurry up!" The commander gave his gun to someone else, adding, "I am just not capable of killing this man."

He didn't kill me! This is the mercy of God and the power of His Word.

station from Amsterdam. Sometimes it was hymn-singing, sometimes it was preaching; always—to my ears—it was dull.

Not to Mama. Religion was her life. We were poor, even by Witte standards; our house was the smallest in the village. But to our door came an unending stream of beggars, itinerant preachers, gypsies, who knew that they would be welcome at Mama's table. The cheese that night would be sliced thinner, the soup stretched with water, but a guest would never be turned away.

Thriftiness was as important in Mama's religion as hospitality. At four I could peel potatoes without a centimeter's waste. At seven the potatoes passed to my little brother Cornelius while I graduated to the heady responsibility of shining shoes. These were not our everyday *klompen:* these were our leather shoes for Sunday, and it was an economic disaster if a pair failed to last fifteen years. Mama said they must shine so the preacher would have to shade his eyes.

Because Mama could not lift heavy loads, Ben did the laundry each week. The clothes had to be hauled in and out of the tub, but the actual washing was done by pumping a wooden handle that worked a set of paddles. This technological marvel was the pride of the household. We would take turns spelling Ben at the handle, pushing the heavy stick blade back and forth until our arms ached.

The only member of the family who did no work was the oldest child, Bastian. Two years older than Ben and six years older than I, Bas never learned to do any of the things other people did. He spent the day standing under an elm tree on the dike road, watching the village go by. Witte was proud of its elms in this tree-poor country: one for every house, their branches meeting to form a green archway over the road. For some reason, Bas never stood beneath our tree. His post was under the third one down, and there he stood all day long, until one of us led him home for supper.

Next to Mama, I think I loved Bas more than anyone on earth. As the villagers passed his elm tree they would call to him to get his shy and wonderful smile in response. "Ah, Bas!" Over the years he heard this phrase so often that at last he began to repeat it, the only words he ever learned.

But though Bas could not talk or even dress himself, he had a strange and remarkable talent. In our tiny sitting room, as in most Dutch parlors in the 1930s, was a small pump organ. Papa was the only one in the family who could read music, and so in the evenings he would sit on the little bench, pumping the foot pedals and picking out tunes from an ancient hymnbook while the rest of us sang.

All except Bas. The minute the music started, Bas would drop down and crawl beneath the keyboard, where he would crouch out of the way of Papa's feet and press himself to the baseboard of the organ. Of course Papa's playing was rough and full of mistakes, not only because he could not hear the music, but also because the years of wielding a hammer on an anvil had left his fingers thick and stiff. Some nights he seemed to hit almost as many wrong notes as right ones.

To Bas it never mattered. He would press against the vibrating wood with rapture on his face. Where he was, of course, he could not see which keys were played or which knobs Papa pulled. But all at once Bas would stand up and gently push against Papa's shoulder.

"Ah, Bas. Ah, Bas," he would say.

And Papa would get up, and Bas would take his place at the bench. He always fussed a little with the hymnal as he had seen Papa do, turning the pages and usually managing to get the whole book upside down. Then, squinting at the page like Papa, he began to play. From beginning to end he would play the songs Papa had played that night. But not as Papa played them—hesitantly, clumsily, full of discords. Bas played them perfectly, without a mistake, with such surpassing beauty that people would stop in the street outside to listen. On summer nights when our door was open, a little crowd would gather outside the house, many of them with tears streaming down their faces. For when Bas played, it was as though an angel sat at the organ.

The big event in our week, of course, was church. Witte is in the polder land of Holland—land that generations of Dutchmen have reclaimed from the sea—and like all villages in the polders is built along a dike. It has only one street, the road leading north and south on top of the dike. The houses are virtual islands, each built on its mound of earth and connected to the road with a tiny bridge spanning the drainage canal. And at either end of town, on the highest, most imposing mounds of all, are the two churches.

There is still a lot of feeling in Holland between Catholics and Protestants, a carryover from the days of the Spanish occupation. During the week the village fishmonger will talk pleasantly with the village ironmonger, but on Sundays the fishmonger will walk with his family northward to the Roman church while the ironmonger will walk with his family southward to the Protestant church, and as they pass on the street neither will acknowledge the other with so much as a nod.

Our family was fiercely proud of its Protestant traditions. My father was glad, I think, that our house happened to be in the northern end of town, because this gave him the entire length of the village in which to demonstrate that we were headed in the right direction.

Because of Papa's deafness, we always sat in the very first pew at church. The pew was too short for the entire family to sit together, and I would manage to lag behind, letting Mama and Papa and the other children go in first. Then I would have to walk back toward the rear of the church to "find a seat." The seat I found was usually far beyond the church door. In the winter I skated down the frozen canals on my wooden *klompen.* In the summer I sat so still in the fields that wild crows would sit on my shoulders and peck gently at my ears.

With a kind of instinct, I knew precisely when the church service would be over and would slip into a corner of the church vestibule just as the first sufferers emerged. I stood near the preacher—who never once missed my presence—and listened for the comments of the congregation about his sermon. Thus I picked up his text, his theme, sometimes even the gist of a story.

This ploy was terribly important, because without it I could not have carried off the most important phase of my weekly adventure. It is the custom in Holland to gather in private homes after church. Three ingredients are always present. Coffee, cigar smoke, and a point-by-point discussion of the sermon. The men in our village could afford these long black cigars only once a week. Each Sunday as their wives brewed strong black coffee, they brought them out and lit up with great ceremony. To this day whenever I catch the smell of coffee and cigar smoke, my heart beats faster; it is an odor associated with fear and excitement: could I once again fool my parents into thinking that I had been to church?

"It seems to me that the preacher used Luke 3:16 just last month," I would say, knowing full well that he had not, but getting across in this way the fact that I knew the text.

Or: "Wasn't that a good story about politicians?" playing out a scrap of conversation I had overheard. "I should think the burgomaster would be mad."

The technique was immensely successful. I blush to think how seldom I attended church as a child. I blush even more when I remember that my trusting, simple-hearted family never suspected.

By 1939 the whole country saw what the Whetstras had seen all along: the Germans were intent on a pattern of conquest that included Holland. In our house we scarcely thought about it. Bas was sick; the doctor called it tuberculosis. Mama and Papa moved onto a mattress in the sitting room. For months Bas lay in their tiny bedroom, coughing, coughing, his flesh shrinking until only bones and skin lay on the bed. His suffering was more dreadful than that of a normal person, because he could not tell us how he felt.

I remember one day just after my eleventh birthday creeping into the sickroom while Mama was busy in the kitchen. Entering that room was strictly forbidden, for the disease was contagious. But that was what I wanted. If Bas was going to die, then I wanted to die too. I threw myself down on top of him and kissed him again and again on the mouth. In July, 1939, Bas died, while I stayed healthy as ever, and I felt that God had betrayed me twice.

Two months later, in September, our government called for a general mobilization. For once, Mama allowed her radio to be used for news. We turned the volume as high as it would go, but still Papa could not hear. So my little sister Geltje stationed herself at the set and shouted salient pieces of information to him.

"ALL RESERVE UNITS ARE ACTIVATED, PAPA."

"ALL PRIVATE CARS ARE COMMANDEERED."

By nightfall the traffic jam had begun, the endless traffic jam that was to be the characteristic feature of the months before invasion. Every automobile in Holland was on the road. There seemed to be just as many going north as there were going south. No one knew where he was supposed to be, but he was getting there as fast as he could. Day after day, wearing my baggy trousers and loose blouse, I stood under the tree where Bas used to stand and watched. Nobody talked much.

Only Mr. Whetstra seemed to find the courage to put into words what we all knew. I could not understand why I was being drawn toward the Whetstras at this time, but frequently I found myself walking past that kitchen window.

"Good afternoon, Andrew."

"Good afternoon, Mrs. Whetstra."

"Out on an errand for your mother? You'd better have a cookie for energy." She picked up a plate of cookies and brought them to the window.

Mr. Whetstra looked up from the kitchen table. "Is that little Andrew? Out to see the mobilization firsthand?"

"Yes, sir." For some reason I put my cookie behind my back.

"Andrew, you must say prayers for your country every night. We are about to go through a very hard time."

"Yes, sir."

"What good can men with popguns do against planes and tanks?"

"Yes, sir."

"They'll be here, Andrew, with their steel helmets and their goosestep and their hate, and all we will have is our prayers." Mr. Whetstra came over to the window and leaned across the sill. "Will you pray, Andrew? Pray for the courage to do all we can, and then having done all, to stand. Will you do that, Andrew?"

"Yes, sir."

"Good boy." Mr. Whetstra drew his head back into the room. "Now get along on your errand."

But as I turned and started down the street, Mr. Whetstra called after me. "You can eat the cookie. Oh, I know, sometimes that old stove of ours smokes something awful. But it's worked fine ever since I got my new window in."

That night, lying on my bed in the loft, I got to thinking about Mr. Whetstra. So he'd known all along. But he hadn't told my father, as every other grown-up in town would have done. I wondered why. I also wondered about his wanting me to pray. What good would

Diary of a Smuggler

CUBA

It's our fourth day in Cuba, and I finally have a few minutes to take a breath and try to take in what I've seen and heard since we arrived. We're actually sitting in the middle of a church service—but now the pastor's giving the sermon, and I don't speak Spanish, so I'm taking the opportunity to scribble a few notes. I don't want to forget any of this.

This church is little more than a wooden hut. Inside, well over one hundred people sit crammed together on makeshift wooden benches and old plastic seats. The window at the back is open, and four men are leaning through, trying to hear the sermon. Everybody is taking studious notes—copying what the pastor writes on the old blackboard in front.

Yesterday we went to visit another pastor. We asked him what the church in Cuba needed most, and he replied: "Bibles. We need them by the thousands. There are never enough. As soon as we get permission for a consignment, they're gone! We are baptizing forty people next week, and we have no Bibles to give them. I've told them to pray." We pulled eight Bibles out of our luggage. His eyes lit up—that's eight prayers answered.

We asked him if the government gives him any problems. He replied, "I think my house is bugged." (We were talking outside on the roof.) "We have a whole regiment of government informers in our church. Some of them have become Christians. They actually do us a favor—they go and report, saying, 'I've seen two healings this week; five people baptized.' They talk to the senior government officials—the people we can't reach!"

that do! God never listened. If the Germans really did come, I planned to do a lot worse to them than pray. I fell asleep dreaming of the feats of daring I would work single-handed against the invader.

By April, Witte was crowded with refugees from the polder land to the east of us. Holland was bombing its own dikes, deliberately flooding land wrested inch by inch from the sea over the centuries, to slow down the German army. Every house except ours, which was too small, held a homeless family from the flooded land, and Mama's soup pot simmered night and day.

But of course the Germans did not come by land. The first planes flew over Witte the night of May 10, 1940. We spent the night in the sitting room, huddled together, not sleeping. All the next day we saw planes and heard the explosions as they bombed the small military airfield four kilometers away. It was my twelfth birthday, but neither I nor anyone else remembered.

Then the Germans bombed Rotterdam. The radio announcer from Hilversum, to whom we had listened since mobilization, wept as he read the release. Rotterdam was gone. In one hour a city had disappeared from the earth. This was the blitzkrieg, the new warfare. The next day Holland surrendered.

A few days later a fat little German lieutenant arrived in Witte in a squad car and set himself up in the burgomaster's house. The handful of soldiers who accompanied him were mostly older men: Witte was not important enough to rate crack troops.

And for a while I really did act out my fantasies of resistance. Many was the night I crept barefoot down the ladder from the loft as two o'clock struck on the town clock. I knew that my mother heard me, because the regular rhythm of her breathing halted as I passed their room. But she never stopped me. Nor did she ask the next morning what had happened to our precious highly rationed sugar. Everyone in the village was amused when the lieutenant's staff car began to give him trouble. His sparks were fouled. His engine stalled. Some said there was sugar in the lieutenant's gas tank; others thought it was unlikely.

Food ran out in the towns before it did in farming villages like ours, and this fact too I used in my child's war against the enemy. One hot day that first summer, I loaded a basket with cabbages and tomatoes and walked the four miles to Alkmaar. A store there still had a supply of prewar fireworks, and I knew the proprietor wanted vegetables.

I pressed my advantage as far as I could and filled my basket with the firecrackers, placing over them the flowers I had brought along for the purpose. The proprietor stood looking at me in silence. Then, with sudden resolution, he reached under the counter and brought up a large cherry bomb.

"I have no more food."

"You'd better get home before the curfew."

That night back in Witte the floorboards of the loft creaked again, and again Mama held her breath. I slipped out, barefoot, into the night. A patrol of four foot soldiers was moving northward up the street toward our house, playing their torches on each of the buildings as they passed. I moved out of the doorway and flattened myself against the side of the house as the marching boots drew closer. The minute the soldiers had passed I sped across the little bridge between our house and the dike road and ran south to the burgomaster's house. It would have been a simple matter to fire the mammoth cherry bomb in the lieutenant's doorway while the patrol was at the other end of the village. But I wanted more adventure than that. I was the fastest runner in the village, and I thought it would be fun to have these old men in their heavy boots run after me. I don't suppose any of them was over fifty, but to my young eyes they seemed ancient.

So I waited until the patrol began its tour back down the street. Just before they got to headquarters, I lit the fuse and ran.

"*Halt!*" A torchbeam picked me up, and I heard a rifle bolt being drawn. I hadn't counted on guns! I zigged and zagged as I ran up the street. Then the cherry bomb exploded, and for a fraction of a moment the soldier's attention was diverted. I darted across the first bridge I could find, raced through a garden, and flung myself down among the cabbage heads. For nearly an hour they hunted for me, shouting gruff syllables to one another in German, until at last they gave up.

Elated by this success, I began discharging volleys in broad daylight. One day I stepped from hiding straight into the arms of a soldier. To run was to admit guilt. Yet in my hands was strong circumstantial evidence: in my left hand were firecrackers, in my right, matches.

"*Du! Komm mal her!*"

My hands clenched around the firecrackers. I did not dare stuff them in my coat pocket; that would surely be the first place he would look.

"Hast du einen Fuerwerkskoerper explodiert?"
"Fuerwerks? Oh no, sir!"

I grabbed the two edges of my coat with my clenched hands and held it wide for him to search. The soldier went over me from my wide trousers to my cap. When he turned away in disgust, the firecrackers in my hand were drenched with perspiration.

But as the occupation dragged on, even I tired of my games. In villages near ours hostages were being lined up and shot and houses burned to the ground, as the real resistance hardened and took shape. Jokes against the Germans ceased to be funny.

All over Holland were the *onderduikers* (literally the under-divers), men and boys in hiding to escape deportation to the forced labor camps in Germany. Ben, sixteen when the war began, dived under a farm near Ermelo the first month, and for five years we had no news of him.

Possession of a radio was made a crime against the new regime. We hid Mama's instrument in a crawl space under the sloping roof, and one by one we would crouch there to listen for the Dutch language broadcasts from England. Later, when the Dutch railroad struck, we would even squeeze railroad workers into that tiny hole, and of course there were always Jews to be hidden for a night on their way to the coast.

As the Germans grew desperate for manpower, Witte's tiny occupation force was withdrawn. Then came the dreaded *razzia.* Trucks would suddenly speed into the villages, at any hour of the day or night, sealing the dike roads at both ends, while squads of soldiers searched every house for able-bodied men. Before I was fourteen I was joining the flight of men and boys into the polders at the first sign of a German uniform. We would run across the fields, crouching low, leaping the canals, making for the swamp beyond the railroad. The railway dike was too high to climb—we would surely be seen—so we would dive into the broad canal that flowed beneath the railroad bridge, to crawl out soaked—panting and shivering. By the end of the war even little Cornelius and Papa, deaf as he was, were joining the race to the swamp.

Between the *razzias,* life was a somber struggle for mere existence. All electricity was reserved for the Germans. With nothing to power the pumps, the rainwater lay deep and stagnant over the polders. In our homes we used oil lamps, making the oil ourselves from cabbage seeds. There was no coal, so Witte cut down its elms. The tree under which Bas had stood was cut the second winter.

But the chief enemy, worse even than the cold and the soldiers, was hunger. We were constantly, naggingly, endlessly hungry. All crops were commandeered for the front as soon as they were picked. My father tended his garden as carefully as ever, but it was the Germans who reaped most of the harvest. For years our family of six lived on rations for two.

At first we were able to add to this allowance by digging the tulip bulbs from our garden and eating them like potatoes. Then even the tulips ran out. Mama would pretend to eat, but many nights I saw her divide her tiny portion among the other plates. Her only consolation was that Bas had not lived to see this time. He never could have understood the ache in his stomach, the dark fireplace, the treeless street.

At last the day came when Mama could not get out of bed. If liberation did not come soon, we knew she would die.

And then in the spring of 1945 the Germans left and the Canadians took their place. People stood in the street weeping for joy. But I was not with them. I was running every step of the five miles

AROUND THE GLOBE
Afghanistan

Population: 22.7 million
Location/Size: Southcentral Asia
251,826 sq. miles
Major Religions: Islam
Level of Persecution: Sharp, rapidly increasing

Freedom of religion is severely restricted in Afghanistan, being primarily determined by evolving, unwritten policies of the various political factions. Most areas of the country see vigorous promotion of Islam, which leads to increasing oppression of the tiny Christian community within the country.

Custom and law require all residents to declare their religion. Afghanis are considered by default to be Muslims. Conversion from Islam to Christianity is illegal and punishable by death. Non-Muslims in the country may practice their faith but not evangelize, and Afghani Christians risk constant danger from their threatening Muslim neighbors.

The church in Afghanistan is presently declining due to warfare and persecution. Christian ministries must find creative ways to enter the country to serve its people.

to the Canadian encampment, where I was able to beg a small sackful of breadcrusts.

Bread! Quite literally the bread of life!

I brought it home to my family with shouts of "Food! Food! Food!" As Mama gnawed the dry crusts, tears of gratefulness to God rolled down the deep lines in her cheeks.

The war was over.

Imagine This

The government of Chiapas has just passed a law that every resident must keep a stone idol in his or her house. You do not have to worship the idol, but it is mandatory to have it in your home, otherwise you will be imprisoned for five years. Do you keep the idol in your home to avoid arrest and continue to witness to others? Or do you refuse to put a false god in your house and face imprisonment?

What Would You Do?

two

The Yellow Straw Hat

And we know that in all things God works for the good of those who love him, and have been called according to his purpose.

Romans 8:28

One afternoon in the summer of 1945, several months after liberation, I came into the house and was met by my little sister, Geltje, with the news that my father wanted to see me.

"He's in the garden," she said.

I walked through the dark kitchen and out into the cabbage patch, blinking my eyes against the bright sunlight. Papa, hoe in hand, *klompen* on his feet, was bent over his cabbages working the little weeds out with patient tenderness. I circled so as to stand in front of him and shouted, "YOU WANTED TO SEE ME, PAPA?"

Papa straightened up slowly. "YOU'RE SEVENTEEN YEARS OLD, ANDREW." I knew instantly what direction the conversation was going to take.

"YES SIR."

"WHAT DO YOU PLAN TO DO WITH YOUR LIFE!"

I wished his voice didn't have to be so loud. And mine in answering him. "I DON'T KNOW, PAPA."

Now Papa was going to ask me why I didn't like smithing. He did. Then he was going to ask why I had not stuck with machine fitting—a trade I had tried to learn during the occupation. He did that, too. I knew that all Witte could hear both his questions and the vague and evasive answers with which I tried to satisfy him.

"IT IS TIME FOR YOU TO CHOOSE A TRADE, ANDREW. BY FALL I WANT YOUR DECISION."

My father leaned back over his hoe, and I knew the conversation was over. I had then perhaps two months to decide on my life's work. Oh, I knew what I wanted all right: to find somehow a life that broke out of the mold. To find adventure. To get away from Witte, from the mental set that was constantly looking backward.

But I also knew that my prospects were not very good. The Germans had come when I was in the sixth grade and taken over the school building, and that was the end of my formal education.

The only thing I could do well was run. That afternoon I took off across the polders, barefoot, running mile after mile along the little footpaths used by the farmers. After five miles I was just getting warmed up. I ran through the town where I had bought the firecrackers. My mind was clear now and functioning well.

I scrambled up the dike that led back to Witte with a mounting sense that I was close to my answer. The solution was clear. There was constant talk in the paper about armed rebellion in the colonies. The Dutch East Indies, so recently liberated from Japan, were now presuming to claim independence from Holland as well. Daily we were reminded that these colonies were Dutch soil— had been for 350 years. Why were our armies not reclaiming them for the Crown?

Why indeed? That night I announced to the household that I knew already what I was going to do.

"What's that, Andy?" said Maartje.

"Join the army."

Mother's instinct was to draw in her breath. "Oh, Andrew!" She had seen too much of armies. "Must we always think of killing?"

But my father and brothers were of a different mind. The very next week I borrowed Papa's bicycle and pedaled to the recruiting office in Amsterdam. By nightfall I was home again, much diminished in my own sight. The army took seventeen-year-olds only in the calendar year in which they turned eighteen. I wouldn't be eighteen until May of 1946!

In January I was back, and this time I was accepted. Before long I was strutting through Witte in my new uniform, oblivious to the fact that the pants were too small, the jacket too big, the whole effect quite top-heavy. But I was going off to take back our colonies for the Queen, and perhaps get a few of those dirty revolutionaries who everyone said were Communists and bastards. The two words automatically went together.

The only people who did not respond with applause were the Whetstras. I walked, top-heavy, past their house.

"Hello there, Andy."

"Good morning, Mr. Whetstra."

"How are your mother and father?"

Was it possible he did not see the uniform? I turned so that the sun glinted from my shiny brass belt buckle. At last I blurted, "I've joined up, you know. I'm going to the East Indies."

Mr. Whetstra leaned back as if to see me better. "Yes, I see. So you're off for adventure. I will pray for you, Andrew. I will pray that the adventure you find will satisfy."

I stared at him, puzzled. Whatever did he mean, adventure that would satisfy? Any kind of adventure, I thought as I looked out over the flat fields stretching away from Witte in every direction, any adventure would satisfy me more than the long sleep of this village.

So I left home. I left home emotionally as well as physically. I worked hard during basic training and felt for the first time in my life that I was doing something I wanted to do.

Oh, how I liked being treated as an adult. Part of my training took place in the town of Gorkum. Each Sunday I would go to church—not because I was interested in the service but because afterward I could count on being invited to dinner. I always

Ethiopia	A Traveler's Story

"OUR FATHER KICKED US AND TOOK OUR BIBLE"

One evening, in the middle of the night, while my sister amd I were praying in our bedroom, our mother heard our prayers. She became very angry and told our father. He was furious. He kicked us and took our Bible. He decided that we should leave the house, but it was already midnight, so he said that we had to leave the house the following morning. He said: "You have another Lord and God, so we cannot live together in the same house. You must leave."

Shaka had to leave, but because I was still at school, he said that I could stay. I was not allowed to have any Christians over, not even Shaka. My father forbade me to attend Christian worship services and meetings. Two months later my father wanted to know what my decision was. I said, "I have decided that Jesus Christ is my personal Savior and that He can change my life. I saw the light." My father said, "You are like your sister, and I don't want to see your face." He kicked me and took a knife to kill me. I ran away in the middle of the night. I left home almost two years ago.

When we left home we stayed with another Christian for a few days and later went to live in the church. We lived in the church for one and a half years, sleeping on the floor. Sometimes we had to go to bed hungry, but we would rather die than ask for food. That was a very tough time for us. When we were hungry, we cried and went to sleep. That was our life. Sometimes other Christians encouraged us, but other times we suffered in silence.

We miss our family, but we hope and believe that they will become Christians too and that we will all live together again one day. We are praying for our parents. We would love to go back to our home.

Our biggest dream is to have God's love revealed to everyone. We want to be witnesses for God.

enjoyed telling my hosts that I had been picked for special commando training in Indonesia.

"Within a few weeks," I would say, dramatically pushing my chair back and taking a long draw from my after-Sunday-dinner cigar, "I shall be in hand-to-hand combat with the enemy." And then, striking a somewhat distant look, I would ask if my hosts would consider writing me while I was overseas. They always agreed, and before I left Holland I had seventy names on my correspondence list.

One of them was a girl. I met her in the usual way, after church—a Reformed service that particular Sunday. She was the most beautiful girl I had ever seen. About my age I guessed, extremely slender, with hair so black it had a tinge of blue in it. But what impressed me most was her skin. I had read about skin as white as snow; this was the first time I had seen it. After a pleasant snooze during the sermon, I went invitation-fishing. Sure enough, I timed my exit just right. Snow White was at the door. She introduced herself.

"I'm Thile," she said.

"I'm Andrew."

"My mother wonders if you would like to have dinner with us."

"Very much indeed," I said, and moments later I left the church with the princess on my arm.

Thile's father was a fishmonger. His home was over his shop, down by the waterfront in Gorkum, and throughout our dinner the pleasant smells of the dockside mingled with the odors of boiled cabbage and ham. Afterward we sat in the family drawing room.

"Cigar, Andrew?" said Thile's father.

"Thank you, sir." I chose one carefully and rolled it in my fingers as I had seen the men in Witte do. Frankly, I didn't like the taste of cigars, but the association with manhood was so strong that I could have smoked rope and enjoyed it. Throughout the coffee-and-cigars, Thile sat with her back to the window, the strong midday sun making her hair more blue than ever. She said hardly a word, but already I knew that this young girl was going to be one of my correspondents and, perhaps, a lot more too.

November 22, 1946: my last day at home. I had already said goodbye to Thile and to the other families in Gorkum. Now it was time to take leave of my own family.

If only I had known it was the last time I would see Mama. I would have been far less of the dashing soldier-going-off-to-war. But I didn't know, and I took Mama's embrace as my due. I thought I looked rather well. At last I had a uniform that fit, I was in excellent physical shape, my hair was cut close army-style.

Just as I was ready to leave, Mama reached under her apron and pulled out a little book. I knew right away what it would be: her Bible.

"Andrew, will you take this with you?"

Of course I said, "Yes."

"Will you read it, Andrew?"

Can you ever say no to your mother? You can do no—but you can't say no. I put the Bible in my dufflebag, as far down as it would go, and forgot it.

Our transport ship, the Sibajak, landed in Indonesia just before Christmas, 1946. My heart raced with excitement at the heavy tropical smells, the sight of naked porters moving up and down the gangplanks, the sounds of the hawkers on the dock trying to get our attention. I shouldered my dufflebag and struggled down the gangplank into the fierce sun of the dockside. I did not guess that within a few weeks I would be killing children and unarmed adults just like the people who crowded around me now.

A few of the hawkers were selling monkeys. Each was held by a little chain, and many had been trained to do tricks. I was fascinated by these little creatures with their serious, ancient faces and stooped to look at one of them more closely.

"Don't touch him."

I straightened up to find myself facing one of my officers.

"They bite, soldier." The officer was smiling, but he was serious. "Half of them have rabies, you know."

The officer moved on, and I withdrew my hand. The little boy who was holding the monkey chased after the officer shrieking at him for ruining the sale. I moved back into the line of debarking soldiers, but right then I knew I had to have a monkey of my own.

Those of us who qualified were separated from the rest of the troops and sent to a nearby island for training as commandos. I liked running the tough obstacle courses: scaling walls, swinging across creeks on vines, crawling into culverts, wriggling under machinegun fire. Even more I liked the hand combat training, where we worked with bayonets, knives, and bare hands. "Hi-

hii! Ho!" It was lunge and parry, thrust with fingers stiff, come at the enemy with drawn knife. For some reason the thought never penetrated that I was training to kill human beings.

Part of the education of a commando was the development of self-confidence. But here I needed no schooling. From childhood I had had a completely unfounded confidence in my ability to do anything I set out to do.

Like drive a Bren carrier, for instance. These were heavy armored vehicles mounted on caterpillar treads, and handling them was difficult even for someone who could drive an automobile—which I could not. But each day as we went out on maneuvers I watched the driver of the carrier on which I rode, until it seemed to me that I had the hang of it.

Unexpectedly, one day I had a chance to find out. Coming out of company headquarters, I ran into an officer.

"Can you drive a Bren carrier, soldier?"

A quick salute and an even quicker, "Yes, sir."

"Well, that one there has to go to the garage. Let's go."

In front of us at the curb was the carrier. Three hundred yards away was the garage. Seven other carriers were parked there, nose to tail, waiting to be serviced. I hopped snappily into the driver's seat while the officer climbed in beside me. I looked at the dashboard. There in front of me was a key, and I remembered that the driver always turned that first of all. Sure enough the engine coughed once and then caught. Now which of those pedals was the clutch? I pressed one of them and it went to the floor, and I knew I had been lucky twice in a row. I put the carrier into gear, let go of the clutch pedal, and with a great kangaroo leap we launched into space.

The officer looked at me quickly but said nothing: no Bren carrier ever starts smoothly. But as I raced full throttle down the company street, I noticed that he was holding on with both hands and bracing his feet. We covered the three hundred yards with only one near-accident—a sergeant who discovered on the spot how great were his powers of flight—and then we came to the line of carriers.

And I knew that I was in trouble.

I didn't know where the brake was.

| Sri Lanka | A Traveler's Story |

THE BIBLE, NOT THE RIFLE:
THE TESTIMONY OF A FORMER TAMIL TIGER

Who would be daring enough to preach the Gospel to the Liberation Tigers of Tamil Eelam (LTTE), the most dreaded militant group in Sri Lanka? *Time* magazine tagged this group "the world's most successful terrorist group." They are committed, well funded, powerfully armed, strategic, and ruthless. They are trained to kill anyone who stands in the way of their schemes.

Pastor Rajeewa has made a bold step in obeying the Lord's call in ministering to this dreaded group. His area of ministry is a village in the northeastern district of Batticoloa. A huge zone in this village is controlled by the Tigers. Bomb blasts and heavy artillery firing vividly depict daily village life. The Tigers have mounted strong barracks with highly trained fighters, which is why "even the government army cannot enter the territory," Pastor Rajeewa comments.

Rajeewa was a former LTTE guerrilla himself. He became a Tamil Tiger because during the civil war, his family was tortured and killed by a band of government soldiers who invaded their village. He was spared from the massacre but was haunted with memories of death. He joined the LTTE when he was a teenager, as a form of revenge. The Tigers taught him Marxism and warfare. He became ruthless in killing people.

Following years of service as a guerrilla, a large void occupied his heart. It was at this time that a villager shared the Gospel with him. During Rajeewa's daily tour of duty, a man approached him with "strange words" about a Savior who died for the sin of mankind. Rajeewa threatened him with death, but the simple villager persisted. This softened Rajeewa's heart.

Every day as Rajeewa was on patrol, the man would approach him with verses from the Bible. As Rajeewa returned to the camp, he thought about those words. Sometimes he would even hear them resounding in his mind.

Continued

Arms flailing and feet flying, I tried every button and lever I could find. Among the things I pushed was the accelerator, and with one last surge of power we plowed into the row of Bren carriers parked at the curb. All seven of them bucked forward, each slamming against the other, until we came to rest, hissing and smoking, our engine at last dead.

I looked at the officer. He stared straight ahead of him, his eyes large, sweat pouring down the sides of his face. He got out of the car, crossed himself, and walked away without once turning to look at me. The sergeant ran up to me and pulled me out of the driver's seat.

"What on earth got into you, soldier?"

"He asked me if I knew how to drive it, sergeant. He didn't ask if I knew how to stop!"

It was probably fortunate for me that we were leaving the next morning for our first combat mission. We were going, rumor said, to relieve a company of commandos that had lost three out of every four of its men.

At dawn we were flown to the front.

And instantly I knew that I had been wrong about this adventure. It wasn't the danger—I liked that—it was the killing. Suddenly targets were no longer pieces of paper stuck up on an earth background, they were fathers and brothers like my own. Often our targets weren't even in uniform.

What was I doing? How had I gotten here? I was more disgusted with myself than I had ever imagined possible.

And then one day the incident occurred that has haunted me all my life. We were marching through a village that was still partially inhabited. This made us bold, for we did not think the Communists would mine a village in which people were still living. Anti-personnel mines were the thing we feared most in the world. They kept us in a state of perpetual fear, lest these jumping, emasculating instruments should explode and leave us groveling and crippled for life. We had been in combat daily for more than three weeks, and the nerves of everyone in our unit were on edge, when about halfway through this peaceful-looking village we stepped into a nest of mines. The company went berserk. Without orders, without reasoning, we simply started shooting. We shot everything in sight. When we came to ourselves, there was not a living thing in the village. We skirted the mined area and walked gingerly through the desolation we had created. At the edge of the village I saw the sight that was to send me nearly mad. A young Indonesian mother lay on the ground in a pool of her own blood, a baby boy at her breast. Both had been killed by the same bullet.

A Traveler's Story
Continued

In 1989, after months of meeting with the villager, Rajeewa surrendered his life to Christ. He secretly left the LTTE and immediately went to Colombo for discipleship and training. In 1990, he committed his life to full-time ministry as an itinerant evangelist. He went back to Batticoloa and started sharing the Gospel with some of his former comrades, as well as with military men. His desire is to see "all of these armed men surrender their lives to Christ, carrying Bibles, not rifles."

He is currently under strict surveillance by his former comrades, and they tried to entice him to become a Tiger again to escape hunger and poverty.

But he continued his ministry in total dependence on God. He was able to construct a small shed as a worship area and train six committed workers to minister with him. They are also former LTTE guerrillas.

Amid trying circumstances, Pastor Rajeewa serves the Lord with hope, willing to sacrifice his life for the sake of the Church and the villagers who need Christ.

I think I wanted to kill myself after that. I know that in the next two years I became famous throughout the Dutch troops in Indonesia for my crazy bravado on the battlefield. I bought a bright yellow straw hat and wore it into combat with me. It was a dare and an invitation. "Here I am!" it said. "Shoot me!" Gradually I gathered around me a group of boys who were reacting as I did, and together we invented a motto that we posted on the camp bulletin board: "Get smart—lose your mind."

Everything we did, those two years, whether on the battlefield or back at the rest camp, was in extremes. When we fought, we fought as madmen. When we drank, we drank until our reason left us. Together, we would weave from bar to bar, hurling our empty gin bottles through the display windows of the local stores.

When I woke up from these orgies, I would wonder why I was doing these things, but the question never got an answer. It occurred to me once that perhaps the chaplain might be able to help. They told me I could find him at the officers' bar, and when I did, he was as tipsy and garrulous as anyone there. He stepped outside to see me, but when I told why I'd come, he laughed and told me I'd get over it. "But if you want, come to services before you fight next time," the chaplain said. "That way you can kill men in a state of grace." He thought the joke was very funny. He went back inside to repeat it to the others.

So I turned to my pen pals. I had kept up with all of the people I had promised to write, and now I ventured to share my confusion with a few of them. In essence they all wrote back the same thing: "You're fighting for your country, Andrew. So the rest doesn't count."

One person alone said more than this. Thile. Thile wrote to me about guilt. That part of her letters spoke straight to my own wretchedness. But then she went on to talk about forgiveness. And there she lost me. My sense of guilt was wrapped around me like a chain, and nothing I did—drinking, fighting, writing letters or reading them—nothing seemed to ease its stranglehold upon me.

And then one day when I was on leave in Jakarta, walking through the bazaar, I spotted a little gibbon tied to a tall pole. He was sitting on top of the pole eating some fruit, and as I went by he jumped onto my shoulder and handed me a section of orange. I laughed, and that was all it took for the excellent Indonesian salesman to come running.

"Sir, the monkey likes you!"

I laughed again. The gibbon blinked twice very deliberately and then showed me his teeth in what could have been a grin.

"How much?"

And that is how I came to acquire a monkey. I took him back to the barracks with me. At first the other boys were fascinated.

"Does he bite?"

"Only crooks," I said.

It was a senseless remark, meaning nothing. But no sooner had I said it than the monkey jumped out of my arms, swung along the rafters, and landed—of all the places in the room he could have chosen—on the head of a heavyset guy who had been winning more at poker than averages allowed. He crabbed sideways, flailing his arms, trying to knock the monkey off his head. The whole barracks was laughing.

"Get him off me!" Jan Zwart shouted. "Get him off!"

I reached out my hand, and the monkey ran to me.

Jan smoothed his hair and tucked in his shirt, but his eyes were murderous. "I'll kill him," he said quietly.

So on the same day I gained one friend and lost another. I hadn't had the monkey many weeks before I noticed that his stomach seemed to be hurting him. One day while carrying him I felt what seemed like a welt around his waist. I put him down on the bed and told him to lie still. Carefully I pulled back the hair until I saw what it was. Evidently when the gibbon had been a baby, someone had tied him with a piece of wire and never taken it off. As the monkey grew, the wire became embedded in his flesh. It must have caused him terrible pain.

That evening I began the operation. I took my razor and shaved off the monkey's hair in a three-inch-wide swathe around his middle. The uncovered welt was red and angry-looking. While the other boys in the barracks looked on, I cut ever so gently into this tender flesh until I exposed the wire. The gibbon lay with the most amazing patience. Even when I hurt him, he looked at me with eyes that seemed to say, "I understand," until at long last I was able to pull the wire away. Instantly he jumped up, did a little cartwheel, danced around my shoulder, and pulled my hair, to the delight of all the boys in the barracks—except Jan.

After that, my gibbon and I were inseparable. I think I identified with him as strongly as he with me. I think I saw in the wire that had bound him a kind of parallel to the chain of guilt still so tight around myself—and in his release the thing I too longed for. Whenever I was not on duty in the daytime, I would take him with me on long runs into the forest. He loped along behind me until he grew tired. Then with a sprint he would dash forward, jump up, and hang on to my shorts, where he would cling until finally I picked him up and put him on my shoulder. Together, we would run for ten, fifteen miles until I would fling myself down on the ground to sleep. Almost always there were monkeys in the trees overhead. My little gibbon would race into the treetops to swing and chatter with the others. The first time this happened, I thought I had lost him. But the minute I stood up to start back,

Diary of a Smuggler

CHINA

I always had doubts as to whether I was truly blessed by God. But when I started this work of delivering Bibles, I was cured of those thoughts. There have been so many times when God has delivered me. Now I know I'm blessed.

Last week I was transporting a large consignment of Scriptures by road, and I was stopped by a Public Security Bureau official. He looked into the back and saw all the books and asked, "What are those?" I never lie, so I said, "They are Bibles." He looked at me, amazed, then began to laugh. I thought he was relishing spending the money he would fine me, and that he would take me to jail. But all he said was "Give me five." I did, and he sent me on my way.

there was a shriek in the branches overhead, a rustling of leaves, and with a thud the gibbon was back on my shoulder.

One day when, laughing and tired, I bore him back into camp, I found a letter waiting for me from my brother Ben. He went on and on about a funeral. It was only slowly that I realized it was Mama's.

Apparently a telegram had been sent—but it had never come. I knew that I was going to cry. I gave the monkey some water and while he was drinking, slipped away from camp. I didn't want even the gibbon with me. I ran and ran until my side throbbed in pain, knowing suddenly how very alone I must always be without her.

And it was that week that Jan Zwart took his revenge on the monkey. One evening I came in from guard duty to be met with the news, "Andy, the little monkey's dead."

"Dead?" I looked up dully. "What happened?"

"One of the boys picked him up by his tail and kept slamming him against the wall."

"Was it Zwart?"

The guy wouldn't answer.

"Where's the monkey now?"

"He's outside. In the bushes."

I found him draped over a branch. The worst of it was, he wasn't quite dead. I picked him up and brought him back to the barracks. His jaw was broken. A great hole gaped in his throat. When I tried to give him water, it ran right out the hole. Jan Zwart watched me warily, prepared for a fight. But I didn't fight. Too many blows in a row had left me stupefied.

Over the next ten days I nursed that monkey day and night. I sewed its throat closed and fed it sugar water. I rubbed its little muscles. I stroked its fur. I kept it warm and talked to it constantly. It was a creature I had released from bondage, and I wasn't going to let it go without a struggle.

Slowly, very slowly, my gibbon began to eat, and then to crawl about on the bed, and at last to sit up and chatter at me crossly if I was slow with the hourly feedings. At the end of two months he was running with me again in the forest.

But he never recovered his confidence in people. That barracks was a place of terror for him. The only time he would stop trembling when people were close was when all four legs and his tail were wrapped around my arm and his head was hidden in my shirt front.

When news came of a major new drive against the enemy, I asked if someone who could drive would borrow a jeep and take me and my gibbon into the jungle. "I want to let him go and then drive away fast." I said, "Will anyone take me?"

"I'll go."

I turned around. It was Jan Zwart. I held his eye for a long time, but he did not blink.

"All right."

As we drove into the jungle I explained to the monkey why I could no longer keep him. At last we stopped. As I put the little gibbon on the ground his wise little eyes stared into mine with what looked like comprehension. He did not try to jump back into the jeep. As we pulled away he sat there on the ground staring after us until we were out of sight.

The next morning, February 12, 1949, our unit moved out at dawn.

It was a good thing I let the monkey go when I did, for I never got back to camp.

I tried to pretend the same bravado on this mission that I had felt on earlier ones. I wore my yellow straw hat as I had before. I shouted as loud, I cursed, I moved forward with my company day after day, but even my defiance seemed to have deserted me.

And then one morning a bullet smashed through my ankle, and I was out of the war.

It happened so suddenly and —at first—so painlessly that I did not know what had happened. We had walked into an ambush. The enemy was on three sides of us, and many times our strength. Why I was shot in the ankle and not in my straw hat I don't know, but as I was running I suddenly fell. I knew I had not stumbled. But I could not get up. And then I saw that my right combat boot had two holes in it. Blood was coming out of both of them.

AROUND THE GLOBE
Bangladesh

Population: 126.1 million
Location/Size: Southern Asia 55,598 sq. miles
Major Religions: Islam
Level of Persecution: Isolated, but growing

Extreme poverty, political turmoil, and natural disasters have plagued this unhappy land. The Bangladesh government does not openly encourage Islamization, but in recent years its policies have begun to take on an increasingly Islamic stance. Some prominent leaders predict that missionaries may not be granted visas in the future, and some speculate that current missionaries might be forced to leave the country.

Despite the extensive ministry of Christian missionaries, Christians comprise only a small percentage of the population. The church is growing in Bangladesh, but Islam remains the dominant religion, preventing Christians from having substantial influence. Nearly all converts are secret believers who fear for their lives if discovered.

"I'm hit," I called, not excited. It was simply a fact, and I stated it as such.

A buddy rolled me into a ditch out of sight. At last medics came with a stretcher. They put me on it and began moving me out, crouching low in the ditch. I still had on my yellow hat and refused to take it off even when it drew fire. A bullet once went through the crown. I just didn't care.

Hours later, still wearing my yellow straw hat, I was stretched out on an operating table in the evacuation hospital. It took two and a half hours to sew up the foot. I heard the doctors discussing whether or not to amputate. The nurse asked me to take the hat off, but I refused.

"Don't you know what that is?" the doctor asked the nurse. "That's the unit's symbol. These are the boys who got smart and lost their minds."

But I hadn't. That was the final irony, the final failure. I hadn't even managed to get my brains blown out. Just a foot. Somehow in all my furious self-destructiveness I had never considered this possibility. I had always seen myself going out in a blaze of contempt for the whole human farce. But to live—and crippled!— that was the meanest fate of all. My great adventure had failed. Worse, I was twenty years old, and I had discovered that there was no real adventure anywhere in the world.

Imagine This

You and your family have been living in China for several years, trying to help a house church grow. But lately you've encountered more and more persecution from the government. Several of the pastors have been arrested and the church body has begun to scatter. Friends around you are telling you and your family to flee to safety. Do you flee from persecution or stay and face the danger around you?

What Would You Do?

three

The Pebble in the Shell

Whatever happens, conduct yourselves in a manner worthy of the gospel of Christ.

Philippians 1:27

I lay on the hospital bed, my right leg so encased in plaster that I could scarcely move.

At first I had visitors from my unit. But the others were getting themselves killed or wounded too. And after all, life was moving on. The doctors told me I would never walk without a cane. It was better not to think about these things; bit by bit my buddies stopped coming.

But not before they had accomplished two things that were to alter events for me.

The first was to mail a letter I had never intended mailing. It was to Thile. I had picked up an odd habit: whenever I came back from a late night on the town or a battle that left me feeling especially dirty, I would write to Thile. I would put down on the paper all the filthy, disgusting things I had seen and done, things I could never really share with anyone; then I would burn it.

Just before I went into my last battle, I had started such a letter to Thile and had left it unfinished in my barracks bag. Well, after I was hit, a helpful buddy went through my bag for personal items before turning it in. And being a resourceful kind of fellow, he looked up Thile's name in my address book and mailed it. You could see he thought he'd done something extra nice.

"Man!" he teased me when he visited me in the hospital. "I've never seen such a list of names! What do you do, write to every family in Holland that has a pretty girl? It took me half an hour to find the last name that went with Thile. You better be careful, man—this could start another war."

Horror must have shown in my face, because he suddenly jumped out of his chair.

"Gee, Andy, I didn't realize it still hurt so bad. And here I am making lousy jokes. I'll come back when you feel better."

For days I tried to remember what I had written in that wretched letter. As near as I could recall it began:

> Dearest Thile,
>
> I'm so lonely tonight. I wish you were here. I wish I could look right into your eyes as I say all these things and know that you still liked me or at least didn't condemn me.
>
> You wrote me once that I should pray. Well, I haven't. Instead I curse. I know words I never even heard in Holland. I tell filthy jokes. The worse I feel the harder I can get the guys laughing. I'm not the person you think I am. This war used to bother me. But it doesn't any more. When I see dead people I shrug. People we have killed, not just soldiers, but ordinary working men, and women, and children.
>
> I have no desire for God. I don't want to pray. Instead of going to church I go to the pub and drink until I don't give a hoot. . . ."

There was more. Much more and much worse. I lay in agony in that hospital ward, trying to remember just what in my drunken fog I *had* written. Well, there was one friend I could say goodbye to. The trouble was, Thile wasn't just "one friend." She was the best friend I'd ever had—and I had wanted her to be so very much more.

Sri Lanka   ## A Traveler's Story

THE WORD OF ENCOURAGEMENT

I had talked for ten hours on Hebrews and was exhausted. It had been my third day on my feet, and I was very weary. My feet throbbed and my bones ached. I felt sick and wondered how I could go on. So I prayed, "Lord, send me a sign of encouragement, please."

I woke up in the morning because someone poked me awake. I groaned because I could see from the blinds that it was not morning. How I needed sleep.

But it was a young leader who was excited. He had just received his own Scriptures two days before. Then he began to speak to me. I concentrated and then lay back, amazed. He was reciting the entire Book of Hebrews from memory. He had not gone to sleep the past two nights, but by torchlight he had memorized the whole book.

By the time he had finished, I was refreshed as if I had slept for a week. What a sign of encouragement!

I thrashed about on the narrow bed, what part of me could move, trying to shut out the picture of Thile reading that letter.

And as I flung out my arm, my hand fell on the book.

That was the second thing the boys had done for me. They had found my mother's little Bible in the bottom of the dufflebag. It was Jan Zwart who brought it to me, leaving it rather shyly on the bedside table just before he left.

"This book was in your things," he said. "I didn't know if you wanted it."

I said thanks, but I didn't pick it up. I doubt if I ever would have, except for the nuns. The hospital to which I had been assigned was run by Franciscan sisters. I soon fell in love with every one of them. From dawn until midnight they were busy in the wards, cleaning bedpans, swabbing wounds, writing letters for us, laughing, singing. I never once heard them complain.

One day I asked the nun who came to bathe me how it was that she and the other sisters were always so cheerful.

"Why, Andrew, you ought to know the answer to that—a good Dutch boy like you. It's the love of Christ." When she said it, her eyes sparkled, and I knew without question that for her this was

INDONESIA

Diary of a Smuggler

The sound of automatic gunfire ripped through the lunchtime air, sending waves of fear into everyone who heard it. This tension has been ever-present in this southern Maluku island of Indonesia since the Muslim/Christian violence began in January of 1999.

It was the first time I had experienced weapons being fired in anger in the middle of a populated city. The soldier who had been questioning our activities turned on his heels and dashed to his quarters in a house nearby. In less than a minute he had re-emerged, and he ran down the road in the direction of the gunfire.

It was my second day in Ambon, and I witnessed for myself the strange, almost surreal, situation that life in this city had become. Everywhere there were gutted buildings—houses, businesses, banks, churches—many of which had been razed.

I looked across at some distant buildings that were still standing, only to realize that the area in between was now a bomb site, a mess of rubble and twisted metal, where maybe twenty houses once stood.

After the shooting started, we drove away from the trouble, deeper into the Christian enclave. Ambon is divided into sectors, and no Muslim or Christian will venture across the unofficial demarcation lines without risking death.

As we came to the main road, there was panic. Women and girls were desperately clawing at the small yellow buses, hammering on the side for the driver to stop and let them on.

As we slowed down, they tried to board our vehicle. I had never seen such fear in people's faces, people who knew that the sound of automatic guns meant that the army was in action and that death was not far away. One girl was recognized and allowed into our vehicle. The other women managed to board buses.

Strangely, the men were not panicking. Some were directing the traffic. "Go, as fast as you can! Get away from here!" they shouted.

the whole answer: she could have talked all afternoon and said no more.

"But you're teasing me, aren't you?" she said, tapping the well-worn little Bible where it still lay on the bedside table. "You've got the answer right here."

So now when my restless hand struck against it, I picked it up. In the two and a half years since my mother had given it to me, I had never once opened it. But I thought about the sisters, their joy, their tranquility: "You've got the answer right there. . . ." I propped the little book on my chest, and with a desultory finger I moved the pages backward until I got to Genesis 1:1.

I read the story of creation and of the entrance of sin into the world. It did not seem nearly as farfetched to me now as it had when our schoolteacher read aloud a chapter each afternoon, while outside canals waited to be

AROUND THE GLOBE
China

Population: 1.25 billion
Location/Size: Eastern Asia
3,690,045 sq. miles
Major Religions: Folk religions
Atheism
Level of Persecution: Sharp, with sporadic change

In a country marked by population control, economic reform, and religious management, the Chinese government's religious policy consists of control and repression. The Three Self Patriotic Movement (commonly called the Three Self Church) is the closely governed "registered" church, and the government has issued repeated crackdowns on the unregistered house churches. Government persecution of Chinese Christians ranges from fines and Bible confiscation to arrest, mistreatment, and even death of Christian evangelists. Muslims and Buddhists in China also contribute to the resistance toward Christianity in the country.

Despite all the persecution and restrictions facing the Chinese Church, the number of Chinese Christians continues to grow. Some speculate that the Chinese Church could become one of the all-time largest mission-sending bases.

jumped. I read on, skipping whole portions, flipping through to get to the story again. At last, many days later, I came to the New Testament. Lying there encased in autograph-covered plaster, I read straight through the Gospels, catching dimly their terrible significance. Could all this really be true?

While I was in the middle of the Gospel According to St. John, a letter was delivered. The handwriting on the envelope was familiar. Thile! With trembling hands I tore it open.

"Dearest Andy," I read—Dearest! The word I had written so many times to her, but never in a letter intended to be mailed—"Dearest

Andy, I have here a letter from a boy who thinks his heart has turned hard. But his heart is breaking and he has shown a little of that heartbreak to me and I am proud that he has." Then followed—when for sheer relief I could read again—of all things a study outline of the Bible! This was the only place, Thile wrote, where human heartbreak could be understood in terms of God's love.

They were wonderful weeks that followed, weeks of reading the Bible together, on opposite sides of the earth. I filled page after page with questions, and Thile went to her pastor and her library and the depths of her own heart to find the answers.

But as the months passed in the hospital, as my cast came off bit by bit, and I saw the ugly shrunken leg and remembered the joys of running that would never be mine again, I found myself holding on to a hard core of resentment, which was just the opposite of the joy Thile and my Franciscan nuns were talking about.

As soon as I was ambulatory, I started leaving the hospital every evening after dinner to hobble painfully to the nearest pub and drink myself into oblivion. The nuns never spoke about it. At least not directly. But on the day before I was to be shipped home my favorite nun, Sister Patrice, pulled a chair up to my bed.

"Andy, I have a story to tell you. Do you know how natives catch monkeys out in the forest?"

My face lit up at the thought of a monkey story. "No. Tell me."

"Well, you see, the natives know that a monkey will never let go of something he wants even if it means losing his freedom. So here's what they do. They take a coconut and make a hole in one end just big enough for a monkey's paw to slip through. Then they drop a pebble into the hole and wait in the bushes with a net.

"Sooner or later a curious old fellow will come along. He'll pick up that coconut shell and rattle it. He'll peer inside. And then at last he'll slip his paw into the hole and feel around until he gets hold of that pebble. But when he tries to bring it out, he finds that he cannot get the paw through the hole without letting go. And, Andy, that monkey will never let go of what he thinks is a prize. It's the easiest thing in the world to catch a fellow who acts like that."

Sister Patrice got up and put the chair back by the table. She paused for a moment and looked me straight in the eye.

"Are you holding on to something, Andrew? Something that's keeping you from your freedom?"

And then she was gone.

I knew perfectly well what she meant. I also knew her sermon wasn't for me. The next day was going to be a great one on two counts: it was my twenty-first birthday, and it was the day the hospital ship sailed for home. To celebrate, I called together all survivors who could still walk or limp of the company I had come to Indonesia with three years earlier. There were eight of us. We had a grand time. We got roaring, shouting, belligerently drunk.

Imagine This

As the leader of the school Bible club, you've held meetings on campus during lunch and after school. In three years the Bible club has grown to over fifty students! Last week the principal announced that the Bible club is no longer allowed to meet on campus. You have witnessed many people come to Christ through the study, but you know that if you continue meeting you might be suspended from school, maybe even expelled.

What Would You Do?

four

One
Stormy Night

I am not ashamed of the gospel, because it is the power of God for the salvation of everyone who believes.

Romans 1:16

"Andrew!" Geltje ran across the little bridge and threw her arms around me. She turned and shouted behind her. "Maartje! Go find Papa! Tell him Andy is home!"

In an instant the tiny front garden was crowded. Maartje ran to kiss me before hurrying out back to fetch Papa. Ben was there, and his fiancée. They had waited to get married, they told me, until I could be at the wedding. Arie, Geltje's new husband, joined us. My young brother, Cornelius, shook my hand gravely. He couldn't keep his eyes off my cane, and I knew he was wondering just how badly hurt I was. In the midst of hugs and kisses, Papa came shuffling around the house, a bit lame himself now. His brown eyes were moist. "ANDREW BOY! GOOD TO HAVE YOU HOME!" Papa's voice was as loud as ever.

"When you feel like it, Andrew," Maartje said after the first greetings were over, "I'll take you out to Mama's grave."

I said that I would like to go right then. The graveyard was just five hundred yards from our house, but to walk even that distance I had to borrow Papa's bicycle, throw my bad leg over the seat, and push myself along, half riding, half walking.

"It's really pretty bad, then?" Maartje asked.

"They don't think I'll ever walk right again."

The ground had not yet fully settled on Mama's grave. There were fresh flowers in a little red vase stuck into the soil. After a while Maartje and I walked home in silence.

That night, though, after it was dark, I announced that I thought I would try taking a walk. No one offered to go with me: each person knew what I wanted to do. I got out the bicycle again and hopped and rolled up the street. The cemetery lay in full moonlight, and it was easy to find the grave. I sat down on the ground and said my last words to my mother.

"I'm back, Mama." It seemed natural talking to her. "I did read your Bible, Mama. Not at first, but I did read it." There was a long silence.

"Mama, what am I going to do now? I can't walk a hundred yards without the pain making me stop. You know I'm no good at smithing. There's a rehabilitation center at the hospital, but what can I learn there? I feel so useless, Mama. And guilty. Guilty for the life I led out there. Answer me, Mama."

But no answer came. The cold moonlight flowed over me and the grave and the rest of us there in that cemetery: the dead and the half-dead. After half an hour I gave up trying to reach into the past. I wheeled myself home.

Geltje was at the kitchen table sewing. "We talked about where you could sleep, Andrew," she said not looking up. "Do you think you could make it up the ladder?"

I looked at the hole in the ceiling above my head; then I made an assault on that ladder. I climbed one rung at a time, putting my good foot up, hauling the other after it. The pain made perspiration stand out on my forehead, but I turned my head so the others did not see. My old bed was waiting for me, clean sheets turned down invitingly. I lay for a long time staring at the sloping ceiling, and at last—far too close to tears for a twenty-one-

Guatemala   A Traveler's Story

POISONED CHEESE, PROTECTED CHRISTIANS

Once I was preaching in Guatemala in a certain area of strong traditional belief. There was intense pressure against believers—so much so that no evangelical was allowed into the area to preach. We were often attacked with stones and expelled from the areas where we preached, but we kept returning to tell them the Good News of Jesus.

One day my family and I went to hold a worship service there. My wife and our eight children accompanied me. I went on a bit farther to another little village while my family remained at this particular place. A couple known to my wife gave her homemade cheese. She gave a piece to each child, and they all ate. Very shortly thereafter they were all convulsing from stomach pain because the cheese had been intentionally contaminated with rat poison! Even the baby, who was still breast-feeding, became ill.

Meanwhile I was preaching the Gospel in another village, with no idea of what had happened to my family. Stones were often thrown at us while we preached but we were never hit. Suddenly, someone came up and gave us the news that my children were all dying! We took them to the doctor, who said they had been poisoned. That night my house was like a hospital.

Continued

year-old man—I fell asleep wondering what had happened to my great adventure.

The next morning, taking only my cane, I hobbled out to get reacquainted with the village. The people I met were polite, but they also seemed embarrassed. They would look uncomfortably at my uniform, then at my foot. "Did you hurt yourself out there in the East Indies or somewhere?" they asked. Obviously the war was unpopular in Holland—as I suppose lost wars always are. It was clear by now that Indonesia would soon be independent, and so it was easiest to pretend that we'd always intended it that way. Returning veterans only made it difficult.

For an odd reason I could not understand, the house where I was headed was the Whetstras'. I found them at home and accepted with pleasure their invitation to a cup of coffee. We sat around the kitchen table while Mr. Whetstra asked me about

Sukarno and the Communists, and at last a more personal question.

"Did you find that adventure you were looking for, Andy?"

I looked down at the floor. "Not really," I said.

"Well," he said, "we'll just have to keep praying."

"For adventure? For me?" I felt the angry flush climbing up the back of my neck. "Sure. I'm a natural for adventure now. When it calls, I'll limp right out to meet it."

Immediately I was ashamed. What had made me answer like that? I left them, feeling I had spoiled a friendship.

Another person I'd been eager to see was Kees. I found him at home, upstairs in his room, bent over a large pile of books. After a rather strained greeting, I picked up one of the books and was amazed to find that it was a theological treatise.

"What's this?" I asked.

Kees took the book from my hands. "I've decided what I'm going to do with my life."

"You're lucky. What is it?" I asked, hardly believing the answer I knew he was going to give me.

"I want to go into the ministry. Pastor Vanderhoop is helping me."

Kees made me squirm, and I got out of there just as soon as I politely could.

The veterans' hospital at Doorn was an enormous complex of treatment centers, dormitories, and rehabilitation units, but its chief quality was boredom. I disliked the exercises, I loathed the trade school, but the thing I hated most was the occupational therapy.

We had to make vases out of floppy, sticky clay. I just never could get the hang of it. The trick was to put the lump of clay precisely on the center of the whirling wheel, then keep the wheel turning while your fingers worked the glob into a useful shape. Somehow I could never find that center. It was so frustrating that on more than one occasion I flung my hunk of clay against the wall.

On first weekend leave I went to see Thile. On the bus to Gorkum I kept telling myself that she could not be as beautiful as I remembered. And then I limped through the door of her father's shop, and she was. Her eyes were blacker, her skin fairer than

Guatemala

A Traveler's Story
Continued

The following day was a Sunday, and Holy Communion was planned for the worship service. I have no idea how I managed to get through it, because my mind was on my dying family at home. The doctor gave us no hope that they would live.

But guess what? No one died, because the Lord rescued them!

I wanted to take the perpetrators to court, but some pastors persuaded me that forgiveness was the better way, so I left vengeance to the Lord.

Two weeks later my whole family had totally recovered.

We have often returned to preach at that place, and we purchased the exact piece of land on which my family was poisoned. We have built a church on that land at great personal sacrifice, and presently more than one thousand people worship Jesus there regularly.

What about the people who poisoned my family? They have all come to Christ, later confessing that they had been pressured by a traditionalist group to do the awful deed.

About 28 percent of the people there are believers now, and although there are still traditional groups as well as satanic groups in the area, they don't attack or threaten us.

anyone else's in the world. Even with her father looking on, our handshake lingered longer than was necessary.

"Welcome home, Andrew."

Thile's father came around the counter wiping fish scales on his apron. He shook my hand fervently. "Tell me all about the Indies!"

As soon as I could, I took Thile away from the fish shop. We spent the rest of the afternoon sitting and talking on a large capstan on the wharf. I told her about my homecoming, about Geltje's husband and Ben's upcoming marriage; I told her about the rehabilitation center, how I hated working with the clay; and though I knew she would be disappointed, I told her that my religious life had come to a dead standstill.

Thile was staring out across the harbor. "And yet," she said gently, "God hasn't come to a standstill." Suddenly she laughed. "I think you're like one of your own lumps of clay, Andy. God has a plan for you, and He's trying to get you into the center of it, and you keep dodging and slithering away."

She turned her dark eyes on mine. "How do you know? Maybe He wants to make you into something wonderful!"

My eyes fell, and I pretended great interest in the cigarette butt I was crushing against the capstan.

"Like what, for instance?" I said.

Thile looked with distaste at the carpet of cigarette ends that I had spread on the pier around us. "Like an ashtray," she said shortly. "How much do you smoke, Andy?"

It had crept up to three packs a day. "I don't know," I said.

"Well, something's making you cough. I don't think it's good for you."

"You're full of plans for my improvement, aren't you?" I hadn't meant to say that. Why did I always ruin things? It was just that suddenly I felt so far away from everyone—even Thile. She didn't know what it was like having to bite the inside of your lip off for fear the pain in your leg would make you cry; or what it was like to have a woman get up on a public bus so that you could take a seat. I left Thile that afternoon knowing I'd said all the things I didn't mean to and none of the things I did.

It was two months before anyone spoke about religion to me again, and then it wasn't Thile but another pretty girl.

It was midmorning on a rather blustery day in September, 1949. We were sitting on our beds, reading and writing letters after morning exercises, when the nurse came in to announce a visitor. I paid no attention until I heard a low whistle rise to the lips of twenty boys. I glanced up. Standing in the doorway, embarrassed and yet pleased, was a striking blonde.

"Not bad," my next-bed neighbor, Pier, whispered.

"I won't take much of your time," the girl began. "I just want to ask you all to join us at our tent meeting tonight. There will be lots of refreshments. . . ."

"What kind?" someone shouted.

". . . And the bus will leave here at seven o'clock, and I hope you can all come."

China   A Traveler's Story

FAITH AND NO BIBLES

"The believers have great faith. They are hungry and thirsty for God. But their need is great. . . . They have no Bibles at all."

Sooki Wei, the young Chinese woman who spoke these words, was not merely expressing a fact, but a plea for help. Although Christians from all over the northwestern province of Shannxi come to her home looking for Bibles, she must often send them away empty-handed.

Chang and Wu—also from northwestern China—face the same hindrances. "We are like the raven that God sent to feed Elijah," said Wu, describing their Bible distribution work. But like Sooki Wei, soon after they receive a shipment of Scriptures, their supplies are exhausted.

Wang, an itinerant evangelist from the central province of Henan, is faced with a similar problem. In 1994, his evangelistic group in southern Henan claimed to have baptized some twenty thousand new converts. According to Wang, another ten evangelism groups from his house-church movement, which are scattered throughout the province, reported similar numbers of conversions.

Yet Wang's group only received two thousand New Testaments last year, falling far short of his group's actual need for effectively discipling this new body of young Christians.

Travel to Sichuan, Gansu, Jilin, or Liunan provinces, and you will invariably hear the same story. The church in China continues to grow rapidly, and the surge of new Christians is outstripping the number of Bibles delivered and distributed to the Chinese church each year.

The boys burst into wild, exaggerated applause with shouts of "Encore! Encore!" as the girl retreated. But when seven o'clock came, every one of us was waiting in the foyer, clean scrubbed, hair stiff with brilliantine. Pier and I were first in line. We were happy, not only because of the night away from the hospital but also because Pier had slipped down to the village and come back with our answer to the question of what refreshments would be served. By the time the bus arrived at the tent grounds, the bottle was half empty. We took seats in the extreme rear of the tent and finished the rest of it.

Most of the boys thought our antics were funny. The people holding the revival service did not. Finally, a funny-looking man with a thin face and deep-set eyes—the kind of person I disliked on sight—took the podium and announced that there were two people in the congregation who were bound by powers they couldn't control.

And then, closing his eyes, he began a long impassioned prayer for the health of our immortal souls. We choked back our laughter till our throats ached from the effort. But when at last, in a pious singsong, he called us "our brethren over whom foreign spirits have gained influence," we could hold it in no longer. We howled, we yelped, we whooped with laughter. Seeing that further prayer was impossible, the man told the choir to sing. The song they chose was "Let My People Go."

Soon the whole congregation was joining in on the refrain. "Let my people go. . . ." Again and again the words swelled up under the big tent.

The meeting ended, the vets trooped out to the waiting bus. But still inside my head the words sang on. "Let them go . . . let me go. . . ."

It is foolish, of course, to suggest that a simple song—a song overheard, not even sung—could become a prayer, and that God would honor it.

And yet the very next day, during dreaded occupational class, a strange thing happened.

In spite of the fact that I had a king-sized hangover, I could do nothing wrong at my wheel. I sat down and slapped a hunk of gray clay on the wheel, then moved it toward the center while my foot worked slowly. A vase rose under my fingers.

Incredulous, I threw another glob of clay onto the wheel. Once again the shape rose effortlessly, matching the form I held in my mind.

Later that day something even more unsettling happened. During afternoon rest period I was flipping through the magazines provided for us, when all at once I reached for the Bible that I kept on my nightstand as a memento of my mother. I had not read it since I'd been back in Holland. But that afternoon I suddenly started reading, and to my astonishment I understood it. All the passages that had seemed so puzzling when I struggled

IRAN

Diary of a Smuggler

It was my first time in Iran, and I was both shocked and impressed. The fact that all women wore scarves, hijaab, and chadors did not bother me so much. What shocked me, however, was the almost total dissatisfaction and discontent of all the women we talked to. "If it were up to us, we wouldn't wear this outfit, but we have to. We're being watched. We have to conform. But after more than twenty years of this regime, we'd love to see a change!"

Conform, don't draw attention to yourself, don't stick out your neck, wait and see what happens—and yes, hope quietly for change. It seems to be the motto for many who through the years have been intimidated into quiet resignation and silence, as if a black blanket had covered the soul of the people.

The new generation, however, is getting restless, feels isolated from the rest of the world, and is desperately looking for alternatives. Many of them would like to leave the country and join relatives or friends in the West, if only they'd get the permission.

I thought about the five young men I had met the previous evening. Once a week they get together in secret to pray and share and study the Word. All of them come from Islamic families. Some of the men have been baptized already; for others the opportunity has not come yet—it's too risky for all parties involved. Their sparkling eyes, open faces, and eager desire to know more about God's Word warmed my heart. What a privilege to share with them that many in the Lord's family pray specifically for them, even without knowing their names. It brought a great smile to their faces. All of them urgently asked for more materials for Bible study; they wanted to have more training. Once a week they met for Bible study, but they weren't satisfied yet. Their hunger for God's Word was remarkable.

through them before read now like a fast-paced action yarn. I read straight through the rest period and had to be called a second time for afternoon tea.

I was still devouring the Bible a week later when the hospital told me I could begin going home for long weekends. I read there, too, stretched out hour on end on my bed in the attic. Geltje would bring me soup, look at me to see if I was all right, then go back downstairs without saying a word.

What was happening to me?

And then the church-going began. I, who never went to church, started now to attend with such regularity that the whole village noticed it: not only Sunday morning, but Sunday evening and Wednesday mid-week service as well. In November, 1949, I was formally mustered out of the army. With part of my separation pay I bought myself a sleek new bicycle and learned to pedal by thrusting with the good leg, coasting with the bad. I still could not take a step without pain, but with wheels beneath me it no longer mattered so much. Now I started attending church services in neighboring towns as well. On Mondays I went to a Salvation Army meeting in Alkmaar. On Tuesdays I pedaled all the way to Amsterdam to a Baptist service. I found a service somewhere every night in the week. At each one I took careful notes on what the preacher said, and then I spent the following morning looking up passages in the Bible to see if all the things he said were really there.

"Andrew!" Maartje came up the ladder, balancing a cup of tea. "Andrew, can I be frank with you?"

I sat up. "Of course, Maartje."

AROUND THE GLOBE
Colombia

Population: 40 million
Location/Size: Northern South America
440,831 sq. miles
Major Religions: Christianity/Catholicism
Level of Persecution: Isolated, static

Coffee and cocaine rank as Colombia's two best-known products, and crime and warfare pervade everyday Colombian life. The Church has suffered greatly at the hands of the drug trade, with many Christians martyred for their stand against crime and violence.

Guerrilla groups, drug cartels, corrupt government bodies, and traditional religions continually test the faith of new believers. Converts are branded as traitors and have at times been marked for assassination; missionaries endure threats, kidnapping, and worse.

Although the Church continues to grow and Christianity has a firm position in society, it has so far failed to witness an end to the severe violence and crime that permeate the land.

"It's just that we're worried about the amount of time you're spending up here all alone. Always reading the Bible. And going to church every night. It isn't natural. What's happened to you, Andy?"

I smiled. "I wish I knew!"

"We can't help worrying, Andy. Papa's worried too. He says—" She stopped as though wondering how much to say. "Papa says it's shell shock." And with that she backed swiftly down the ladder.

I thought about what she'd said. Was I in danger of becoming a religious fanatic? I had heard of people who lost their minds and went around quoting Scriptures at everyone. Was I going to get like that?

And still my strange compulsion swept me on, biking from church to church, studying, listening, absorbing. Pier wrote me once, asking me to meet him for a good old-fashioned drinkfest, but I didn't answer the letter. I intended to, but I found it weeks later stuck in the back of a biography of Hudson Taylor.

And on the other hand I began spending a lot of time with Kees, and with my old schoolteacher, Miss Meekle, and with the Whetstras, and of course, more than ever with Thile. Every week I cycled down to Gorkum to talk over with Thile the things I was reading and hearing. It was too cold now to sit out on the wharf. So we tended the fish shop and, between customers, talked.

At first Thile was thrilled about the things that were happening to me, but as the weeks stretched into months and I continued my hot-paced rounds of churches, she began to be alarmed. "You don't want to burn yourself out, Andy," she'd say. "Don't you think you ought to pace yourself a bit? Read some different kind of books. Go to the movies now and then."

I couldn't bother. Nothing in the world interested me except the incredible voyage of discovery on which I had set out. From time to time, also, Thile asked if I had found a job. This was a more serious problem. Obviously until I had a job I couldn't even suggest to Thile the dream I had had so long for her and me. I set out job-hunting in earnest.

Before I found one, though, a fragile little event occurred that changed my life far more radically than the bullet that had torn through bone and muscle a year before. It was a stormy night in the dead of winter, 1950. I was in bed. The sleet blew across the polders as it can only blow in Holland in mid-January. I pulled the covers higher under my chin, knowing that outside the sleet was driving almost parallel to the ground. There were many voices in that wind. I heard Sister Patrice. "The monkey will never let go. . . ." I heard the singing under the big tent. "Let my people go. . . ."

What was it I was hanging on to? What was it that was hanging on to me? What was standing between me and freedom?

The rest of the house was asleep. I lay on my back with my hands under my head staring at the darkened ceiling and all at once, very quietly, I let go of my ego. With a new note in the wind yelling at me not to be a fool, I turned myself over to God— lock, stock, and adventure. There wasn't much faith in my prayer. I just said, "Lord, if You will show me the way, I will follow You. Amen."

It was as simple as that.

Imagine This

Living as a Christian in Colombia with your family, you are approached by armed guerrilla rebels. They tell you that your family must plant a drug crop in one year or you will all be killed. You believe they are serious because you have witnessed their aggressive attacks in the past. Do you participate with the drug trafficking and align yourself with the guerrillas? Do you flee the area, leaving behind other Christian brothers and sisters?

What Would You Do?

five

The Step of Yes

> Trust in the LORD with all your
> heart and lean not on your own
> understanding; in all your ways
> acknowledge him, and he will make your
> paths straight.
>
> Proverbs 3:5—6

I went to sleep that night with the sounds of the winter storm yelling at me. Curiously enough, although I had just thrown away every shred of self-defense, I felt secure in a way I had never before known.

In the morning I woke up with such joy welling in me that I had to tell someone. I couldn't tell my family; they were worried enough about me already. That left the Whetstras and Kees.

The Whetstras understood right away. "Praise the Lord!" Philip Whetstra shouted.

The phrase made me uncomfortable, but the tone of his voice warmed my heart. The Whetstras did not seem to think I had done anything strange or abnormal. They used words like "born again," but in spite of the odd language, I got the idea that the step I had taken was along a well-traveled road.

Kees also, when I told him, recognized the experience at once. He was sitting at his desk, surrounded by his inevitable books. He gave me a scholarly look. "There's a name for what's happened to you," he said, tapping a particularly forbidding-looking volume. "It's called a crisis conversion. I'll be interested, Andrew, to see if a response-in-depth follows it."

To my surprise, though, when I went to see Thile, she did not seem as pleased as the others. Wasn't this the kind of thing people did at mass rallies? she asked.

Poor Thile, she was about to have another shock worse than the first. A few weeks later—in the early spring of 1950—I went to Amsterdam with Kees to hear a well-known Dutch evangelist, Arne Donker. Toward the end of his sermon, Pastor Donker interrupted himself.

"Friends," he said, "I've had the feeling all night that something very special is going to happen at this meeting. Someone out there in the audience wants to give himself to the mission field."

Theatrics, I thought. He's got someone planted out here who's going to jump up now and run forward and add a little emotion to the evening. But Mr. Donker continued to peer out over the audience.

The silence in the meeting hall under his stare grew oppressive. Kees felt it too. "I hate this sort of thing," he whispered. "Let's get out of here!"

We edged our way to the end of our row. Heads turned eagerly. We both sat down.

"Well," said Mr. Donker at last, "God knows who it is out there. He knows the person for whom is waiting a life of perpetual risk and danger. I think probably it's a young person. A young man."

Now all over the hall people were turning and looking around as if to spot whom the preacher meant. And then, in obedience to some summons I shall never understand, both Kees and I were on our feet.

"Ah, yes," the preacher said. "There you are. Two young men! Splendid! Will you boys come forward?"

With a sigh, Kees and I walked down the long aisle to the front of the meeting hall, where we knelt, as if in a dream, to hear Mr. Donker say a prayer over us. As he prayed, all I could think of was what Thile would say. "Really, Andrew!" She would be shocked and hurt. "You *are* going down the sawdust trail, aren't you?"

But worse was still to come. After he had finished his prayer, the preacher told Kees and me that he wanted to see us after the service. Reluctantly, and half suspecting him of being a hypnotist, we stayed behind. When the hall was empty, Mr. Donker asked us our names.

"Andrew and Kees," he repeated. "Well boys, are you ready for your first assignment?" Before we had a chance to protest, the preacher went on.

"Good! I want you to go back to your own hometowns—where do you come from, boys?"

"Witte."

"Both from Witte? Excellent! I want you to go back to Witte and hold an open-air meeting in front of the burgomaster's house. You'll be following the biblical pattern—Jesus told the disciples to spread the good news 'beginning at Jerusalem.' They had to start their preaching in their own backyard. . . ."

The words exploded one by one in my mind like mortar shells. Did this man know what he was asking?

"Oh, I'll be with you, boys!" Mr. Donker went on. "Nothing to be alarmed about. It's all in getting used to it. I'll speak first. . . ."

I was barely listening. Instead, I was remembering how much I disliked street preachers of any stripe. More words drifted into my conscious.

". . . So we have a date, then. Saturday afternoon in Witte."

"Yes, sir," I said, intending to say no.

"And you, son?" Mr. Donker asked Kees.

"Yes, sir."

Kees and I rode the bus home in stunned silence, each secretly blaming the other for having got us into such a spot.

Not a soul in Witte missed that meeting. Even the town dogs turned out for the show. We stood with the evangelist on a little platform made of boxes and looked out over a sea of familiar faces. Some were laughing outright, some only grinning. A few—like the Whetstras and Miss Meekle—nodded encouragement.

The next half hour was a nightmare. I don't remember a thing that Kees and Mr. Donker said. I only remember the moment when

China | A Traveler's Story

TORTURED INTO CHRIST

One night last October I was visiting the house church of my friend. I guess you could say I was looking for God. My girlfriend had run off with a richer man, and my heart was full of schemes of revenge, some of which were quite violent.

But at my workplace I was befriended by a man who invited me to a religious meeting.

At the meeting there were about fifty people present. A real mixture. Some looked quite wealthy and well dressed. I could not help noticing there were many attractive young women there also. They were singing and clapping without fear. And then a man who must have been about forty began to speak from the Bible. I remember him talking about prayer and the words "ask, seek, knock."

Then the police burst in.

There were seven officers, and they went to the man who was speaking. "This is an illegal meeting," they declared. "You are all under arrest."

The police had a swagger about them. Clearly they thought they had complete control over these people's lives. My luck was really out. They picked five of us (including me), plus the pastor, and hauled us down to the station.

My friend tried to intervene on my behalf, saying, "He is not one of us." But they paid no attention. As we were swaying against each other in the van, he leaned over and said, "If you get into real trouble, call on Jesus and He will help."

At the station we were all placed in separate rooms. "I'm not a Christian," I said to the two interrogators. They just kept smoking and replied, "Okay, have it your way, but you are a criminal. Besides, we will know soon enough if you really are a Christian or not."

Continued

Mr. Donker turned toward me and waited. I stepped forward, and a terrifying silence rose to meet me. Another step and I was at the edge of the platform and glad for the loose Dutch trousers that hid my knocking knees.

I couldn't remember a thing I had planned to say. So all I could do was tell about the way I felt dirty and guilty coming home from Indonesia. And how I had carried around the burden of what I was and what I wanted out of life, until one night during a storm I laid it down. And I told them how free I had felt ever since—that is, until Mr. Donker here had trapped me into saying I wanted to become a missionary.

A Traveler's Story
Continued

I asked them, "How do you mean?"

He said simply, "When we beat Christians up, they don't curse like the others." Then his face changed, and he barked orders at me. "Stand up, feet together, arms straight out by your sides. Put your knees together and half crouch."

I saw what they were up to. They were putting me in the crucifix position. After five minutes, I was shaking with the effort of holding my arms at right angles to my torso, and my thighs were giving way, too, in the crouch position.

One of the interrogators began burning his cigarette into the palms of my hands. I was so shocked I screamed and collapsed on the floor. At once they both pounced on me, kicking me with their shoes. I could hear the crunch of ribs breaking.

The amazing thing was, at that moment, I prayed, "Jesus, if you are God, get me through this." Immediately it was as if my body was a sluice for cool water. And with the coolness came a rush of compassion for my interrogators. To be honest, I said to myself, "What a stupid thing to feel for these horrid men who are beating me." I knew this was the force of Jesus within me, but it did not make sense.

The torture was not over. They strung me up by the thumbs, and that was awful because both of them dislocated.

In the morning they let me go with a warning. "Don't you dare go to a Christian meeting again." But I said to them, "Before I go, I want to thank you."

They echoed, mystified, "Thank us?"

I said, "Thank you for making me a Christian. Your cruelty forced me to call on Jesus, and to my surprise, He came into me and gave me compassion. I see you not as powerful men, but as sad sadists fighting a losing battle for your self-respect."

They were stunned. Again, so was I. Who was this speaking through me? It was as if a new spirit of boldness as well as love was flowing through me.

Now I am free. I only want to do one thing—tell others about Christ. I intend to get some Bible training, and then I will depart for another province to spread the Word. All China must hear of Jesus. If I live to be eighty, then I have fifty-five years left to spread His Gospel. That's not too long to reach the whole country.

I expect I will be tortured again. But since I was tortured into Christ, I can, with His help, endure being tortured for Christ!

"But you know," I said to my hometown, "I might surprise him at that. . . ."

I almost dreaded my next date with Thile. It's hard to tell the girl you hope will marry you that you've suddenly decided to be a missionary. What kind of a life was that to offer her? Hard work, little pay, maybe disagreeable living conditions in some far-off place.

How could I even suggest such a life to her, unless she herself were heart and soul committed to the idea as well?

And so the following week I started my campaign to make a missionary out of Thile. I told her about the moment at the meeting when the conviction had hit me and how sure I had been since of God's hand in this choice.

Strangely enough, the hardest thing for Thile to accept seemed to be not the rigors of mission life, but the fact that I had walked forward in front of all those people.

"One place I agree with Mr. Donker, though," she said. "The place to start any ministry is at home. Why don't you get a job right around Witte and consider that your mission field at first? You'll discover quickly enough whether or not you're meant to be a missionary."

This made sense. The largest industry anywhere near Witte was the huge Ringers' chocolate factory in Alkmaar. Geltje's husband, Arie, worked there, and when I asked him, he said he would put in a good word for me with the hiring office.

The night before I biked to Alkmaar to apply for a job, I had a wonderful dream. The factory was full of despondent, unhappy people who noticed at once that I had something different. They crowded around me, demanding my secret. When I told them, truth dawned on their faces. Together we knelt. . . .

I was really sorry when I had to wake up.

I sat on the wooden bench outside the hiring office at Ringers'. The cloying smell of chocolate hung in the air, heavy and unappealing.

"Next!"

I walked through the door as briskly as I could; I had left my cane at home. Walking was still painful for me but—except when I was tired—I had learned to step on the injured ankle without limping. The personnel director was scowling at the application form in front of him.

"Medical discharge," he read aloud. He looked at me suspiciously. "What's the matter with you?"

"Nothing," I said, feeling the blood rush to my face. "I can do anything anyone here can do."

"Touchy, aren't you?"

But he gave me a job. I was to count the boxes at the end of one of the packaging assemblies, then wheel them to the shipping room. A slack-faced boy led me through a maze of corridors and stairways and at last pushed open the door to an enormous assembly room where perhaps two hundred girls were ranged around a dozen conveyer belts. He left me at one of them.

"Girls, this is Andrew. Have fun!"

To my astonishment, a chorus of whistles greeted this introduction. Then, shouted suggestions. "Hey, Ruthie, how would you like him?" "Can't tell by looking." Then followed perversion and bathroom talk. Even my years in the army had not prepared me for the language I heard that morning.

The leader of the foul wisecracking, I discovered, was a girl named Greetje. Her favorite subject was sodomy: she speculated aloud on which animal would find a soul mate in me. I was grateful when my cart was full and I could escape for a few moments to what seemed like the sanctuary of male company in the shipping room.

Too soon, it was unloaded and I had to run the gamut of whistles in the big room again. "This may be a mission field, Lord," I thought as I took the receipt for the boxes to the timekeeper's window in the center of the room. "But it's not mine. I'll never learn to talk to these girls. They'd take anything I said and twist it around until——"

I stopped. For smiling at me through the glass partition of the timekeeper's booth were the warmest eyes I had ever seen. They were brown. No, they were green. And she was very young. Blonde, slender, she couldn't have been out of her teens, and she was handling the most responsible job on the floor: the work orders and finished-work receipts. As I handed mine through the window, her smile broke into a laugh.

"Don't mind them," she said gently. "This is the treatment they give every newcomer. In a day or two it'll be someone else."

My heart flooded with gratitude.

She handed me a new shipping order from the pile in front of her, but still I stood there, staring at her. In a room where the rest of the women wore enough powder and rouge to make up a circus, here was a girl without a trace of makeup. Only her own fresh young coloring set off those eyes that were never the same shade twice.

The more I looked at her, the more I was sure I had seen her before. But the question would sound like a cliché. Reluctantly, I went back to the assembly line.

The hours seemed to drag. By the end of the long day on my feet, every step on my ankle was agony. Try as I would, I began to limp. Greetje spotted it at once.

"What's the matter, Andy?" she shrieked. "You fall out of bed?"

"East Indies," I said, hoping to shut her up.

Greetje's yelp of triumph could be heard all over the room. "We got a war hero, girls! Is it true what they say about Sukarno, Andy? Does he like them very young?"

It was the worst mistake I could have made. For days—long after I would have lost the value of novelty for them—the girls questioned me about what they imagined to be the exotic life of the East.

More than once I would have quit the job in sheer boredom at their one-track conversation—except for the smiling eyes behind the glass partition. I took to going there even when I had no receipt to deliver. Sometimes along with a receipt I'd slip a note of my own: "You're looking very nice today," or "Half an hour ago you frowned. What was the matter!" I kept wondering how she felt about the talk she overheard, and what she was doing in a place like this anyhow. And always, I was haunted by the feeling that I knew her.

I worked at the factory a month before I got up courage to tell her, "I'm worried about you. You're too young and too pretty to be working with this crowd."

The girl threw back her head and laughed. "Why, Grampa!" she said. "What old-fashioned ideas you have! Actually"—she leaned close to the little window—"they're not a bad crowd. Most of them just need friends, and they don't know any other way to get them."

She looked at me as though wondering whether to confide in me. "You see," she said softly, "I'm a Christian. That's why I came to work here."

I gaped in astonishment at my fellow missionary. And all at once I remembered where I had seen this face before. The veterans' hospital! This was the girl who had invited us to the tent meeting! And that was the place where. . . .

I stumbled over my words in my eagerness to tell her all that had happened, and how I had come here to Ringers' on the same mission as her own. Her name, she told me, was Corrie van Dam. And from that day on, Corrie and I were a team. My job of collecting the finished boxes took me up and down the rows of packagers, where I could keep a lookout for anyone with problems. I would pass the word to Corrie, who could speak to the girl in private when she came to the window for her next work order.

In this way we eventually found a small nucleus of people interested in the same things we were. The British evangelist Sidney Wilson was holding "youth weekends" in Holland then, and we started attending these.

One of the first people to come with us was a blind and badly crippled girl, who worked on the same belt with Greetje. Amy read Braille and showed me how she punched out letters to the other blind people with a little hand Braille-writer. I bought one too, and a copy of the Braille alphabet, and would leave Braille notes on the moving belt of chocolates for Amy's quick fingers to find.

Of course, this was too much for Greetje to leave alone.

"Amy!" she would bellow down the row of working girls. "How much is he offering this time?"

For a long time Amy took the jibes in good humor. But one day I came back from the shipping room to see her blinking her milky eyes as though to keep back tears.

"I can see," Greetje was booming, "how you might not be sure."

She caught sight of me and grinned maliciously. "All men are alike in the dark, eh, Amy?" she shouted.

I stopped still in the doorway. I had prayed that morning, as I always did while biking to work, that God would tell me what to say to people. The order I seemed to be getting now was so unexpected I could hardly believe it, and yet so clear that I obeyed without thinking.

"Greetje," I called across the room, "shut up. And shut up for good!"

Greetje was so startled, her jaw literally dropped open. I was startled myself. But I had to follow up or lose the initiative.

"Greetje," I called, still shouting across the great hall, "the bus leaves for the conference center at nine Saturday morning. I want you to be on board."

"All right."

Her answer came just that quickly. I waited to see if a joke was coming, but I noticed that now it was Greetje who was blinking her eyes. As I went back to loading boxes, I noticed that the entire room was strangely silent. Everyone was a little awed at what was happening.

And on Saturday, Greetje was aboard the bus. That surprised me most of all. She was her old self, though, and let us know that she was coming only to find out what really went on after the lights went off.

At the conference grounds Greetje stayed very much to herself. During the meetings she kept up a steady stream of sotto voce comments as people told how God was making a difference in their lives. In between meetings Greetje read a romance magazine.

Sunday afternoon the bus brought us back to Alkmaar, where I had left my bicycle at the depot. Greetje lived in the next town to Witte. I wondered what my chances were of persuading her to ride along with me on the back of my bike. It would be a wonderful opportunity to have her uninterrupted attention.

"Can I give you a lift home, Greetje? Save you the bus fare?"

Greetje pursed her lips, and I could tell she was weighing the disadvantage of having to ride with me against the price of the bus ticket. Finally, she shrugged and climbed onto the little jump seat at the rear of my bike. I gave Corrie a wink and pushed off.

As soon as we were out in the country, I intended to face Greetje with her need for God. But to my astonishment, the clear command that came this time was: "Not one word about religion. Just admire the scenery."

Ethiopia | A Traveler's Story

"I SLEPT UNDER A TREE FOR THREE MONTHS"

The moment I accepted Christ as my personal Savior, people told my parents that their son had changed his religion. They called me and we discussed my conversion. Finally they gave me a choice: "Choose between us and Jesus." I decided to follow Jesus. My parents, brothers, and sisters started beating me with sticks and finally chased me out of the house. For three months I slept under a tree. Finally some Christians found out that I slept in the open air, and they gave me some bread. For the last five years I've been living like this, traveling from one Christian's house to the next, sleeping a few nights here and a few nights there.

When my parents expelled me from home, I was in ninth grade, but with the assistance of other Christians, I have completed twelfth grade. While I was attending school I was not able to buy clothes, textbooks, etc. The university doesn't want to accept me because my results are not up to standard. So I am just simply sitting and waiting. If I were to go back to my family, they would tell me to deny Jesus.

Again I could scarcely believe I was hearing correctly. But I obeyed. During the entire trip I did not say a word to my captive about religion. Instead, I talked about the tulip fields we were passing and discovered that she too had eaten tulip bulbs during the war. When we got to her street, I actually got a smile from her.

Next day at the factory Corrie met me with shining eyes. "What on earth did you say to Greetje? Something terrific must have happened!"

"How do you mean? I didn't say a word."

But sure enough, all morning long Greetje didn't crack a dirty joke. Once Amy dropped a box of chocolates. It was Greetje who knelt down and retrieved the pieces. At lunchtime she plunked her tray down beside mine.

"Can I sit with you?"

"Of course," I said.

"You know what I thought?" Greetje began. "I thought you would high-pressure me into 'making a decision for Christ,' like they said at those meetings. I wasn't going to listen. Then you didn't say a word. Now . . . don't laugh, will you?"

"Of course not."

"I began to wonder, 'Does Andrew think I've gone so far there's no turning back? Is that why he doesn't bother talking to me?' And then I began to wonder if maybe I *had* gone too far. Would God still listen if I said I was sorry? Would He let me too start all over again, like those kids claimed? Anyhow, I asked Him to. It was a pretty funny prayer, but I meant it. And, Andy, I began to cry. I cried almost all night, but this morning I feel great."

It was the first conversion I had ever watched. Overnight Greetje was a changed person. Or rather she was the same person with a tremendous addition. She was still a leader, she still talked all the time—but what a difference. When Greetje stopped telling smutty stories, many of the other girls stopped too. A prayer cell was started in the factory, with Greetje in charge of attendance. If someone's child was sick, if a husband was out of work, Greetje found out about it, and woe to the worker who didn't put some money in the hat. The change in this girl was complete and it was permanent. Night after night in my loft bed back in Witte, I went to sleep thanking God for letting me have a part in this transformation. That factory was a different place. And it all came about through obedience.

One day when I pedaled through the main gate, I had a surprise waiting for me.

"Mr. Ringers wants to see you," Corrie said.

"Mr. Ringers!" I must be in real trouble—maybe he'd found out I was pushing religion on company time. A secretary held open the door to the president's private office. Mr. Ringers was sitting in an enormous leather armchair and waved me into another. I sat down on the edge of the cushion.

"Andrew," said Mr. Ringers, "do you remember the psychological tests we finished about two weeks ago?"

"Yes, sir."

"The tests show that you have a rather exceptional I.Q."

I had no idea what an "I.Q." was, but since he was smiling, I smiled too.

"We have decided," he went on, "to put you into our management training course. I want you to take two weeks off. Walk through the factory and examine every job you see. When you find one you like, let me know—we'll train you for it."

When at last I found my voice, I said, "I already know the job I'd like. I'd like to be that man who talked to me after I finished the tests."

"A job analyst," said Mr. Ringers. His keen eyes bored into mine. "And I suppose," he said, "that while discussing jobs, you wouldn't object if the subject of religion came up?"

I felt my face turning scarlet.

"Oh, yes," he said. "We know about the proselytizing you've been doing upstairs. And I might add that I consider your kind of work considerably more important than manufacturing chocolates."

He smiled at the relief on my face. "I don't know any reason, Andrew, why you can't do both. If you can help me to run a better factory while getting recruits for God's kingdom, why I'll be satisfied."

Thile was ecstatic at my new job. She hoped I would find it so interesting that I would forget the missionary idea. But I couldn't. Although I loved the new work, I felt more and more persuaded that I was being called to something else. In return for my analyst's training I agreed to stay on at Ringers' two years. When that time was up, I knew I would have to leave.

Seeing that my mind was made up, Thile stopped arguing and pitched in to help me. Her own church was the Dutch Reformed, which had many overseas missions. She wrote to each of them, asking what the qualifications were for serving. From them, all the same answer came back: ordination was the first step to being a missionary.

But when I wrote to the Dutch Reformed seminary, I discovered that making up the schooling I had missed during the war and then studying theology would take twelve years. Twelve years! My heart sank at the news. Nevertheless, I enrolled at once in some correspondence courses.

Books were the greatest problem. I had no savings of any kind. And now, with Greetje in charge of good works at the factory, any guilders that Geltje did not need for the household were swiftly put to good use.

I was pondering the problem over a cigarette one evening when it occurred to me that I was holding the answer in my hand. I looked at the slender white tube with the smoke curling pleasantly from its tip. How much did I spend for these things every week? I figured it up and was enlightened. Enough for a book, every week of the year. Enough to own the volumes I was reading now a few pages at a time in the rear of a bookstore.

It wasn't easy, stopping. I guess I liked to smoke as much as any Dutchman, which is a great deal indeed. But I did stop, and gradually, on the little table between Cornelius' bed and mine, a library began to grow. A German grammar, an English grammar, a volume of church history, a Bible commentary. They were the first books, besides the Bible and the hymnbook, that anyone in our family had ever owned. For two years I spent every spare moment reading.

When Miss Meekle learned what I was doing, she offered to coach me in English, and I gratefully accepted. She was a wonderful teacher: kind when I was discouraged, enthusiastic when my own resolve weakened. If her pronunciation seemed a bit different from the English I heard occasionally on Mama's wireless, I put it down to faulty electronics and carefully imitated Miss Meekle.

But though Miss Meekle was pleased that I was completing my education, she was less sure about seminary. "Do you really think you need to be ordained in order to help people?" she would say. "You're twenty-four years old. At this rate you'll be in your mid-thirties before you even begin. Surely there's useful work for laymen in the missions? I'm not telling you, Andrew. I'm just asking the question."

And of course it was the question I asked myself almost every day. One weekend I was discussing it with Sidney Wilson. Enough of us now attended his weekends from Ringers' that we would reserve the whole conference center for ourselves. As I grumbled about the delays and formalities of education, he began to laugh.

"You talk like the people at WEC," he said.

"WEC?"

"Worldwide Evangelization Crusade," he said. "It's an English group that trains missionaries to go out to parts of the world where the churches don't have programs. They feel like you about waiting."

Church missions, he explained, were run on budgets. A mission board waited until it had the money, or at least knew where it was coming from, before they sent a man out. Not WEC. If they thought God wanted a man in a certain place, they sent him there and trusted God to worry about the details.

"Same with the men they send," Mr. Wilson went on. "If they think a man has a genuine call and a deep enough commitment, they don't care if he hasn't a degree to his name. They train him at their own school for two years and then send him out."

That part appealed to me, but I wasn't so sure about the lack of financing. I had known several people who "trusted God" for their needs, but most of them were really beggars. They didn't come right out and ask for money; they hinted at it. They were known around Witte as "the hint missionaries," and it was said of them that they didn't live by Faith, but by Feelers. No, what I had seen of them was grubby and undignified. If Christ were a King and these were His Ambassadors, it surely did not speak well of the state of His exchequer.

Surprisingly, it was Kees—who had been studying for ordination for so many years—who was the most interested when I told him what Mr. Wilson had said. "Carry neither purse, nor script, nor shoes," Kees quoted. "Theologically that's very sound. I'd like to know more about the WEC."

And a few months later we had a chance to. Sidney Wilson phoned me one day at Ringers' to say that a man from WEC headquarters was visiting in Haarlem.

"His name is Johnson, Andy. Why don't you go see him—while he's here?"

So the next weekend I biked down to Haarlem. It was just as I thought. Mr. Johnson was thin and gaunt, and his clothes shrieked of missionary barrels.

But when he talked about the work the mission was doing all over the world, his sallow face came alive. It was obvious that he

VIETNAM

Diary of a Smuggler

On a recent Sunday morning I was "smuggled" into a youth meeting on the back of a motorbike. I found myself in a crowded room with fifty young men and women. A piano, a set of drums, a guitar, and tambourines played Christian choruses you'd know, including some sung in English and projected on the wall.

I leaned over to the pastor and asked, "Isn't it dangerous for you to sing so loudly in such a crowded community?"

He replied, "Because the people in this area know our good works, they leave us alone."

Continued

gave the credit for all accomplishments to the WEC training school up in Glasgow, Scotland, and to its teachers, most of whom served without pay. They included doctors of theology and Biblical exegesis and other academic subjects, but on the faculty were also master bricklayers and plumbers and electricians, for these students were being trained to start missions where none existed. And even this, he said, was not the real emphasis. The true aim of the school was a simple one: to turn out the best Christians these students were capable of being.

I went to see Kees as soon as I got back to Witte. Together we took a bike ride across the polders. Kees's questions were sharp and practical, the kind he would be asking if he planned to drop everything and enroll tomorrow. How much were the fees? When did the next session begin? What were the language requirements? I had not been interested enough to ask. So I gave Kees the address of the WEC headquarters in London and waited for the news I knew I would be hearing. Sure enough, a few days later Kees told me he had made application for admission to the Glasgow school.

Because of his qualifications, Kees was accepted almost at once. I would get home from Ringers' to find long, glowing letters from Glasgow, describing his life there, the courses he was taking, the discoveries in Christian living he was making. I had already been at the factory longer than the two years I had promised Mr. Ringers when he trained me for the new job. Surely this WEC school was the right place for me too.

And still I hung back. I seemed to have so many points against me. I didn't have Kees's learning. And hide it though I might from others, I had a crippled ankle. How could I be a missionary if I couldn't even walk a city block without pain!

Did I really intend to be a missionary—or was it only a romantic dream with which I indulged myself? I had often heard Sidney Wilson speak of "praying through." He meant by this, sticking with a prayer until he got an answer. Well, I was going to try it. One Sunday afternoon in September, 1952, I went out on to the polders where I could pray aloud without being embarrassed. I sat on the edge of a canal and began talking to God casually, as I might have talked with Thile. I prayed right through coffee-and-cigar hour, right through Sunday afternoon, and on into the evening. And still I had not reached a point where I *knew* I had found God's plan for my life.

"What is it, Lord? What am I holding back? What am I using as an excuse for not serving You in whatever You want me to do?"

And then, there by the canal, I finally had my answer. My "yes" to God had always been a "yes, but." Yes, but I'm not educated. Yes, but I'm lame.

With the next breath, I did say "Yes." I said it in a brand-new way, without qualification. "I'll go, Lord," I said, "no matter whether it's through the route of ordination, or through the WEC program, or through working on at Ringers'. Whenever, wherever, however You want me, I'll go. And I'll begin this very minute. Lord, as I stand up from this place, and as I take my first step forward, will You consider that this is a step toward complete obedience to You? I'll call it the Step of Yes."

I stood up. I took a stride forward. And in that moment there was a sharp wrench in the lame leg. I thought with horror that I had turned my crippled ankle. Gingerly I put the foot on the ground. I could stand on it all right. What on earth had happened? Slowly and very cautiously I began walking home, and as I walked, one verse of Scripture kept popping into my mind: "Going, they were healed."

Diary of a Smuggler

VIETNAM

Continued

This is a praying church. I was so impressed with some of the young leaders who told of a decision they reached about two years ago. They realized that the house churches and the open churches were not in unity. They also were convicted that they were not praying enough for those who persecuted them. So early in 1997 these young leaders invited the Body of Christ to fast and pray for forty days. And they did. The church began to greatly expand through conversions. Not surprisingly, their persecutors turned up the heat! The last two years have seen more intense harassment, interrogations, and arrests than it has seen for a number of years. A second forty-day fast began in August 1998, and even more believers participated.

Just as impressive is the church's commitment to training and discipling. The introductory training program, open to any Christian who has a desire to serve the Lord, lasts a week. During that time potential leaders learn how to witness and preach. Then they are sent back to their home community with the charge to establish a cell group which becomes part of their house-church community. Thousands have taken this training course.

No wonder the church in Vietnam is growing. These gentle, tenacious believers are bold, and they expect miracles, pray and fast, train their key leaders in biblical theology and practice aggressive evangelism under persecution.

I couldn't remember at first where it came from. Then I recalled the story of the ten lepers, and how *on their way* to see the priest as Christ had commanded, the miracle happened. "Going, they were healed."

Could it be? Could it possibly be that I too had been healed?

I was due at a Sunday evening service in a village six kilometers away. Normally, I would have ridden my bicycle, but tonight was different. Tonight I was going to *walk* all the way to the meeting.

I did too. When it came time to go home, a friend offered me a ride on his motorbike.

"Not tonight, thank you. I think I'll walk."

He couldn't believe it. Nor, later, could my family believe that I had actually been to the service; they had seen my bicycle leaning against the wall and assumed that I had changed my mind.

The next day at the chocolate factory I walked each employee back to his post at the end of our interview instead of sitting rooted to my chair as I had done in the past. Halfway through the morning my ankle began to itch, and as I was rubbing the old scar, two stitches came through the skin. By the end of the week the incision, which had never healed properly, at last closed.

The following week I made formal application for admission to the WEC Missionary Training College in Glasgow. A month later the reply came. Dependent on space opening up in the men's dormitory, I could start my studies in May, 1953.

Corrie had news for me, too, my last day on the job. She also was leaving Ringers': she had been accepted in a nurse's training program. I looked into her eyes sparkling with her surprise and decided finally that they were hazel. We held hands just for a moment, then quickly said goodbye.

Ahead of me now was the task I dreaded above all others: breaking the news to Thile that I had enrolled in a school sponsored by no church, supported by no organization, lacking all of the recognized, dignified, time-honored accompaniments that for her were part of education—and indeed of religion itself. We spent a miserable afternoon walking along the waterfront in the lovely springtime of Gorkum. Thile said very little. I had arguments marshaled for all the objections she would raise. But instead of arguing she grew more and more silent. The only time she sounded angry was when I mentioned the healing of my leg. I made the mistake of calling it a little miracle.

"That's a little strong, isn't it, Andrew?" she flared up. "People have injuries get better every day, and most of them don't go around making wild claims."

I didn't stay for dinner with Thile's folks that night. They all needed time, I thought, to get used to the new plans. That was it;

Thile just needed time. Eventually she would come to see why this was right.

Meanwhile, I set about raising money for my trip. I sold the few things I owned—my bicycle and my precious shelf of books—and purchased a one-way ticket to London, where I was to meet the directors of the WEC before heading for Glasgow. When I had paid for the ticket, I had left a little over thirty British pounds, the fee for the first semester.

I was to leave for London on the 20th of April, 1953. But just before that date three things happened in such rapid succession that they left me reeling.

The first was a letter from Thile. She had written, she said, to the board of missions of her

AROUND THE GLOBE
Comoros Islands

Population: 592,000
Location/Size: Southeastern African islands
863 sq. miles
Major Religions: Islam
Level of Persecution: Sharp, static

According to African Christian leaders, these four volcanic islands are the world's most difficult to evangelize. Christians are not recognized by the government and are forbidden from meeting or publicly expressing their faith. Though the church enjoys a somewhat tolerant atmosphere, sporadic persecution has been intense.

Believers also suffer from the poverty that pervades the nation. Travel, evangelism, and church planting are hampered by the lack of evangelistic resources available to them. The Comorian church remains small, but it does continue to grow. In fact, church growth is currently outpacing that of the general population.

church asking their opinion of the school in Glasgow. They had replied that it was a nonaccredited, unaffiliated enterprise that had no standing in any mission circle with which they were involved.

This being the case, Thile went on, she would prefer neither to see nor to hear from me as long as I was associated with this group. She signed the short letter, Thile. Not: Love, Thile. Just, Thile.

As I stood in the doorway holding the letter, trying to take in what it meant in my life, Miss Meekle crossed the little bridge to our house.

"Andrew," she said, "there's something on my mind. Something I've wanted to tell you for a long time. Only I didn't quite know how to do it." She took a deep breath and plunged in. "You see, Andrew, I've never actually *heard* any English. But I've read a lot of it," she added hastily, "and a lady I write to in England says my grammar is perfect." She paused miserably. "I just thought I'd tell you." And she fled.

I was still digesting these two pieces of information when, two days later, a telegram arrived from London: "Regret to inform you expected vacancy has not materialized. Request for admission denied. You may re-apply 1954."

Three blows in a row. There was no room for me in the school. I probably could not speak the language in which the courses were taught. And if I went I would lose my girl.

Every reasonable sign seemed to point away from the school in Glasgow. And yet, unmistakable inside me, sublimely indifferent to every human and logical objection, was a little voice that seemed to say "Go." It was the voice that had called to me in the wind, the voice that had told me to speak out in the factory, the voice that never made sense at a logical level.

The next day I was kissing Maartje and Geltje goodbye, shaking hands with Papa and Cornelius, and running down the road for the bus that would take me on the first leg of a journey that is still going on.

Imagine This

You have been dating someone for several years, and you plan to be married. Until recently, you and your girlfriend were both Muslims. But a few months ago, you accepted Jesus as your Savior. You are certain that you will be disowned if your family knows of your conversion, and you will definitely be unable to marry the woman you love.

What Would You Do?

SIX

The Game of the Royal Way

That is why, for Christ's sake, I delight in weaknesses, in insults, in hardships, in persecutions, in difficulties. For when I am weak, then I am strong.

2 Corinthians 12:10

I stepped off the train in London, holding the piece of paper on which I had written the address of the Worldwide Evangelization Crusade headquarters.

Outside the train station, tall red buses and high black taxicabs spun dizzily past on the wrong sides of the street. I walked up to a policeman, held out the paper, and asked how I might get to this address. The officer took the paper and looked at it. Then, nodding, he stretched out his arm and for several minutes rattled off directions. I stared at him dumbfounded: I could not understand one single word. In embarrassment I took back the paper, said "Dank ou," and walked away in the direction of his first arm wave.

I tried several other policemen, with no better results. At last there was nothing for it: I had to spend a bit of precious cash on a taxi. I found one parked at the curb, handed the driver the piece of paper, and closed my eyes as we whirled off in the left-hand lane. A few moments later he stopped. He pointed to my piece of paper, then to a large building badly in need of paint.

I picked up my suitcase, made my way up the steps, and rang the doorbell. A woman opened the door. I explained as carefully as I could who I was and why I was here. The lady looked at me with a vacant stare that assured me that she had not caught even the drift of my remarks. She signaled with her hand that I was to come in, showed me a straight chair in the hallway, and then disappeared. When she came back she had in tow a man who spoke some Dutch. Once again I explained who I was and where I was headed.

"Ah, yes, of course. But didn't you get our cable? We wired you three days ago that there was no room up in Glasgow just now."

"I got the cable, yes."

"And you came anyhow?"

I was happy to see that the man was smiling.

"A place will open for me when the time comes," I said. "I am certain of it. I want to be ready."

The man smiled again and told me to wait a moment. When he returned, he had the news I was hoping for. It would be all right for me to stay here at headquarters for a short while, provided I was willing to work.

And so began one of the hardest two-month periods of my life.

The physical work I was required to do was not difficult: I was to paint the WEC headquarters building. As soon as I got used to the ladder, I enjoyed the job tremendously. I didn't even take a holiday for the coronation of Queen Elizabeth. The staff members kept shouting up to me to come down and see the events on television. But I preferred my perch high above the street where I could see flags on every roof and watch the plane formations flying over.

What made the two months difficult was learning English. I worked so hard on the language that my head continually ached. The people at WEC all practiced what they called Morning Quiet Time—they got up long before breakfast to read their Bibles and pray before the business of the day began or any words were spoken. I liked the idea immediately. I was up with the first bird song, dressed, and out in the garden with two books in my hand. One was an English Bible; the other was a dictionary. It was doubtless an excellent technique, but it did have some disadvantages. My English during that period was filled with thees, thous, and ver-ilys. One time I passed on a request for butter by saying, "Thus sayeth the neighbor of Andrew, that thou wouldst be pleased to pass the butter."

But I was learning. After I had been in England six weeks I was asked by the director to lead the evening devotional. At the end of seven minutes I ran out of English words and sat down. Two weeks later I was asked to speak again. This time I chose as my text Christ's words to the blind man on the road to Jericho. "Thy faith hath saved thee." It was a foolish choice, because the sound "th" for a Dutchman is anathema.

"Dy fade had saved dee," I announced, and then for fourteen minutes by the clock I tried to prove my point to the grand amuse-ment of the other workers.

At the close of my little sermon they all gathered around. "You're getting better, Andy," they said, pounding me joyously on the back. "We could almost understand what you said! And fourteen min-utes! That makes you twice as good as when you spoke for seven!"

"So this is our Dutchman. . . . I think his sermon was very fine indeed."

The voice came from the back of the room. Standing in the door-way was a middle-aged, balding, plumpish, pink-faced man I had not seen before. I was struck instantly by the sparkle in his eyes: they were half closed as if he were thinking of some mischief to do.

"Andrew, I don't believe you've met William Hopkins," the WEC director said. I walked to the rear of the room and extended my hand. William Hopkins took it in both of his own large hands, and when he was through, I knew that I had been thoroughly greeted.

"He looks strong enough," Mr. Hopkins said. "If we can get him the papers, I think he will do very well."

I must have looked puzzled, because the director explained that the time had come when I would have to leave the headquarters building. The painting job was finished, and my bed was needed for a returning missionary. But if Mr. Hopkins could get me British working papers, I could get a job in London and start saving money toward books and other expenses in Glasgow. Whenever practical matters of this kind arose, I learned, people always turned to William Hopkins.

"Go get your things, Andrew m'boy," Mr. Hopkins said. "You're invited to come live with Mrs. Hopkins and meself for a few days until we find some work."

It didn't take long to pack one suitcase. While I was putting away my toothbrush and razor, one of the WEC workers told me a little about Mr. Hopkins. He was a successful contractor, yet he lived in penury. Nine-tenths of his income he gave away to various missions. WEC was only one of his great-hearted concerns.

Within a few moments I was standing at the front door saying goodbye to the staff.

"The building looks beautiful, Andy," the director said, shaking hands.

"Dank ou."

"Let's hear that 'th'."

"Thee-ank ee-ou."

Everyone laughed as William Hopkins and I walked down the steps to his truck. The Hopkins' living quarters on the Thames River were about what I would have expected: simple, warm, homey. Mrs. Hopkins was an invalid. She spent most days in bed, but she did not object to my intrusion.

"You make yourself at home here," she greeted me. "You'll discover where the cupboard is, and you'll learn that the front door is never on the latch." Then she turned to her husband, and I saw in her eyes the same sparkle I had seen in his. "And don't be surprised should you find a stray in your bed some night. It *has* happened. If by chance it happens again, there's blankets and pillows in the living room, and you can make a bedroll by the fire."

Before the week was over I was to discover how literally these words were meant. One evening when I came back to the house, after another long and fruitless wait at the work-permit office, I found both Mr. and Mrs. Hopkins sitting in the living room.

"Don't bother to go up to your room, Andrew," Mrs. Hopkins said. "There's a drunk in your bed. We've had our tea, but we saved you some."

Colombia ## A Traveler's Story

BLAMED AND ACCUSED TO DEATH

A Christian teenager and his father were forced by the Armed group to go to a specific place to see if the Violence group was there. They went but did not detect the presence of any other group. Upon their return they had to report to the Armed group. They said they hadn't seen the Violence group. Given the information, the Armed group went into the specified area, but it just so happened that the Violence group was there. There was an enormous battle, and two of the Armed group fighters were killed. Both believers were blamed and accused of lying, being told that they actually had seen the Violence group, but that they had purposely not said so. This was not true. They had not seen them because of the camouflage. Afterward, the father left the region. The teenager remained implicated in what had happened.

A month later, the Armed group came to look for the father and son to avenge the deaths of their men. Since they couldn't find the father, they took the young man and tortured him terribly. They castrated him, pulled out his nails, and plucked out his eyes. It was ghastly. I couldn't look at the scene . . . neither could his mother. They threw him into the San Jorge River, where he was found hacked to pieces.

Because of the presence of the armed groups in the region, we are not free to speak about most things resulting from the surrounding conflict.

As I ate my meal in front of the fire, she told me about the man in my bed. Chiefly to get out of the rain, he had come into the little store-front mission Mr. Hopkins ran, and Mr. Hopkins had brought him home. "When he wakes up, we'll find him some food and some clothes," Mrs. Hopkins said. "I don't know where they'll come from, but God will supply."

And God did. On this and on dozens of similar occasions while I stayed with the Hopkinses, I saw God meet their practical needs in the most unusual ways. Never once did I see anyone go hungry or coatless from their house. It wasn't that they had money. From the profits of Mr. Hopkins' construction business they kept just enough to supply their own modest needs. Strangers—such as myself and the beggars and streetwalkers and drunks who passed continually through their doors—had to be fed by God. And He never failed. Perhaps it was a neighbor dropping by with a casserole, "Just in case you're not feeling up to cooking tonight, ducky." Perhaps it was an old debt unexpectedly paid, or one of the previous bed-tenants returning to see if he could help. "Yes, son, you can. We have an old man in the bed upstairs tonight who has no shoes. Do you think if we measured his feet you might find him a pair?"

I had intended to stay with the Hopkinses only a day or two, until I got my working papers and found a job. But though Mr. Hopkins and I went back to the labor ministry again and again, the work permit was never granted.

And meanwhile, I had been asked by the Hopkinses to stay on in their home, and it happened like this. The first morning after I arrived there Mr. Hopkins went off to work early, Mrs. Hopkins had to stay in bed, and I was left to myself. And so I found a mop and scrubbed the kitchen floor. Mopping the bathroom, I found the soiled clothes bin and did the washing. By afternoon the clothes were dry, so I ironed them. Then when Mr. Hopkins was still not back, I cooked dinner.

I was used to doing these things at home: anyone in my family, male or female, would have done the same. But the Hopkinses, when they discovered what I had done, were thunderstruck. Either they were not used to the practical Dutch, or they were not used to having their own needs noticed, but at any rate they acted as though I had done something remarkable and asked me then and there to stay on as one of the family.

And so I did. I became chief cook and bottlewasher, and they became my English mother and father. Like many, many others, I was soon calling them Uncle Hoppy and Mother Hoppy. Indeed, in many ways Mrs. Hopkins reminded me of my own mother, both in her uncomplaining acceptance of pain and ill health, and in the door "never on the latch" to the needy.

As for Uncle Hoppy, knowing him was an education all by itself. He was a man utterly without self-consciousness. Sometimes when I drove with him in his truck to various construction sites around the city, I would beg him—since he was president of the company— at least to put on a tie and buy himself a coat with elbows in it.

But Uncle Hoppy would laugh at my embarrassment. "Why, Andy, nobody knows me here!"

In his own neighborhood, though, it was no better. I would catch him at the door heading for church in work-boots and a two-days' growth of beard. But when I would scold him, he would fix me with reproachful eyes. "Andy, m'boy! Everybody knows me here!"

Uncle Hoppy's own store-front mission was something of a puzzle to me. Its doors were always open, and occasionally a stray derelict would wander in, but only for a snooze or a bit of warmth; when it came time for services, Uncle Hoppy usually found the chairs empty. This didn't stop him. I remember one day hearing him preach an entire sermon to the empty chairs.

"You missed our appointment this time," Uncle Hoppy said to the people who somehow had not found their way in. "But I'll meet you out on the street, and when I do, I'll know you. Now listen to what God has to say to you. . . ."

When the sermon ended, I objected. "You're too mystic for me," I said. "When I get to preach someday, I want to see real people out there."

Uncle Hoppy only laughed. "Just you wait," he said. "Before we get home we will meet the man who was supposed to be in that chair. And when we do, his heart will be prepared. Time and place are our own limitations, Andy; we mustn't impose them upon God."

And sure enough, as we were walking home we were approached by a streetwalker, and Uncle Hoppy plunged into the conclusion of his sermon just as though she'd sat spellbound through the first forty minutes. That night I slept in front of the fire again, and by morning this indefatigable contractor and his wife had a new convert to Christianity.

At last one day came a letter from Glasgow: the long-awaited vacancy had opened up. I was to report in time for the fall term.

We did a triumphal march around Mother Hoppy's bed—Uncle Hoppy, a stray vagabond, and I—until suddenly all of us at once realized that it meant saying goodbye. I left London in September, 1953, for the missionary training school in Scotland.

This time I had no trouble finding my way to the address I wanted. I walked up the hill carrying my suitcase until I came to Number 10 Prince Albert Road. The building itself was a tall two-story house on the corner. A low stone wall ran around the property. I could see the stump-ends of iron railings in it, melted for scrap during the war no doubt. Over the entrance on a wooden archway were the words "Have Faith In God."

This I knew was the main purpose of the two-year course at Glasgow: to help the student learn all he could about the nature of faith. To learn from books. To learn from others. To learn from his own encounters. With fresh enthusiasm I walked under the arch and up the white pebbled path to the door.

My knock was answered by Kees. How good it was to look into that solid Dutch face again. After we had slapped one another's shoulders many times, he seized my bag and ushered me to my top-floor room. He introduced me to my three roommates, showed me the fire escape, and pointed out where the rest of the forty-five young people slept—men in one of the attached houses, women in the other.

"And ne'er the twain shall meet," Kees said. "We're hardly supposed to talk to the girls. The only time we can see them is at dinner."

Kees sat with me through the formal introduction to the director, Steward Dinnen. "The real purpose of this training," Mr. Dinnen told me, "is to teach our students that they can trust God to do what He has said He would do. We don't go from here into the traditional missionary fields, but into new territory. Our graduates are on their own. They cannot be effective if they are afraid or if they doubt that God really means what He says in His Word. So here we teach not so much ideas as trusting. I hope that this is what you are looking for in a school, Andrew."

"Yes, sir. Exactly."

"As for finances—you know of course, Andy, that we charge no tuition. That's because we have no paid staff. The teachers, the London people, myself—none of us receives a salary. Room and board and other physical costs for the year come to only ninety pounds—a little over two hundred and fifty dollars. It's as low as

Vietnam   *A Traveler's Story*

IMPRISONED TO SET OTHERS FREE

In his home in central Vietnam, Nam Loc shared the Gospel one-on-one to every villager. His witness won thousands of people to Christ. It also earned the wrath of his detractors, who conspired with police authorities in filing trumped-up charges against him. First he was accused of stealing idols from converts' homes. He was arrested, chained, and dragged away from his home to a tiny prison cell that he shared with two other prisoners.

There he immediately witnessed to his prisonmates. His first day in prison was not one of despair, because as he shared, one weary soul, battered by life's difficulties, found rest and peace with God.

One day the authorities came with a tempting proposition—freedom. But he rejected it. Why? His freedom could only be gained on one condition—he must become a spy for the government and identify who his fellow believers were. But Nam would have rather remained a captive in prison than betray his fellow brothers and sisters in the faith.

His stubborn defiance was rewarded with a heavier charge—a political one that effectively prolonged his prison term to seven to nine years. He was accused, again spuriously, of burning a portrait of Ho Chi Minh—the founder of the Communist movement in Vietnam.

Solitary confinement came next. For five months he neither saw nor talked to anyone. Completely detached from everything, he passed the days singing praises to God. One after another, he sang hymns he knew from memory. Prison officials got so enraged that they violently beat him every time he sang.

He was beaten. Yes. But only physically. For even as his body suffered, his determination remained strong. He kept sharing Jesus with other prisoners.

But how did he do this? Through his chamber ran a water pipe that was connected to other prison cells. An idea came to his mind. He bore a hole in it from which he spoke to his fellow prisoners about Jesus Christ. Many heard his message, and they believed in Jesus!

Nam did not serve his entire prison sentence. After nine months he was released from prison through the petition of a Communist general!

And he is doing it again, telling people about the wonderful love of Jesus, his Savior. Another prison term? Maybe. When that happens, Nam can resume his interrupted water-pipe evangelism.

this because the students do the cooking, cleaning, everything, themselves. But we do request the ninety pounds in advance. Now I understand you will not be able to do this."

"No, sir."

"Well, it's also possible to pay in installments, thirty pounds at the start of each session. But for your sake and for ours we like to insist that the installments be paid on time."

"Yes, sir. I altogether agree."

I did agree too. This was going to be my first experiment in trusting God for the material needs of life. I had the thirty pounds I had brought from Holland for the first semester's fee. After that I really looked forward to seeing how God was going to supply the money.

During the first few weeks, however, something kept happening that bothered me. At mealtimes the students would frequently discuss inadequate funds. Sometimes after a whole night in prayer for a certain need, half of the request would be granted, or three-quarters. If an old people's home, for example, where students conducted services, needed ten blankets, the students would perhaps receive enough to buy them six. The Bible said that we were workers in God's vineyard. Was this the way the Lord of the vineyard paid His hired men?

One night I went out for a long, solitary walk. On several occasions students had warned me not to "go into Patrick." Patrick was the slum sitting at the bottom of our hill. It was, they said, the home of addicts, drunks, thieves, even murderers, and walking its streets was unsafe. And yet this area drew me now as if it had something to say.

All around me were the dirty gray streets of Patrick. Litter blew across the cobblestones. The September air was already raw. Before I had gone five blocks I was accosted two times by beggars. I gave them all the money I had in my pockets and watched as they moved without pretense toward the nearest pub. I knew that these drifters, begging in the streets of the Glasgow slums, would receive a better income than the missionaries-in-training at the top of the hill.

I could not understand why this bothered me so. Was I greedy? I didn't think so. We had always been poor, and I had never worried about it. What was it then?

And suddenly, walking back up the hill toward the school, I had my answer.

The question was not one of money at all. What I was worried about was a relationship.

At the chocolate factory I trusted Mr. Ringers to pay me in full and on time. Surely I said to myself, if an ordinary factory worker could be financially secure, so could one of God's workers.

I turned through the gate at the school. Above me was the reminder "Have Faith In God."

That was it! It wasn't that I needed the security of a certain amount of money, it was that I needed the security of a relationship.

I walked up the crunchy pebblewalk feeling more and more certain that I was on the verge of something exciting. The school was asleep and quiet. I tiptoed upstairs and sat by the bedroom window looking out over Glasgow. If I were going to give my life as a servant of the King, I had to know that King. What was He like? In what *way* could I trust Him? In the same way I trusted a set of impersonal laws? Or could I trust Him as a living leader, as a very present commander in battle? The question was central. Because if He were a King in name only, I would rather go back to the chocolate factory. I would remain a Christian, but I would know that my religion was only a set of principles, excellent and to be followed, but hardly demanding devotion.

Suppose on the other hand that I were to discover God to be a Person, in the sense that He communicated and cared and loved and led. That was something quite different. That was the kind of King I would follow into any battle.

And somehow, sitting there in the moonlight that September night in Glasgow, I knew that my probing into God's nature was going to begin with this issue of money. That night I knelt in front of the window and made a covenant with Him. "Lord," I said, "I need to know if I can trust You in practical things. I thank You for letting me earn the fees for the first semester. I ask You now to supply the rest of them. If I have to be so much as a day late in paying, I shall know that I am supposed to go back to the chocolate factory."

It was a childish prayer, petulant and demanding. But then I was still a child in the Christian life. The remarkable thing is that God honored my prayer. But not without first testing me in some rather amusing ways.

The first semester sped by. Mornings we spent in the classrooms studying systematic theology, homiletics, world religions, linguistics—the type of courses taught in any seminary. In the afternoon we worked at practical skills: bricklaying, plumbing, carpentry, first aid, tropical hygiene, motor repair. For several weeks all of us, girls as well as boys, worked at the Ford factory in London, learning how to take a car apart and put it together. In addition to these standard trades, we were taught to build huts out of palm fronds and how to make mud jars that would hold water.

And meanwhile we took turns in the kitchen and the laundry and the garden. No one was exempt. One of the students was a doctor, a German woman, and I used to watch her scouring garbage pails as though she were preparing a room for surgery.

The weeks passed so fast that soon it came time for me to head out on the first of several training trips in evangelism. "You're going to like this, Andy," said Mr. Dinnen. "It's an exercise in trust. The rules are simple. Each student on your team is given a one-pound banknote. With that you go on a missionary tour through Scotland. You're expected to pay your own transportation, your own lodging, your food, any advertising you want to do, the renting of halls, providing refreshments—"

"All on a one-pound note?"

"Worse than that. When you get back to school after four weeks, you're expected to pay back the pound!"

I laughed. "Sounds like we'll be passing the hat all the time."

"Oh, you're not allowed to take up collections! Never. You're not to mention money at your meetings. All of your needs have got to be provided without any manipulation on your part—or the experiment is a failure."

I was a member of a team of five boys. Later when I tried to reconstruct where our funds came from during those four weeks, it was hard to. It seemed that what we needed was always just there. Sometimes a letter would arrive from one of the boys' parents with a little money. Sometimes we would get a check in the mail from a church we had visited days or weeks earlier. The notes that came with these gifts were always interesting. "I know you don't need money or you would have mentioned it," someone would write. "But God just wouldn't let me get to sleep tonight until I had put this in an envelope for you."

Contributions frequently came in the form of produce. In one little town in the highlands of Scotland we were given six hundred eggs. We had eggs for breakfast, eggs for lunch, eggs as hors d'oeuvres before a dinner of eggs with an egg-white meringue dessert. It was weeks before we could look a chicken in the eye.

But money or produce, we stuck fast to two rules: we never mentioned a need aloud, and we gave away a tithe of whatever came to us as soon as we got it—within twenty-four hours if possible.

Another team that set out from school at the same time we did, was not so strict about tithing. They set aside their ten percent all right, but they didn't give it away immediately, "in case we run into an emergency." Of course they had emergencies! So did we, every day. But they ended their month owing money to hotels, lecture halls, and markets all over Scotland, while we came back to school almost ten pounds ahead. Fast as we could give money away, God was always swifter, and we ended with money to send to the WEC work overseas.

There were times before the end of the tour, however, when it looked as though the experiment was failing. One weekend we were holding meetings in Edinburgh. We had attracted a large group of young people the first day and were casting about for a way to get them to come back the next. Suddenly, without consulting anyone, one of the team members stood up and made an announcement.

"Before the meeting tomorrow evening," he said, "we'd like you all to have tea with us here. Four o'clock. How many think they can make it?"

A couple dozen hands went up, and we were committed. At first, instead of being delighted, the rest of us were horrified. All of us knew that we had no tea, no cake, no bread and butter, and exactly five cups. Nor did we have money to buy these things: our last penny had gone to rent the hall. This was going to be a real test of God's care.

And for a while it looked as though He was going to provide everything through the young people themselves. After the meeting several of them came forward and said they would like to help. One offered milk; another, half a pound of tea; another, sugar. One girl even offered to bring dishes. Our tea was rapidly taking shape. But there was one thing still missing—the cake. Without cake, these Scottish boys and girls wouldn't consider tea tea.

So that night in our evening prayer time, we put the matter before God. "Lord, we've got ourselves into a spot. From somewhere we've got to get a cake. Will You help us?"

That night as we rolled up in our blankets on the floor of the hall, we played guessing games: How was God going to give us that cake? Among the five of us, we guessed everything imaginable—or so we thought.

Morning arrived. We half expected a heavenly messenger to come to our door bearing a cake. But no one came. The morning mail arrived. We ripped open the two letters, hoping for money. There was none. A woman from a nearby church came by to see if she could help. "Cake," was on the tip of all our tongues, but we swallowed the word and shook our heads.

"Everything," we assured her, "is in God's hands."

The tea had been announced for four o'clock in the afternoon. At three the tables were set, but still we had no cake. Three-thirty came. We put on water to boil. Three-forty-five.

And then the doorbell rang.

All of us together ran to the big front entrance, and there was the postman. In his hand was a large box.

"Hello, lads," said the postman. "Got something for you that feels like a food package." He handed the box to one of the boys. "The delivery day is over, actually," he said, "but I hate to leave a perishable package overnight."

We thanked him profusely, and the minute he closed the door the boy solemnly handed me the box. "It's for you, Andrew. From a Mrs. William Hopkins in London."

I took the package and carefully unwrapped it. Off came the twine. Off came the brown outside paper. Inside, there was no note—only a large white box. Deep in my soul I knew that I could afford the drama of lifting the lid slowly. As I did, there, in perfect condition, to be admired by five sets of wondering eyes, was an enormous, glistening, moist, chocolate cake.

With this kind of experience behind me, I was not really surprised to find waiting for me when we got back to school, a check from the Whetstras that was exactly enough, when converted into pounds, to pay my second term's fee.

The second term seemed to go even faster than the first, so much was there to grasp and to ponder. But before that term was over, I had received money to keep me there a third, this time from—of all places—some buddies at the veterans' hospital. And so it went throughout the second year too.

I never mentioned the school fees to anyone, and yet the gifts always came at such a moment that I could pay them in full and on time. Nor did they ever contain more than the school costs, and—in spite of the fact that the people who were helping me did not know one another—they never came two together.

God's faithfulness I was experiencing continually, and I was also finding out something about His sense of humor.

I had made a covenant with God never to run out of money for school fees. My covenant said nothing about running out of soap. Or toothpaste. Or razor blades.

One morning I discovered I was out of laundry soap. But when I reached into the drawer where I kept my money, all I could find was sixpence. Laundry soap cost eightpence.

"You know that I have to keep clean, God. So will You work it out about the two pennies?" I took my sixpence and made my way to the street where the shops were, and sure enough, right away I saw a sign. "Twopence off! Buy your SURF now." I walked in, made my savings, and strolled back up the hill whistling. There was plenty of soap in that box to last, with care, until the end of school.

But that very night a friend saw me washing out a shirt and shouted, "Say, Andrew, lend me some soap, will you? I'm out."

Of course I let him have the soap and said nothing. I just watched him pour out my precious Surf, knowing somehow that he wasn't going to pay it back. Every day he borrowed a bit more of that soap, and every day I had to use just a little bit less.

And then it was toothpaste. The tube was really finished. Squeezed, twisted, torn apart, and scraped—finished. I had read somewhere that common table salt makes a good dentifrice. And no doubt my teeth got clean, but my mouth wore a permanent pucker.

And razor blades. I had not thrown away my used blades, and sure enough the day came when I had to resurrect them. I had no hone, so I stropped them on my bare arm. Ten minutes a day on my own skin: I remained clean shaven—but it was at a price.

Throughout this time I sensed that God was playing a game with me. Perhaps He was using these experiences to teach me the difference between a Want and a Need. Toothpaste tasted good, new razor blades shaved quicker—but these were luxuries, not necessities. I was certain that should a real need arise, God would supply it.

And a true need did arise.

It was necessary for foreigners in Britain to renew their visas at periodic intervals. I had to have mine renewed by the thirty-first of December, 1954, or leave the country. But when that month rolled around, I did not have a cent to my name. How was I going to get the forms down to London? A registered letter cost one shilling—twelve pennies. I did not believe that God was going to let me be thrown out of school for the lack of a shilling.

And so the game moved into a new phase. I had a name for it by now. I called it the Game of the Royal Way. I had discovered that when God supplied money He did it in a kingly manner, not in some groveling way.

Three separate times, over the matter of that registered letter, I was almost lured from the Royal Way. I was, that last year, head of the student body and in charge of the school's tract fund. One day my eye lit first on the calendar—it was the twenty-eighth of December—and then on the fund. It happened to contain several pounds just then. Surely it would be all right to borrow just one shilling.

And surely not, too. Quickly I put the idea behind me.

And then it was the twenty-ninth of December. Two days left. I had almost forgotten how bitter salt tasted and how long it took to strop a razor blade on my arm, so intrigued was I over the drama of the shilling. That morning the thought occurred to me that perhaps I might *find* those pennies lying on the ground.

SUDAN

Diary of a Smuggler

Within one day, we went from freezing-cold Holland to the heat of the Sudanese desert. Sudan has two things in abundance: sand and dust. Fortunately, in the city there are also trees and bushes. But in the refugee camps at the edge of the city, inhabited by women and children who have fled or been driven from southern Sudan by the war, we did not see a single blade of grass, not the smallest of trees, not even weeds.

It's a land of surprises, a land of contrasts. During our stay, we were repeatedly confronted with contrasts. While my wife was visiting the wife of one of the brethren who was in prison because of his faith, I was able to proclaim the Gospel openly in the chapel of another prison. I was moved as I listened to one of the prisoners giving his testimony. He had found Jesus right there. All this is possible in Sudan.

On the way home we met a woman from Austria whose husband had died two days before we met her. While my wife and I listened to her sad story, our thoughts returned to one woman we met in Sudan. She, too, has known grief. After she and her husband became Christians, they experienced much opposition and persecution. Her husband, who suffers from a heart condition, is in prison, and she is alone in caring for their six children.

And yet she was not complaining; on the contrary, her eyes shone. She had witnessed the strength that God gives her every day. What a contrast there was between these two women.

We were reminded of the words of Jesus in Mark 10:29-30: "I tell you the truth . . . no one who has left home or brothers or sisters or mother or father or children or fields for me and the gospel will fail to receive a hundred times as much in this present age (homes, brothers, sisters, mothers, children, and fields—and with them, persecutions) and in the age to come, eternal life."

This is the truth of Sudan. We saw it in the lives of the people we met. They chose the better part and God did not abandon them!

I had actually put on my coat and started down the street before I saw what I was doing. I was walking along with head bowed, eyes on the ground, searching the gutter for pennies. What kind of Royal Way was this! I straightened up and laughed out loud there on the busy street. I walked back to school with my head high but no closer to getting the money.

The last round in the game was the most subtle of all. It was December 30. I had to have my application in the mail that day if it was to get to London on the thirty-first.

At ten o'clock in the morning, one of the students shouted up the stairwell that I had a visitor. I ran down the stairs thinking that this must be my delivering angel. But when I saw who it was, my heart dropped. This visitor wasn't coming to *bring* me money, he was coming to *ask* for it. For it was Richard, a friend I had made months ago in the Patrick slums, a young man who came to the school occasionally when he just had to have cash.

With dragging feet I went outside. Richard stood on the white-pebble walkway, hands in pockets, eyes lowered. "Andrew," he said, "would you be having a little extra cash? I'm hungry."

I laughed and told him why. I told him about the soap and the razor blades, and as I spoke I saw the coin.

It lay among the pebbles, the sun glinting off it in just such a way that I could see it but not Richard. I could tell from its color that it was a shilling. Instinctively I stuck out my foot and covered the coin with my toe. Then as Richard and I talked, I reached down and picked up the coin along with a handful of pebbles. I tossed the pebbles down one by one, aimlessly, until at last I had just the shilling in my hand. But even as I dropped the coin into my pocket, the battle began. That coin meant I could stay in school. I wouldn't be doing Richard a favor by giving it to him: he'd spend it on drink and be thirsty as ever in an hour.

While I was still thinking up excellent arguments, I knew it was no good. How could I judge Richard when Christ told me so clearly that I must not. Furthermore, this was not the Royal Way! What right had an ambassador to hold on to money when another of the King's children stood in front of him saying he was hungry. I shoved my hand back into my pocket and drew out the silver coin.

"Look, Richard," I said, "I do have this. Would it help any?"

Richard's eyes lit up. "It would, mate." He tossed the coin into the air and ran off down the hill. With a light heart that told me I had done the right thing, I turned to go back inside.

And before I reached the door the postman turned down our walk.

In the mail of course was a letter for me. I knew when I saw Greetje's handwriting that it would be from the prayer group at Ringers' and that there would be cash inside. And there was. A lot of money: A pound and a half—thirty shillings. Far more than enough to send my letter, buy a large box of soap, treat myself to my favorite toothpaste—and buy Gillette Supers instead of Blues.

The game was over. The King had done it His way.

AROUND THE GLOBE
CUBA

Population: 11.2 million
Location/Size: Caribbean island
42,804 sq. miles
Major Religions: Christianity/Catholicism
Spiritist religion
Level of Persecution: Harassment, declining

Although the Castro regime officially declared Cuba to be an atheist state, the Roman Catholic Church is still the largest organized religion in the country. The government has clearly stated itself to be neutral on the subject of the Church, but it persists in imposing severe restrictions on meetings, street evangelism, and church construction. Pastors often experience arrest, churches are infiltrated by informants, and believers face constant discrimination.

Currently the Cuban Church enjoys unprecedented revival and a new day of freedom. Cuban Christians still face numerous challenges from the government, but the threat of martyrdom has begun to subside in recent years. The Church is exploding in numbers and now possesses the opportunity to permeate the nation with Christianity.

It was spring, 1955. My two years at the Missionary Training College were almost over, and I was eager to start work. Kees had graduated the year before and was in Korea. His letters were full of the needs and opportunities there, and the director asked me if I would consider joining him.

And then one morning—quietly, without fanfare, as God's turning points so often come—I picked up a magazine, and my life has never been the same since.

The week before graduation I went down into the basement of Number 10 to get my suitcase. There on top of an old cardboard box in the musty cellar was a magazine that neither I nor anyone else at the school ever remembered seeing before. How it got there I shall never know.

I picked it up and flipped through it idly. It was a beautiful magazine, printed on glossy paper and bright with four-color pictures. Most of them showed masses of marching youths parading the streets of Peking and Warsaw and Prague. Their faces were animated, their steps vigorous. The text, in English, told me that these young people were part of a worldwide organization ninety-six million strong. Nowhere was the word Communist used, and only occasionally did the word Socialist appear. The talk was all of a better world, a bright tomorrow. And then, toward the back of the magazine, there appeared an announcement of a youth festival to be held in Warsaw that coming July. Everyone was invited.

Everyone?

Instead of putting the magazine down, I stuck it under my arm and carried it with my suitcase back to my room. That night with no idea where it would lead, I dropped a line to the Warsaw address mentioned in the magazine. I told them frankly that I was training to be a Christian missionary, and that I was interested in going to the youth festival to exchange ideas: I would talk about Christ, and they could talk about socialism. Would they be willing for me to come under these circumstances? I posted the letter, and back bounced an answer. Most certainly they wanted me to come. Since I was a student, reduced rates were available. A special train would be leaving from Amsterdam. My identification was enclosed. They looked forward to seeing me in Warsaw.

The only person in the world I told about this trip was Uncle Hoppy. He wrote back, "Andrew, I think you should go. I am enclosing fifty pounds sterling for your expenses."

And in that moment—just as I left Scotland to head back home for Holland—a dream began to take shape. It had flashed formlessly in and out of my thoughts since the days at Ringers', always vaporous and ill-defined—until now.

It began my last day at the factory. There was a single card-carrying Communist employed at Ringers', a short, stout woman whose close-cropped gray hair stood up on her head like a brush. She had a standard pronouncement on everything from our wages ("slave") to the Queen (an "oppressor"). My evangelistic efforts, when she detected them, pushed the button in her that released such statements as: "God-is-the-invention-of-the-exploiter-class." Being an utterly humorless person herself, she never realized that people were laughing at her. In twenty years at the factory she had not made a single convert.

I found her a pathetic, rather than a laughable, figure and at lunchtime would often go to the table where she sat alone. The day I left Ringers' I stopped by the bench where she worked to say goodbye.

"You're getting rid of me at last!" I said, hoping at least to keep our parting friendly.

"But not of the lies you've told!" she flared back at me. "You've hypnotized these people with your talk of salvation and pie-in-the-sky! You've blinded them with. . . ."

I sighed and settled myself for the opiate-of-the-people lecture. But to my surprise, the angry voice faltered.

"Of course, they believed you," she went on less certainly. "They're untrained. They haven't been taught dialectical argument. They think just what they *want* to think.

"After all"—her voice was so low I could scarcely hear—"if you could choose, who wouldn't choose, well God—and all that."

I glanced at her swiftly and thought I saw the unthinkable: I thought I saw tears in her eyes.

Imagine This

You drive up to the border of Saudi Arabia with a suitcase filled with Bibles. You realize that if you are caught, you will be arrested. When you cross the border, a guard stops your car. He asks you what is in your suitcase.

What Would You Do?

seven

Behind the Iron Curtain

So do not be ashamed to testify about our Lord, or ashamed of me his prisoner. But join with me in suffering for the gospel, by the power of God, who has saved us and called us to a holy life.

2 Timothy 1:8-9

Coming back to Witte after two years in England was like living through one of those experiences that "has happened before." Just as when I returned from Indonesia, everything in the village that hot morning in July, 1955, was so precisely as it had been when I left it that at first I had the uncomfortable feeling that no time had elapsed at all. Geltje was out in the garden hanging up clothes when I stepped across the little bridge onto our plot of land. Here, though, there was a difference: a little boy was playing on the front stoop—Geltje's son.

"Hi!" I called around him. "Anybody home? It's Andy!"

And once again, everyone suddenly appeared. There were the shouts and hugs, the catching up, the attack on the problem of logistics: who would sleep where when Uncle Andrew was home.

The next several days were spent visiting friends. I went to see Mr. Ringers at the factory. I visited Miss Meekle, who threw her hands into the air with astonishment at my English, and with Kees's family. I called on the Whetstras, where I discovered to my surprise that they were about to move to Amsterdam. They had done well in their flower-export business and wanted to be closer to the big shipping offices.

Last of all, I went down to Ermelo to visit my brother Ben and his wife. Very casually I asked him if he had heard anything about Thile.

"Yes," he said, just as casually. "I read last year that she'd been married. A baker, I believe."

And because there seemed nothing more to say, neither of us said anything at all.

The train for Warsaw left Amsterdam July 15, 1955. I was astonished at the number of students who had been attracted by the festival. Hundreds of young men and women milled about the station. For the first time I began to believe the extravagant figures I had read in the magazine.

My suitcase was heavy. In it were just a few clothes—a change of linen and some extra socks. Most of the bag was filled with small thirty-one-page booklets entitled "The Way of Salvation." If the Communists had attracted me to their country with literature, I was going to carry in literature of my own. Karl Marx had said, "Give me twenty-six lead soldiers and I will conquer the world," meaning of course the twenty-six letters of the alphabet. Well, this game could be played both ways: I was going to Poland with editions of this powerful little book in every European language.

And so, with the suitcase almost tearing away from its handle, and my new corduroy pants squeaking at every step, I climbed aboard the train. A few hours later I was standing in Warsaw's Central Station, waiting for my hotel assignment. I felt very alone. I knew not a single person in all of Poland, nor a single word of the language. From all over the world thousands upon thousands of young people were converging on Warsaw for purposes opposite my own. As we waited, I found myself praying, and I wondered if mine were the only prayers offered in this enthusiastic, laughing, confident throng.

My "hotel" turned out to be a school building that had been converted into a dormitory especially for this occasion. I checked in and was assigned to a mathematics classroom that held thirty beds. As soon as possible I left the hotel and went out into the Warsaw streets, wondering what I was supposed to do next. Rather aimlessly I boarded a public bus and suddenly, as we wove our way through traffic, I knew what I was supposed to do. I had learned a little German during the occupation, and I knew that there was a large German-speaking minority in Poland. So, taking a deep breath, I said aloud in German: "I am a Christian from Holland." Everyone near me stopped talking. I felt horribly foolish. "I want to meet some Polish Christians. Can anyone help me?"

Silence. But then, as she rose to leave the bus, a fat woman pressed her face near mine and whispered an address in German. Then she said the words "Bible shop."

My pulse raced. A Bible shop? In a Communist country? I found the address, and sure enough there it was: a Bible shop plain as day. The window was filled with Bibles, red-letter editions, foreign translations, pocket Testaments. But the shop was barred with a heavy grill, and the door was padlocked. There was a notice pasted on the door, which I carefully copied word for word and took back to the hotel.

My group leader smiled. "It's a notice of vacation," he said. "'Closed for holidays. Will open again July 21st.'"

So I had to wait.

Our routine for the three weeks was established early. We were supposed to go on the official sightseeing tour in the morning and to listen to speeches in the afternoon and evening.

I followed the routine for a few days. It was clear that we were being shown a well-scrubbed face of Warsaw. New schools, thriving factories, high-rise apartments, overflowing shops. It was all very impressive. But I wondered what I would see if I managed to get off by myself, alone.

One morning I decided to try just that. I rose early and, before the rest of my group came down for breakfast, was out of the building.

What a day it was. Up and down the broad avenues of Warsaw I walked, saddened by the signs of war violence everywhere. Whole blocks were bombed out, blocks the sightseeing tours had avoided. Slum areas abounded, meat shops with long queues, men and women with rags for clothes. One scene in particular stands out in my memory. There was a bombed-out section of town in which families lived like rabbits in a warren. These people had dug their way into the basements and were making their homes in them. I saw a little girl playing barefoot in the dust and debris. I had a Polish booklet with me, which I handed to her, along with a small banknote. She looked at me in surprise and ran up the mound of rubble. In a moment a woman's head appeared, sticking up out of the ground. She stumbled forward, holding the tract and the bill. Behind her came a man. They were filthy, and they were both drunk.

I tried speaking to them in German and in English and even in Dutch, but they just looked at me blankly. I told them in pantomime to read the booklet, but from the way they held it I realized at last that they could not read. They simply kept shaking their heads, and at last with a smile and a shake of my own I left them.

Sunday came. This was a big day on the agenda. We were to take part in a demonstration at the stadium. Instead, I went to church.

Newspapers in Holland had carried so many stories about the house arrest of Polish church leaders and the closing of seminaries that I had had the impression that all religion in Poland had gone underground. Obviously this was not so. The Bible shop was apparently still operating. I had passed Catholic churches with the doors wide open. Were there, I wondered, Protestant churches still functioning too?

I didn't want to ask at the school for directions to a church, since I was supposed to be at the rally. So I slipped out and found a taxicab. "Good day," I said in Polish. The driver smiled back and rattled off a long happy sentence. But "good day" was all the Pol-

Vietnam | A Traveler's Story

"A CHICKEN LAID OUR BIBLES"

My grandfather had an amazing memory. When other members of his family came to join him in rural Gansu province, he taught us about Christ from the fragments of verses he learned from a pastor.

In 1995 my grandfather gathered us all together. He said he had bad news. "I have taught you of Christ for over fifteen years from the memory of a pastor who died so I might have faith. But I have no more to teach you. I committed about five hundred verses of the Scripture to memory from that pastor, and I have expounded each of them to you a hundred ways since then. It is time for us to find the rest of the sacred texts."

We all looked at each other. This sounded impossible. We did not even know that what we were looking for was called a "Bible." For all we knew, there may have been thousands of different scriptures. In fact, that's what we assumed, since that's what the Daoists have.

We said to him, "But who will find us these texts?"

He replied, "God will; we must pray."

We prayed . . . and prayed . . . and prayed. For two years we prayed. Nothing happened. But for the faith of my grandfather, I think some of us would have moved to another faith. He was firm: "God is testing us to see if we are really His. We must keep trusting and keep faithful."

Continued

ish I had learned, and when I asked him in German to take me to a church, his face fell. I tried English and he looked blanker still.

I folded my hands as in prayer, then opened them as if reading. Next I crossed myself and shook my head. No, not a Catholic service. Again I pantomimed reading the Bible. The driver was smiling again. He started across town, and sure enough he had understood: we stopped at a red brick building that boasted two spires. Ten minutes later I was seated at a Reformed Church service behind the Iron Curtain.

I was surprised at the size of the congregation; the church was about three-quarters full. I was surprised, too, at the number of young people. The singing was enthusiastic, the sermon apparently Scripture-centered, as the preacher was constantly referring to his Bible. When the service was over, I waited in the rear of the sanctuary to see if I could find anyone who spoke a language I spoke. My clothes must have marked me as a foreigner, for before long I heard the word:

"Welcome."

I turned and found myself looking into the face of the pastor. "Could you wait a moment?" he said in English. "I should like to speak with you."

And I with him!

After most of the congregation had left, the pastor and a handful of young people volunteered to answer my questions. Yes, they worshiped openly and with considerable freedom, as long as they stayed clear of political subjects. Yes, there were members of the church who were also members of the Communist Party. Well, the regime had done so much for the people that one just closed an eye to the rest. "It is a compromise, yes," said the pastor with a shrug of his shoulders, "but what can you do?"

"What church do you belong to at home?" one of the young men asked in excellent English.

"Baptist."

"Would you like to go to a Baptist service?"

"Very much indeed."

He got out pencil and paper and wrote down an address for me. "There's a service tonight," he said.

And that evening, after learning from the rest of the Dutch delegation how boring the day's endless speeches had been, I set out by taxi once again, this time armed with a specific address.

The service was already in progress when I arrived. There was a smaller turnout here. The people were less well-dressed, and there were almost no teenagers. But an interesting thing happened. Word was passed to the minister that a foreigner was in the congregation, and I was immediately asked to come up on the platform and speak to them. I was astonished. Did they have this amount of freedom?

"Is there anyone here who speaks German or English?" I asked, not realizing that I had discovered a technique I would use often in the future. It happened that there was a woman in the congregation that night who spoke German. Through her I preached my first sermon behind the Iron Curtain. It was short and insignif-

One Sunday a few of us were praying, and a chicken came into our house. She clucked and made a great noise and then promptly laid an egg. We did not know where she had come from, so my grandfather tied some money to the leg of the chicken. It was only about 10 cents. The chicken strutted off with an injured air from the whole experience. We knew she would return to her owner.

Less than an hour later there was a loud cry on the street. Someone was yelling, "Who tied money to my chicken? Who tied money to my chicken?" The voice sounded angry, but my grandfather replied without hesitation, "It was me."

The man came into our little house. A well-dressed man who had soft hands and was very well groomed followed him. He said in a cultured voice, "I am a high ranking member of the Communist party in Beijing."

Our hearts sank. What was he going to do?

"I have never heard of such honesty in all my life," he said. "This is astonishing. I have just come from Beijing to visit my brother after being betrayed and deceived. I lost lots of money."

He turned to my grandfather and said, "My government desperately needs your spirit of scrupulous honesty. If only there were more like you in China. Tell me, what makes you so honest?"

My grandfather answered him in two words: "Jesus Christ!"

The Communist official seemed to smile to himself and then asked, "Can I do anything for you?"

My grandfather, with the boldness of a long life, said, "We would like to find the sacred texts of Christ!"

The official looked at him, puzzled. "What do you mean 'sacred texts'? Don't you mean a Bible?"

It was the Communist official who told us what a Bible was.

Again the boldness of my grandfather staggered me. He asked the official, "Can you help us get a copy?"

The official smiled openly now. He made no promise, but merely said, "I will see what I can do."

The official went back to Beijing, but nothing happened. Months went by. We continued to pray. Then a young man appeared in the village, asking for us. He pulled out from his totebag seven brand-new Bibles.

We asked him, "How did you know to come here to us?"

He said, "I am part of a network of house churches, and one of our leaders was arrested in Beijing last year. While he was in jail, he was visited by a high-ranking public official, who said, 'If I let you go, will you promise to deliver a Bible to an old man and his family in Gansu?' Our leader said he would see to it. The next day he was released and given a piece of paper with your grandfather's address on it."

That's why we say, "A chicken laid our Bibles!"

icant except for one inescapable fact: here I was, a Christian from the other side of the Iron Curtain, standing up and preaching the Gospel in a Communist country.

At the end of my little talk the pastor said the most interesting thing of all. "We want to thank you," he said, "for *being* here. Even if you had not said a word, just seeing you would have meant so much. We feel at times as if we are all alone in our struggle."

That night, lying on my cot in the mathematics classroom, I got to thinking about how different these two churches had been. One, apparently, was following the route of cooperation with the government: it attracted larger crowds, it was acceptable to young people. The other, I felt, was walking a lonelier path. When I asked if Party members attended their services, the answer was "Not that we *know* about!" I was learning so much so fast that it was difficult to assimilate it all.

I had been in Poland nearly a week! At last it was the twenty-first of July, the day the Bible shop reopened. I left the hotel early and walked through the almost empty avenues until I got to the address on New World Street.

Just before nine o'clock a man hurried down the street, stopped in front of the Bible shop, bent over, and inserted a key in the lock.

"Good morning," I said in Polish.

The man stood up and looked at me. "Good morning," he said a trifle distantly.

"Do you speak either English or German?" I asked in English.

"English." He looked up the street. "Come in."

The proprietor switched on lights and began raising shades. While he worked I introduced myself. The proprietor grunted. Then it was his turn. He showed me his shop: his many editions of the Bible, the wide range of prices available. And all the while he was eliciting fragments of information from me, trying to establish just who I really was.

"Why are you in Poland?" he asked suddenly.

"If one member suffers, all suffer together," I quoted from First Corinthians.

The proprietor looked at me steadily. "We have not been talking about suffering," he said. "On the contrary, I have been telling you how free we are to publish and distribute Bibles." And with that he started to tell a story that would illustrate, he said, how well Christians got along with the regime. Even Stalin, before his recent death, had smiled on the work of the Bible shop.

One day, he said, two officials came into the shop and handed him a written order. To celebrate Stalin's birthday, every shop was to display his picture in its window surrounded by a selection of its choicest wares.

"Of course," the proprietor said, "I was eager to cooperate. I went shopping that very day and found just what I wanted: a very large color picture of Stalin, arms folded, looking downward with an affectionate smile on his lips. I placed the picture in my window. Then I chose my most expensive Bible and opened it to some words of Christ written in red, just below the approving eyes of Stalin. Everyone seemed to like my display, for soon a crowd gathered and every face was smiling. The People's Police arrived. 'Take that down!' they ordered. 'Oh no, sir,' I said. 'I could not do that, for here are my orders from the Government in black and white.'"

I was laughing, but the proprietor was not. There was not even a twinkle in his eye. It was my first encounter with the dry double entendre that plays such a part in the life of the Christian community behind the Iron Curtain. Hastily I arranged my features to match the sober expression of his own.

As we talked several customers came in. I was interested to see how busy the little shop was. When we were alone again, I asked the proprietor if there were Bible stores in other Communist countries. "Some yes, some no," he said. He began dusting the shelves. "I understand that in Russia Bibles are very scarce indeed. In fact, they tell me fortunes are being made there. A man smuggles ten Bibles into Russia and sells them for enough to buy a motorcycle. He drives the motorcycle back into Poland or Yugoslavia or East Germany and sells it for a fat profit, with which he buys more Bibles. That's just hearsay of course."

All that morning I visited with the Bible shop owner, and when it came time to say goodbye, I did it regretfully. Walking

Diary of a Smuggler

CUBA

Alfonso pastors a growing church in Havana, but the burden of his heart is for Cuba's children. We had spoken in secret last autumn when I went to deliver Bibles, children's materials, and supplies to some churches in Cuba.

When we last visited pastor Alfonso, we took him a selection of Christian children's comics and storybooks. Other teams have delivered children's picture Bibles, Sunday school materials, and practical supplies. Without these, Cubans would have very few Christian resources, since none are available on the island. Apart from the high cost of living, acute shortages of basic necessities have inflated prices, so most Cubans live in great poverty.

"We have learned to trust God for everything, and we have seen Him answer in miraculous ways. You tell me Cubans know how to pray. My response is that we have had to learn, otherwise we would have starved," shared another pastor.

When we entered Cuba our suitcases brimmed with Bibles, clothes, and other basic necessities, but God so often goes one step further to show how much He cares about individuals. We happened to give pastor Alfonso a large bag full of soap we had brought, since it is virtually unaffordable in Cuba. When his wife saw the soap, her eyes lit up. "This Christmas we wanted to give our Sunday school children a bar of soap each as a gift. We have been praying for God to supply the means for us to buy them, but He's just given us the soap!"

I remembered my trip to buy that soap. Having decided on economy bars, I was filling my shopping basket when I changed my mind and chose the luxury brands instead. For once in their lives, I thought, I wanted them to have the best. But it was God, wanting to bless those who have nothing.

back to the school, I tried to make sense of the visit. Here was a store selling Bibles openly to anyone who wanted one—hardly an example of the religious persecution we had so often heard about in Holland. And yet my friend was as circumspect in his talk as if he were carrying on an illegal trade. There was an uneasiness, a tension in the air that told me all was not as it seemed.

As yet I had not attempted the principal thing I had come to do. I wanted to hand out my "twenty-six lead soldiers" openly on the street, to see what would happen.

So for several days running I stood on corners, I went to the marketplace—bright with fresh summer vegetables—I rode the trams, and everywhere I handed out my booklets.

I had never seen trams as crowded as these. There were riders on the platforms, on the couplings, on the hubs. I remember once squeezing onto a rear platform, holding my tracts over my head so they would not be crushed. A peasant woman near me looked up at the pamphlets and crossed herself.

"Ja. Ja," she said in German, "this is what we need in Poland."

That was all. But I knew that we had really met, she the Catholic from Eastern Europe, I the Protestant from the West. There on the crowded tramway platform we had met as Christians.

As the days passed and no evil consequences followed the distribution of my booklets in public for all to see, I began to feel exhilarated about the possibilities in this unexpected mission field. And then one day I discovered how deep my own defeatist attitudes still ran. I believed that I had passed out Christian literature in every conceivable setting. But one morning in the daily Quiet Time that I had observed ever since London days, I thought about the military barracks just up the street from the school. Not only had it never occurred to me to pass out booklets to the soldiers there, but the very sight of their uniforms made me quicken my steps in the other direction.

How blind could you get! I of all people ought to have known that the uniform doesn't make the man. The day before the festival ended I walked up to the group of six Red soldiers standing guard and handed each of them a booklet. The men glanced at the booklets, at me, then at each other. I told them I was Dutch and found that one of them spoke German.

"It must make you very bitter, the American occupation," one of them said.

"The what?"

"The occupation of Holland by the American Air Force."

I was in the midst of trying to explain that we were not an occupied country when the soldiers all suddenly came to attention. Up walked an officer, barking orders in Polish as he came. The six soldiers wheeled smartly and marched away double time. But I noticed that they carried their booklets with them.

"What was it you gave these men?" said the officer in German.

"This, sir." I handed him one of the little books. He looked at it carefully. Two hours later it was I who broke away. We were scheduled to leave the next day, and I had a dozen travel forms to fill out. As we parted, the officer, a Russian Orthodox by birth, wished me Godspeed and a safe journey.

The next morning was our last in Warsaw. I was up even earlier

AROUND THE GLOBE
Ethiopia

Population: 62.5 million
Location/Size: Eastern Africa
446,953 sq. miles
Major Religions: Orthodoxy/Christianity
Islam
Protestant Christianity
Level of Persecution: Sporadic, static

Severe persecution plagued the Ethiopian church during the Marxist regime of Mariam, but it has since slacked off markedly. The new atmosphere of freedom promotes increased opportunities for evangelism to which both the national church and foreign missionaries are responding.

Despite the political freedom currently enjoyed by the Church, other religious groups (most notably, Islam) have prompted a sharp rise in harassment and discrimination against Christians.

The Ethiopian Church is growing at a moderately fast rate and could exceed one hundred million by the middle of this century. Given adequate resolution of conflicts with Islam, Christianity could permeate the entire country.

than usual and out on the street at sunup. I found a bench on one of the broad avenues, wiped off the dew, and sat down with my pocket Testament on my knee. I had a special purpose in coming out so early. I wanted to pray for each person I had encountered on my trip. For a long time that morning I pictured the places and the people I had seen. On three Sundays I had visited Presbyterian, Baptist, Roman Catholic, Orthodox, Reformed, and Methodist churches. Five times I had been asked to speak during a service. I had visited a Bible shop, talked with soldiers and an officer, with people on street corners and on trolley cars. I prayed for each one.

And as I sat praying I heard the music.

It was coming toward me down the avenue. Martial, smart, with a sound of voices singing. And then I saw it—the perfect climax to the visit: the Parade of Triumph that ended the festival.

This was the other side of the picture. For over against the one little Bible shop and the occasional Christian I had met, was this mammoth counterfact: the tremendous strength of the regime.

Here they came now, the young Socialists, marching down the avenue. Not for a moment did I believe they were there under coercion. They marched because they believed. They marched eight abreast: healthy, vital, clean-cut. They marched singing, and their voices were like shouts. On and on they came for ten minutes, fifteen minutes, rank after rank of young men and young women. . . .

The effect was overwhelming. These were the evangelists of the twentieth century. These were the people who went about shouting their good news.

And part of the news was that the old shackles and superstitions of religion, the old inhibiting ideas about God, no longer held. Man was his own master: the future was his to take.

What should we of the West do about them, these thousands of young people still marching past me, clapping now with a terrifying rhythm?

Kill them? This was the answer the Nazis had offered.

Let them win by default? Much as I loved and respected the WEC and its training college, it had never once sent a man behind the Iron Curtain.

What should we do then? What should *I* do?

The Bible in my lap lay open, pages ruffling in the morning breeze. I put down my hand to hold them still and found that I was looking at the book of Revelation. My fingers were resting on the page almost as though they were pointing. "Awake," said the verse at my fingertips, "and strengthen what remains and is on the point of death. . . ."

Suddenly I realized that I was seeing the words through a blur of tears. Could it be that God was speaking them to me right now, telling me that my life work was here behind the Iron Curtain, where His remnant Church was struggling for its life? Was

I to have some part in strengthening this precious thing that remained?

But that was ridiculous! How could I? As far as I knew, back then in 1955, there was not a single missionary working in this largest of all mission fields. What could I, one person without funds or organization, do against an overwhelming force like the one passing in front of me now?

Imagine This

You were arrested for your faith in Christ, and you have been in prison for several years because of it. Each day you face beatings and attacks from prison guards who tell you that if you confess the names of your church members and deny your faith, they will let you free. You feel exhausted and at the end of your rope, but you know that if you share the names of your Christian brothers and sisters, they will be arrested and beaten.

What Would You Do?

eight

The Cup of Suffering

If one part suffers, every part suffers with it; if one part is honored, every part rejoices with it. Now you are the body of Christ, and each one of you is a part of it.

1 Corinthians 12:26–27

Our train pulled into Amsterdam right on schedule. I got off with the rest of the crowd, corduroy trousers still squeaking, but carrying a suitcase that was considerably lighter than it had been going to Warsaw.

I did not go directly to Witte. Instead, I went to see the Whetstras in their new Amsterdam home.

It was a beauty: a handsome brown brick house in a pleasant, tree-lined street near the river. Parked in front was a shining new Volkswagen, light blue, which Mr. Whetstra had also written me about. I put my suitcase down on the sidewalk and tried the little car's door.

"Well, son, what do you think of her?"

I turned around to find Mr. Whetstra smiling at me. He took me for a short spin around the waterfront.

"But enough of showing off," he said. "You must tell us about your visit to Poland."

So for the rest of the afternoon I told the Whetstras about my trip. I told them, too, about the Bible verse that apparently had been given me in such an uncanny way.

"But how would I go about strengthening anything?" I said. "What kind of strength do I have?"

Mr. Whetstra shook his head. He agreed with me that one lone Dutchman was scarcely an answer to the kind of need I had been describing. It was Mrs. Whetstra who understood.

"No strength at all!" she answered me joyously. "And don't you know that it is just when we are weakest that God can use us most? Suppose now that it wasn't you but the Holy Spirit Who had plans behind the Iron Curtain? You talk about strength. . . ."

My return to Witte was coupled with a pleasant surprise.

Neighbors dropped in all evening with questions, the basic ones all of us were asking in 1955 when travel behind the Curtain was just beginning and the Communist world was still cloaked in mystery. But finally the last guest clomped across our little bridge, and it was time for bed. I stretched, reached for my nearly empty suitcase, and started to follow Cornelius up the ladder to the loft.

"Just a minute, Andy," said Geltje.

I stopped.

"We have something to show you!"

I got down off the ladder and followed Geltje into the room off the parlor that had once been Mama's and Papa's. Every inch of it was filled with memories: Bas's wasted form beneath the blanket; Mama during the last months of the war—too weak to lift her head from that pillow. . . .

"With the new room for Papa finished over the shed, Andy," Geltje was saying, "we've decided you should have this for your headquarters."

I couldn't find my breath. In my wildest dreams of bliss, I had never imagined a room of my own. In this small house I knew at what sacrifice Arie and Geltje were making me this gift.

"UNTIL YOU'RE MARRIED!" Papa boomed from the living room. Papa was beginning to make frequent remarks about his twenty-seven-year-old bachelor son. "JUST UNTIL YOU'RE MARRIED!"

I somehow found words to say. A room of my own! That night after the rest of the family had gone to bed, I closed my own door and went around my room just feeling my furniture.

"Thank you for a chair, Lord. Thank you for a bureau. . . ." I would build a desk. I'd put it there, and I'd spend hours here in my room, studying and working and planning.

I had not been home a week before the invitations began to come in. Churches, clubs, civic groups, schools; everybody wanted to know about life behind the Iron Curtain.

I accepted them all. In part I needed the payment they offered. But I had an even stronger reason. Somehow I felt sure that through the speeches I was going to be shown what I was to do next.

And that's what happened.

A church in Haarlem where I was to speak had posted advertisements all over town stating that my subject was to be "How Christians Live Behind the Iron Curtain." I would never have presumed to speak on such a topic after a three-week visit to one city. But at least the announcements did draw a crowd—the hall was jammed. And they drew something else: a group of Communists.

I recognized them right away—some of them had been on the trip—and I wondered what heckling I might be in for. To my surprise, however, they made no move either during the speech or during the question period that followed. But afterward one of the women came up to me. She had been a leader of the Dutch delegation in Warsaw.

"I didn't like your talk," she said.

"I'm sorry. I didn't think you would."

"You told only part of the story," she said. "Obviously you haven't seen enough. You need to travel more, visit more countries, meet more leaders."

I said nothing. What was she leading up to?

"In other words, you ought to take another trip, and that's what I've come to suggest." I held my breath. "I am in charge of selecting fifteen people from Holland to take a trip to Czechoslovakia.

They'll be gone four weeks. There'll be students and professors and people in communications, and we'd like someone from the churches. Would you come?"

Was this God's hand? Was this the next door opening in His plan for me? I decided to put the question before Him once again in terms of money. I knew I didn't have funds for such a trip. "If You want me to go, Lord," I said in a flash prayer beneath my breath, "You will have to supply the means."

"Thanks," I said aloud, "but I could never afford such a trip. I'm sorry." I began to pack away the pictures of Warsaw I had brought with me.

I could feel the lady staring at me.

"Well," she said finally, "we can work that out."

I looked up. "What do you mean?"

"About the expenses. For you, there will be no charge."

And so began my second trip behind the Iron Curtain. It was much like my visit to Poland except that the group was smaller and I had a lot more trouble getting off by myself. I kept wondering what it was God wanted me to learn in Czechoslovakia.

And toward the end of the four weeks I found the answer. Everywhere we had been told about the religious freedom that people enjoyed under communism. Here in Czechoslovakia, our guide told us, there was even a group of scholars, paid by the State, who had just finished a new translation of the Bible and were even now working on a Bible dictionary.

"I would very much like to visit these men," I said.

So that afternoon I was taken to a large office building in the heart of Prague. It was the Interchurch Center—the headquarters for all Protestant churches in Czechoslovakia. My first impression was astonishment at the size of the physical facilities that the Church was able to maintain. I was led into a suite of offices where scholarly looking gentlemen in black coats sat behind heavy tomes and piles of paper. These were the men, I was told, who had worked on the new translation. I was very impressed. But gradually some amusing facts began to emerge. I asked if I might see a copy of the new translation, and was shown a bulky, much-fingered manuscript.

"Oh. The translation has not been published yet?" I asked.

"Well, no," said one of the scholars. His face seemed sad. "We've had it ready since the war, but. . . ." He glanced at the tour director and let his sentence drift off.

"What about the Bible dictionary? Is that ready yet?"

"Almost."

"But what good will it do to have a dictionary of the Bible and no Bible? Are there earlier translations?"

The scholar looked again at the tour director as if trying to decide how much he could say.

"No," he finally blurted out. "No. It's very difficult. Very difficult to find Bibles here nowadays."

The tour director considered the interview over. I was shepherded out without having a chance to ask more questions. But the damage had been done. I had glimpsed the subterfuge. Rather than make a frontal attack on religion in this devout nation, the new regime was playing the game of Frustration. It was sponsoring a new translation of the Bible—a translation that never quite got published. It was sponsoring a new dictionary of the Bible— only there were no Bibles to go with the dictionary.

The next day I asked our guide to take me to the Interdenominational Book Store at Jungmanova No. 9. I was determined to see for myself how difficult it was to buy a Bible. The shop was well stocked with music, stationery, pictures, statues, crosses, books that were more or less related to religion. In any similar shop in Holland there would be an entire section of the store devoted to different editions of the Scriptures.

"May I see a red-letter Bible, please?" I asked the saleswoman. By now I had discovered that, between English and German, I rarely had any trouble communicating.

The saleswoman shook her head. "I'm sorry, sir. Those are out of stock right now."

"Well, how about a standard black-and-white edition?"

But these too, it seemed, were temporarily unavailable.

"Ma'am," I said, "I have come all the way from Holland to see how the Church is faring in Czechoslovakia. Are you going to tell

A Traveler's Story

JESUS BECOMES LORD OF A YOUNG COMORIAN MUSLIM'S LIFE

My name is Rashid. I grew up in a small village on Mayotte. My grandfather is the Kadi and my father the Muezzin [the person who calls the people to the mosque] of that village.

One day I saw a very beautiful girl who was the daughter of a local pastor. I tried to make an appointment with her and asked her to be my friend. Instead of going out with me, she invited me to her home.

When I came to her home, her father explained the Bible to me and later gave me my own Bible. Whenever I went to their house to see the girl, I did not get the opportunity to speak to her. She was constantly busy in the kitchen, and I could never get time with her. Her father always kept me busy by explaining the Bible to me.

I listened to everything he said but did not really know what to do with the Bible. When he gave it to me, I first wanted to throw it away on my way home. I was on the verge of throwing it into the sea when I decided to hide it instead. I thought if I read it I might get an appointment with the girl. However, every time I went to their home, I just learned about the Bible and did not get to spend time with the girl. Eventually, I really became interested in the Bible.

For three months I studied the Bible. I started going to church and made lots of friends. I thought I had been going to church because of the friendly girl. Later when I asked myself why I was really going to church, I realized it was because I had a hunger for the Word of God.

me that I can walk into the largest religious bookstore in the country and not be able to buy a single Bible?"

The saleswoman excused herself and disappeared into the back of the store. There was a rapid and somewhat excited discussion behind the curtain, followed by the sound of paper rattling. And then the manager himself appeared, carrying a parcel already wrapped in brown paper.

"Here you are, sir." I thanked him. "It's that new translation that makes Bibles scarce," the manager said. "Until that comes out, new Bibles just aren't being printed."

It was our last day. Big plans had been made for us. We were to go out of Prague on a tour of model communities in the countryside. Then we were to come back for dinner, a press conference, and final goodbyes.

I might possibly have suffered through this schedule for the sake of politeness, except for one thing: it was Sunday. It was my last chance to worship with Czech believers without having a "guide" hovering nearby.

I had planned my escape for days. I had noticed that the rear door of our tour bus had a faulty spring: even in "closed" position there was a gap over a foot wide between it and the doorjamb. By holding my breath. . . .

As the bus pulled away from the hotel that last day, I was in the last seat. At every traffic light I sized up my chances for slipping out that door unseen. But too many heads were turning, taking in the sights of the city. At last came a chance when every neck was craned forward, staring at the heroic bronze figure of a man on horseback. I never learned who it was, for as the tour director began describing it, I sucked in my breath, squeezed through the opening, and stepped down into the street. The air brakes hissed, and the powerful motor revved up. I was alone in Prague.

Half an hour later I was standing in the vestibule of a church I had spotted on a previous tour of the city, watching people come in. I was particularly anxious to see how a church could function without Bibles. Occasionally someone carried a hymnal, more rarely a Bible. But one thing that puzzled me—many people brought looseleaf notebooks. What were they for?

The service began. I took a seat in the back and immediately had a surprise. Almost everyone seemed farsighted! The owners of the hymn books held them out at arm's length, high in the air. Those with looseleaf notebooks did the same. And then I realized: the people with books were sharing them with those who had none. In the notebooks were copied, note by note and word by word, the favorite hymns of the congregation.

It was the same with the Bibles. When the preacher announced the text, every Bible owner in the congregation found the reference and held his book high so that friends nearby could follow the reading. As I watched those men and women struggling literally to get close to the Word, my hand closed over the Dutch Bible in my coat jacket. How much for granted I had always taken my right to own this Book. I thought that I would never reach for it again without remembering the old granny in front of me now, standing almost on tiptoe, squinting as she strained to see the words in the Bible her son held aloft.

After the service I introduced myself to the preacher. When I mentioned that I had come from Holland chiefly to meet with Christians in his country, he seemed overwhelmed.

"I had heard," he said, "that Czechoslovakia was going to begin opening its borders. I didn't believe it. We've been—" he looked around—"almost imprisoned since the war. You must come and talk with me."

Together we went to his apartment. It was only later that I learned how dangerous a thing for him this was in the Czechoslovakia of 1955. He told me that the Government was trying to get a total grip on the Church. It was the Government that selected theological students—choosing only candidates who favored the regime. In addition, every two months a minister had to renew his license. A friend had recently had his renewal application denied—no explanation. Each sermon had to be written out ahead of time and approved by the authorities. Each church had to list its leaders with the State. That same week in Brno five brethren were on trial because their church did not permit the naming of leaders.

It was time for the second service at the church.

"Would you come and speak to us?" he asked suddenly.

"Is that possible? Can I really preach here?"

"No. I did not say 'preach.' One must be careful with words. As a foreigner you can't preach, but you can bring us 'greetings' from Holland. And," my friend smiled, "if you wanted to, you could bring us 'greetings' from the Lord."

My interpreter was a young medical student named Antonin. First I brought greetings from Holland and the West. That took a couple of minutes. And then for half an hour I brought greetings to the congregation "from Jesus Christ." It worked so well that Antonin suggested we try the device again in another church. All in all, that day I preached four times and visited five different churches. Each was memorable in its own way, but the last one

VIETNAM

Diary of a Smuggler

One of the first things I learned as I worked with the house-church movement in Ho Chi Minh City is how to move around on motorcycles. In a city with five million people and one million motorbikes, it is inevitable that a person rides one while visiting.

This was my experience. I was told the day before to go in front of a famous hotel and wait for my ride. I didn't know who would pick me up or where he would bring me. All I knew was that I had to be to the hotel by 7:30 A.M.

At exactly 7:30 A.M., a motorbike stopped nearby. When our eyes met, the driver nodded curtly. I took it to mean that he was my assigned guide, but I really had no way of knowing.

It took us twenty minutes to reach the house where the class I was going to was located. Last year the class was in a different location, but the police visited the place and even took a picture of the pastor. They had to look for another safe place.

The new place was out of harm's way. The small factory downstairs provided a good cover for the meeting. Whatever sounds that were made upstairs were muffled by the hammering and sawing being done in the shop below.

Security is very important in this kind of work. On the first day, the orientation did not deal with the topics to be covered in the class, but on what to do when there are unexpected "visitors." The thirty students were informed about the exit doors. They were even assigned which door to take so as not to create confusion when the emergency came.

Precautionary measures were instituted in the program as well. There was no singing, no loud praises or prayer. But if you think that all these security measures hampered the work or doused the enthusiasm of the students, think again.

Everything seemed normal; I didn't sense the nervousness that otherwise would have characterized such a gathering. In fact, all students had their pens and pencils poised, ready to scribble their notes and insights on paper. They were all ears and eyes on Pastor Joseph.

How I wished that our Bible classes in the free world elicited the same reaction. If only the free Christians knew that attending a Bible class in Vietnam is this dangerous, they would begin to appreciate the freedom they have and perhaps no longer take it for granted.

most of all. For it was there that I received the Cup of Suffering.

It was seven o'clock in the evening, already dark on that November day. I knew that by now the tour group would be really anxious about me. It was time I tried to find them.

But even as I was thinking this, Antonin asked me if I would visit just one more church, "where I think they especially need to meet someone from Outside."

So once more we traveled across Prague until we came to a small out-of-the-way Moravian church. I was astonished at the number of people there, especially young people. There must have been forty persons between the ages of eighteen and twenty-five. I spoke my greetings and then answered questions. Could Christians in

AROUND THE GLOBE
Indonesia

Population: 212.1 million
Location/Size: Southeastern Asian islands
752,410 sq. miles
Major Religions: Islam
Christianity
Level of Persecution: Sporadic, but growing

In theory, the Indonesian constitution recognizes freedom of religion and guarantees freedom of religious expression. However, in practice, religious choice is restricted to Islam, Protestantism, Catholicism, and Hindu-Buddhism. Of the followers of each choice, Muslims are clearly favored.

In coming years it's likely there will be recurring violence and tension between Muslims and Christians. Yet despite the growing hostility against Christians and radical actions taken by certain groups, many Muslims are increasingly curious about Christianity, and the Church has enjoyed a substantial harvest. The Church is currently growing and will likely number more than sixty-five million by the middle of the century.

Holland get good jobs? Did anyone report you to the Government when you went to church? Could you attend church and still get into a good university?

"You see," Antonin told me, "it's unpatriotic to be a Christian in Czechoslovakia these days. Some of these people have been blackballed at work. Many have missed out on education. And that"—he took a small box from the hands of a young man who stood beside him—"is why they want you to have this."

The young man was speaking to me very earnestly in Czech.

"Take this to Holland with you," Antonin translated, "and when people ask you about it, tell them about us and remind them that we are part of the Body, too, and that we are in pain."

I took the box and opened it. Inside was a silver lapel ornament in the shape of a tiny cup. I had seen several of the young people wearing them and had wondered what they were.

Antonin was pinning it to my jacket. "This is the symbol of the Church in Czechoslovakia. We call it the Cup of Suffering."

When Antonin had left me at the hotel, I thought again about those words. I realized that we in Holland were as insulated from the real facts of modern Church history as were the Christians in Czechoslovakia. The Cup of Suffering was the symbol of a reality that we had to share.

Right now, however, I had another reality to face. Where would I rendezvous with my group? They were not at the hotel—nor did anyone there know where the farewell dinner was to have been held. I went to a restaurant where we had eaten several times. "No, monsieur, the group from Holland did not eat here tonight."

"Well, is it too late for me to have a sandwich?"

"Of course not, monsieur."

I had taken one bite of the sandwich when the door of the restaurant flew open and the tour director walked in. She glanced swiftly around the room, then sighted me. Her shoulders collapsed in an involuntary sigh of relief. But the next instant her face flushed with anger. She fairly ran to my table, flung a bill at the waiter, and indicated the door with a jerk of her head. It was obvious that she did not trust herself to speak.

Outside waiting for us at the curb was a government car—a long black limousine with its engine running, driven by a most unpleasant looking man. He got out as we approached, opened the door, and then locked it behind us. Where were they taking me? Remembering the Hollywood version of such scenes, I tried to keep track of where we were going.

And as I did, the humor of the situation came to me. Because we were going to the hotel.

Just before the car stopped, the tour director spoke her first words. "You have held the group up half a day. We have called every hospital, every police station. We finally called the morgue. Unfortunately, you were not there! Where have you been?"

"Oh," I said, "I got separated. And so I walked around. I really am sorry for the trouble I've caused you."

"Well, I want to tell you officially, sir, that you are no longer welcome here. Should you attempt to enter this country again, you will discover as much for yourself."

And so I did. A year later I applied again for a visa to Czechoslovakia and was turned down. I tried once more two years after that and again was refused. It was five years before I was allowed back inside that beautiful land. And meanwhile I had seen such persecution of Christians that Czechoslovakia by contrast seemed a place of freedom and liberty.

Imagine This

You are a Christian living in China and are about to apply to a university. A friend of yours recently applied, but was denied acceptance because she is a Christian. You are required to state your religion on the application, and you know you will likely be denied acceptance if you state that you are a Christian.

What Would You Do?

nine

The Foundations Are Laid

Consider it pure joy, my brothers,
whenever you face trials of many kinds,
because you know that the testing of
your faith develops perseverance.

James 1:2-3

The next few months seemed to be pure frustration. The trips to Poland and Czechoslovakia had come about almost without my thinking about them. But now when I began to make inquiries about return visits to these places and trips to other Iron Curtain countries, I encountered month after month of officialdom: questionnaires, delays, forms in triplicate—but never a visa.

Even my own little room posed problems. In Czechoslovakia I had thought so often about that room waiting for me at home and longed to be back in it. Now I discovered a drawback I could never have anticipated. Perhaps it was the very fact that it was so snug and comfortable; at any rate the room itself came to symbolize for me the fact that I was very much alone.

Day after day as I sat in that room drafting letters to consulates, I would dream of a wife who would share both the room and the vision of work behind the Curtain. On more lucid days I would laugh at myself: if missionary work was a poor life to offer a beautiful girl—the girl in my dreams was gorgeous—what would she say to this new mission field I had glimpsed, where separation and secrecy and uncertainty would be the best I could offer? These, as I say, were objections that reason raised; the girl herself, being a dream girl, never mentioned them.

Money was another problem. Although neither Geltje nor Arie ever mentioned the subject, I knew that I should be participating in the expenses of the household. Shortly after I had come back from my trip to Poland, the Dutch magazine *Kracht Van Omhoog* had asked me to write a series of articles for them about my experiences behind the Iron Curtain. I was no writer, and I did nothing about the invitation. But now as I sat in my little room with my empty wallet on the homemade desk in front of me, I seemed to hear God say, "Write those articles for *Kracht Van Omhoog.*"

I was mystified by the command. Surely it could have nothing to do with the need for money about which I had just then been praying: the magazine offered no payment.

But that sense of insistence was there, and in sheer obedience I sat down and wrote about what I had observed not only in Poland but also in Czechoslovakia. I mailed the articles the next day, along with some photographs. The editor acknowledged them with his thanks—but without money as I expected—and I dismissed the whole matter from my mind.

And then one morning there was another letter from *Kracht Van Omhoog*. A strange thing was happening: although nowhere in the article had I mentioned money or indicated that I was even considering another trip to these places, from all over Holland readers were sending in money. It was never very much, just a few guilders at a time. But the editor wanted to know where he should send them.

And thus began the most amazing story of supply. The first gifts from my unknown friends were small because my needs were small. I wanted to help Geltje with the household expenses; my old jacket was worn out; I had promised Antonin that I would try to mail him a copy of the Czech Bible. And to meet these small needs there was a small income from readers of *Kracht Van Omhoog*. Later as my work expanded and there was greater need, so too did contributions from readers increase. It was only when there was need for really large sums, years later, that God turned elsewhere for our funds.

But something far more important than money came out of the first contact with *Kracht Van Omhoog*. In the mail one morning came a letter from the leader of a prayer group in the village of Amersfoort. The Holy Spirit, the letter said, had instructed them to get in touch with me; they didn't know why—but could I pay a visit to Amersfoort?

I was immediately intrigued. If the Holy Spirit was directing people's actions so minutely today, this was the very thing I needed to know more about. I went to Amersfoort. The group of about a dozen men and women met in the home of a man named Karl de Graaf, a builder of dikes.

I had never met a group like this. Instead of a planned program for the evening, with a leader and a study topic as with the other prayer groups I had attended, these people seemed to spend most of their time listening. There was an occasional prayer said aloud—in no particular order around the room—but these prayers were more like outbursts of love and praise for God than thought-out petitions. It was as though every individual in that room sensed that God was very close, and in the delight of His company wanted nothing, needed nothing, except occasionally to express the joy bubbling up inside.

Occasionally, in the listening, expectant stillness, one of the group would apparently hear something else: some instruction, some piece of information, that came from outside his own knowledge. This too would be spoken aloud. "Joost's mother, in America, needs our prayers tonight." "We thank You, Lord, that our prayer for Stephje has just now been answered." I was so caught up in this new kind of prayer experience that when the others got up to go and Mrs. de Graaf led me to my room, I could scarcely believe the clock on the dresser: it was four-thirty in the morning.

Several days later I was working in my room on a new article for *Kracht Van Omhoog* when Geltje knocked on the door.

"There's someone to see you, Andrew. I don't know him."

I went out to the front stoop, and there was Karl de Graaf. "Hello!" I said, surprised.

"Hello, Andy. Do you know how to drive?"

"Drive?"

"An automobile."

"No," I said, bewildered. "No, I don't."

"Because last night in our prayers we had a word from the Lord about you. It's important for you to be able to drive."

"Whatever on earth for?" I said. "I'll never own a car, that's for sure."

"Andrew," Mr. de Graaf spoke patiently, as to a slow-witted student, "I'm not arguing the logic of the case. I'm just passing on the message." And with that, he was striding across the bridge to his waiting car.

The idea of learning to drive seemed so farfetched that I did nothing about it. But a week later the dike builder drove up to the door again.

"Have you been taking your driving lessons?"

"Well—not exactly. . . ."

"Haven't you learned yet how important obedience is? I suppose I'm going to have to teach you myself. Hop in."

That afternoon I sat behind the wheel of a motor vehicle for the first time since that disastrous morning eleven years earlier when I had driven the Bren carrier full speed down the company street. Mr. de Graaf returned again and again, and so skilled a teacher was he that a few weeks later I took my driving test and passed it the first time around—a rare thing in Holland. I still could see no reason why I—who didn't even own a bicycle anymore—should be carrying an automobile driver's license around in my pocket. But Mr. de Graaf refused to speculate. "That's the excitement in obedience," he said. "Finding out later what God had in mind."

And then occurred the event that for a while drove everything else from our minds. In the fall of 1956 came the Hungarian Revolt and with it the flight to the West of hundreds of thousands of terrified and disillusioned people, not only from Hungary but from Yugoslavia and East Germany and every other Communist country. These refugees were herded into vast camps near the borders where conditions were said to be unthinkable. A man spoke in front of the burgomaster's house in Witte, asking for volunteers to help in the camps. I went in the first bus to leave Holland.

The volunteers occupied only the front of the bus; the rest of the bus was filled with food, clothing, and medicine to be divided equally among the largest refugee camps, located in West Germany and Austria.

Nothing I had heard prepared me for what we found. Ten families in a room was commonplace, some of them trying to preserve a vanished way of privacy by hanging up their blankets for walls during the daytime.

We plunged into this sea of need like swimmers on the edge of the ocean, passing out clothing and medicine, writing letters, trying to locate separated families, making visa applications. And of course, whenever I could, I held prayer services. And it was here that I made an astonishing discovery. Most of these people knew literally nothing about the Bible. Those who had grown up under the old regimes were largely illiterate. The younger ones, who had been raised under communism, were better educated but of course not in the Bible.

And so I began, working mostly through interpreters, holding a few small classes in the most basic kind of Bible education. I knew from experience how powerful this knowledge can be, but I was scarcely prepared for its effect on lives in which it was totally new. People who had been sunk in despair became pillars of strength for a whole barracks. I saw bitterness change to hope, shame to pride.

I remember one old couple, escapees from Yugoslavia. The wife was smelly and fat and had chin hairs an inch long. She at least tried to keep the area around their beds picked up and tidy, but her husband, unsettled by the move from his ancestral farm, just sat on the edge of his cot, rocking endlessly back and forth day after day.

They began attending the Bible class I taught in their barracks. At first they appeared thunderstruck at what they heard. The old man wept as he listened, letting tears fall unchecked into his lap.

Ethiopia   ## A Traveler's Story

"I SAW A VISION OF JESUS"

I was born into a family who practiced witchcraft, and they dedicated me to an evil spirit. One night an evil spirit came to me where I was sleeping and insisted that I should kill myself. Then I saw a vision that looked like a fire that came from heaven. I looked at it in amazement. The fire descended onto our house, setting it ablaze, and finally it penetrated the house and stood behind me. The moment the fire was behind me, it looked like the Son of Man—a beautiful man. He started to speak to me. "What did the evil spirit say to you?" He asked. "He said I should commit suicide." The Son of Man said to me, "You must not kill yourself; you'll be My witness."

After the incident I went to Addis Ababa and worked in a relative's house. My family in Addis belonged to the Coptic church, and although they didn't read the Bible, they had one on their bookshelf. I took it and started reading the Gospel of John in the New Testament. I started to wonder who this Jesus was

whom I had never heard of before. As I was about to clean the room I had another vision. The vision was of Jesus, the same Jesus I saw before. He said to me: "You will be My witness; start going to church and accept Me, for I am your Savior." I cried and cried and cried. I became very afraid and considered myself a Pentie [derogatory name referring to a Pentecostal]. "I have really become a Pentie; I don't want to be a Pentie," I thought to myself. I fell asleep and all night long I heard the words: "Jesus, Jesus, Jesus . . ." The next morning I went to the church and accepted Jesus as my personal Savior.

The moment my family heard about this, they expelled me from the house, saying, "If you've become a Pentie, you have betrayed us, and we don't want to see you. Leave our house."

This happened eight years ago. Since then I've been serving the Lord. In the name of Jesus, I will never go back to my old way of life.

By about the fourth class I noticed that the woman's chin hairs were gone, and the husband had begun to shave.

Tiny details, of course, except for what they said about two people awakening to a sense of themselves as beloved children of God.

"If only," said the old man after the class one day, and then he stopped.

"If only what?" the interpreter prodded.

"If only I had known all of this years ago, back home, back in Yugoslavia."

That too was becoming my dream.

The clothing and other supplies we had brought to the camps had long since run out, and we returned to Holland to try to collect more. While I was home I went once more to the Yugoslavian consulate to apply, as I had before, for a visa.

Once again there were forms in triplicate to fill out, photographs (which I now ordered by the score) to affix, the unpromising: "This will take some time to process." Only once in filling out the application blank did I hesitate. There it was, halfway down the page, the familiar space for "occupation." I had the feeling that mine had weighed against me before in these applications. But what was the phrase we had been taught in Glasgow? Walk in the Light, nothing hidden, nothing concealed, everything open and transparent for all to see. And so, as I had before, I wrote MISSIONARY in block letters, and left the completed forms on the desk.

When our bus was filled again with blankets and clothing, powdered milk and coffee and chocolate, we set out again for the refugee camps. I was working in West Berlin when the telegram came about Papa. He had died in his garden.

I caught the next train home. The simple little funeral was held at the graveside. As is the custom in land-hungry Holland, Mama's grave was reopened and Papa's casket lowered to rest on top of hers.

Now the old house was empty indeed. How I missed the booming voice that had filled it from floor to rafters. How I missed the round-shouldered form bent so patiently over the rows of lettuce and cabbages, missed his love for growing things.

I went back to Germany and threw myself harder than ever into the work with the refugees. The Hungarian Revolt had brought the newest wave of escapees, but actually the camps in West Berlin were old ones, forgotten by the world until this latest event made headlines. In these camps had lived for years the leftovers of the second world war, the homeless, the displaced, the stateless thousands created by the Nazi madness. To me, these people were the saddest of all, especially the children. I met eleven- and twelve-year-olds who had never seen the inside of a real house. Two single persons received greater allotments of space and clothing than a married couple, so marriage was rare, and most of the children were illegitimate. For months I worked to get a group of these youngsters into Holland. I knew plenty of families ready to take them—Geltje and Maartje would have taken some—but again and again the children failed to pass the health requirements. In those cold, damp barracks TB was endemic. The posters on the walls offering entry into Sweden or the United States for young adults free of disease were a mockery to the sick who made up ninety percent of every camp.

It was while I was in the midst of this hopeless and heart-breaking work that one morning during the Quiet Time that was now an integral part of every day wherever I was, I had the most remarkable impression. It was just as though I heard a voice tell me: "Today you are going to get the visa for Yugoslavia."

I was incredulous. I had almost forgotten about my pending applications for travel there and other places, so wrapped up had I been with the camps. Still, I found myself glancing out the window of the volunteer hostel, watching for the morning mail. When I saw the carrier coming, I ran down to meet her. "A letter for you from Holland!" she said and fished around in her bag.

I took the letter from her. The address in Witte was crossed out, and above it, in Geltje's handwriting, was the street and number of the hostel in Berlin. In the left-hand corner of the envelope was the seal of the Yugoslavian embassy at The Hague. "Thank you!" I said, and right there on the corner I ripped the letter open and stared uncomprehending at its contents. The Yugoslav government regretted to inform me that my application for a visa had been denied. That was all. No explanation.

What did it mean? Surely I had received some kind of advance knowledge about this letter. But my message had been that the visa was granted. Could it be that I was to go to the Yugoslavian consulate in Berlin and make a new application? I ran up to my room, snatched up a set of photographs, and headed for the tramway. Within an hour I was once more filling out those long

Diary of a Smuggler

PERU

Our trip to Peru was one of awesome pleasure and beauty, yet deeply marked by the contrasts this nation holds. One city we visited was Ayacucho. The city is spread out like a large patchwork of streets and roads containing small homes and shanties—a picture of struggling humanity. It is a city of one hundred thousand people with a population of fifteen thousand orphans, children without hope. The Shining Path terrorists killed many of their parents. Some parents, due to financial struggle, were unable to provide for their children. The children were abandoned and forced to live on the streets and fend for themselves. If they were fortunate enough, they were able to live in the small school and orphanage.

At the school and orphanage we were hailed as honored guests, and we were entertained with a formal program of singing school kids and recited Bible verses. Our hearts were moved with compassion as we watched these little children, who formerly had no hope, now find their hope and trust in Jesus. Their education here will allow them the ability to get a job and contribute to the society of Ayacucho. It was a great pleasure to distribute candy and sweets to these school kids, along with needed clothes and Bibles for future distribution.

We also spent time in a village called Pampa Marca. Here, various pastors came from great distances to be commissioned to continue to preach the Word throughout the Andes. During the church service we were informed that we were the first white people they had ever seen! After that we distributed Bibles to all the pastors present, not being one short or one over—just the exact amount needed. How good God is to His children.

triplicate forms. And once more I came to the line: "Occupation." This was the one, I suspected, that was causing all the trouble.

"Lord," I said under my breath, "what shall I put here?"

And all at once I was recalling the words of the Great Commission: "Go ye, and teach all nations. . . ." Then, I was a teacher, wasn't I? On the application form I wrote TEACHER and handed the forms across the desk.

"If you will have a seat over there, sir, I will examine your application right now."

The official disappeared into another room. I waited an anxious twenty minutes during which time it seemed to me that I could hear the chatter of a telegraph key. But it must have been a mistake, because the clerk came back all smiles to wish me a happy journey into his country.

I had to tell someone the good news. My folks? We didn't have a telephone, and it was awkward going through the neighbors. The Whetstras? That was it! I'd telephone the Whetstras.

I placed a station-to-station call and got Mr. Whetstra himself on the line.

"This is Andrew calling. How lucky to find you home in the middle of the day."

"I thought you were in Berlin."

"I am."

"We were so sorry to hear about your father."

"Thank you. But this call is good news, Mr. Whetstra. I just had to tell you. I have in my hand two pieces of paper. One is a letter from the Yugoslavian consulate in Holland turning down my request for a visa, and the other is my passport, stamped with a visa by the Yugoslav people here. I've got it, Mr. Whetstra! I'm going behind the Curtain as a missionary!"

"Andrew, you'd better come home for your keys."

"I'm sorry, Mr. Whetstra, this is a bad connection. I thought you said *keys*."

AROUND THE GLOBE
Iran

Population: 67 million
Location/Size: Southwestern Asia
630,578 sq. miles
Major Religions: Islam
Level of Persecution: Sharp, growing

Persecution and restrictions have sharply increased for Iranian believers in recent years. Although the constitution protects religious rights of Christians, Jews, and Zoroastrians, all have been harassed, and a few have even been martyred. Authorities frequently detain pastors and routinely interrogate and beat Muslim converts. Radicals regularly threaten Christian leaders with death.

Because Christian missionaries are not permitted in the country, individual missionaries must work underground. Believers rely on secret satellite TV receivers to hear the Gospel, and many Iranians remain unreached by the Gospel message.

Despite growing persecution, the Church is growing, but it is still small and unlikely to represent a substantial share of the country in the near future.

"I did. To your Volkswagen. We've talked it all over, and there's no untalking us. Mrs. Whetstra and I decided months ago that if you got the visa, you also got our automobile. Come home and pick up the keys."

Once in Amsterdam I really did try to talk them out of it. Such a big gift: I just didn't see how I could accept it.

"What about your business?" I asked them.

"Our business?" Mr. Whetstra spoke the words scornfully. "Andrew, you are on the King's business! No, we've prayed about it, and these are our orders."

And so that same afternoon, misgivings still struggling with delight, I went with Mr. Whetstra to get the papers signed over and became the still-unbelieving owner of an almost-new, beautiful blue Volkswagen.

The only disagreeable part of the experience was driving into Witte.

I tried to enter town unnoticed, but you can't slip unobserved into a little Dutch town like Witte with a bright blue Volkswagen. The entire village immediately gathered around, wanting to know whose car it was, and—as I had guessed would happen—not liking it when I told them it was my own. What was the son of a blacksmith doing with an automobile?

"Religion is a good business, eh, Andy?" said one man rubbing the material of his own coat between his fingers. He winked broadly.

Everyone laughed, and although I told them again and again that it was a gift from the Whetstras, I could see that they still didn't like it: the blacksmith's son shouldn't be driving a car. The families of Witte had often given me pennies from their grocery money for my work in the refugee camps. That money stopped now. My relationship with my hometown was never quite the same again.

But I had work to do. I spent several days planning my itinerary, scouring Amsterdam for any kind of Christian printed matter in Yugoslav languages, and going over the car for places to conceal what I found. I spent a little time, too, wondering how God was going to supply the money for this trip.

The end of March was my target date. Before then I drove down to see Karl de Graaf. I couldn't wait to see his face when he saw the car—the visible proof of what he'd known only by faith till then.

But Mr. de Graaf showed no surprise whatever. "Yes," he said, "I thought you'd have it by now. Because," he went on, drawing an envelope from his pocket, "God has told us that you will be needing an additional sum of money these next two months. And here it is."

He placed the envelope in my hand. I didn't even open it. By now I knew enough of this remarkable group to be sure that the envelope contained precisely the amount I would need for the trip. And so with a heart full of thanks I said goodbye to him, to the Whetstras, to my family, and left Holland for Yugoslavia, behind the Iron Curtain.

Imagine This

You have spent the last three years as a pastor for a small church in Colombia. Recently, guerrilla warfare has become increasingly hostile. Several members of your congregation have been murdered or kidnapped. You've noticed two young guerrilla members hanging around the church in the past couple of months. How do you respond to them?

What Would You Do?

ten

Lanterns in the Dark

We were under great pressure, far beyond
our ability to endure, so that we
despaired even of life. Indeed, in our
hearts we felt the sentence of death.
But this happened that we might not
rely on ourselves but on God

2 Corinthians 1:8 — 9

Just ahead was the Yugoslav border. For the first time in my life
I was about to enter a Communist country on my own instead of
in a group invited and sponsored by the government. I stopped
the little VW on the outskirts of the tiny Austrian village and took
stock.

The Yugoslav government in 1957 permitted visitors to bring
in only articles for their personal use. Anything new or anything
in quantity was suspect because of the black market thriving all
over the country. Printed material especially was liable to be confiscated at the border, no matter how small the quantity, because
coming from out of the country, it was regarded as foreign propaganda. Now here I was with car and luggage literally bulging
with tracts, Bibles, and portions of Bibles. How was I to get them

past the border guard? And so, for the first of many times, I said the Prayer of God's Smuggler:

"Lord, in my luggage I have Scripture that I want to take to Your children across this border. When You were on earth, You made blind eyes see. Now, I pray, make seeing eyes blind. Do not let the guards see those things You do not want them to see."

And so, armed with this prayer, I started the motor and drove up to the barrier. The two guards appeared both startled and pleased to see me. I wondered how much business came their way. From the way they stared at my passport, it might have been the first Dutch one they had ever seen. There were just a few formalities to attend to, they assured me in German, and I could be on my way.

One of the guards began poking around in my camping gear. In the corners and folds of my sleeping bag and tent were boxes of tracts. "Lord, make those seeing eyes blind."

"Do you have anything to declare?"

"Well, I have my money and a wristwatch and a camera. . . ."

The other guard was looking inside the VW. He asked me to take out a suitcase. I knew that there were tracts scattered through my clothing.

"Of course, sir," I said. I pulled the front seat forward and dragged the suitcase out. I placed it on the ground and opened the lid. The guard lifted the shirts that lay on top. Beneath them, and now in plain sight, was a pile of tracts in two different Yugoslavian languages, Croatian and Slovene. How was God going to handle this situation?

"It seems dry for this time of year," I said to the other guard, and without looking at the fellow who was inspecting the suitcase, I fell into a conversation about the weather. I told him about my own homeland and how it was always wet on the polders. Finally, when I could stand the suspense no longer, I looked behind me. The first guard wasn't even glancing at the suitcase. He was listening to our conversation. When I turned around he caught himself and looked up.

"Well, then, do you have anything else to declare?"

"Only 'small' things," I said. The tracts were small after all.

"We won't bother with them," said the guard. He nodded to me that I could close the suitcase and with a little salute handed me back my passport.

My first stop was Zagreb. I had been given the name of a Christian leader there, whom I shall call Jamil. The name had come from the Dutch Bible Society, which listed him as a man who occasionally ordered Bibles in quantity. However, they had not heard from him since Tito had become premier in 1945. I hardly dared hope that he would still be living at the same address, but with no other choice, I had written a carefully worded letter stating that toward the end of March a Dutchman might visit his country. And now I was driving into Zagreb looking for his address.

To underline the wonders of that first Christian contact in Yugoslavia, I shall have to tell what happened to my letter, even though of course I did not know the whole story until later. It had been delivered to the address all right, but Jamil had long since moved. The new tenant did not know his whereabouts and returned the letter to the post office. There it was held up for two weeks while a search was made for Jamil's new address. On the very day I entered Yugoslavia it was finally delivered. Jamil read it, puzzled. Who was this mysterious Dutchman? Was it safe to try contacting him?

With nothing better than a vague feeling that he should do *something*, Jamil boarded a tram and went to his old apartment house. But then what? Jamil stood on the sidewalk wondering how to proceed. Had the Dutchman already arrived and gone about asking for a certain Jamil? Did he dare go to the new tenant with the suspicious story that someday an unknown Dutchman might call asking for him? What on earth should he do?

And it was at that moment that I pulled up to the curb and stopped my car. I stepped out not more than two feet away from Jamil, who of course recognized me at once from my license plates. He seized my hands, and we put our stories together.

Jamil was overjoyed at having a foreign Christian in his country. He repeated the theme I had heard first in Poland, that my "being there," meant everything. They felt so isolated, so alone. Of course he would help me set up contacts with the believers in his country. He knew just the man to translate for me. So a few days later, with a young engineering student named Nikola as my guide and interpreter, I set off in my blue Volkswagen to bring "greetings" to the Yugoslavian Christians.

On this first car trip behind the Iron Curtain I discovered that I had energy I never dreamed of. My visa was good for fifty days. For seven straight weeks I preached, taught, encouraged, distributed Scripture. I held more than eighty meetings during those fifty days—speaking as many as six times on a Sunday. I preached in large cities, hamlets, isolated farms. I spoke openly in the North, covertly in the South, where Communist influence was strongest.

At first glimpse it did not seem to me that the Church in Yugoslavia was under any particular persecution. I had to register with the police when I moved into a new district, but I was free to visit believers even in their homes. Churches operated openly. After a while I abandoned the pretext of bringing "greetings" and simply began to preach. No one objected. Except for certain restricted areas, mostly along the borders, I was free to travel wherever I chose within the country, with no government guides to check on my activities.

This amounted to a real kind of freedom, much more than I had expected. But bit by bit as I got to know Yugoslavia better, I became aware of the slow wearing-down process the government was exerting on Christians. The effort seemed to be centered on the children. Leave the old folks alone, but wean the young people away from the Church.

One of the first churches Nikola and I visited was a Roman Catholic one in a small village not far from Zagreb. I noticed that there was not a single person under twenty in the entire congregation, and I asked Nikola about it. In answer he introduced me to a peasant woman who had a ten-year-old son.

"Tell Brother Andrew why Josif is not here," said Nikola.

"Why is my Josif not with me?" she asked. Her voice was bitter. "Because I am a peasant woman with no education. The teacher tells my son there is no God. The government tells my son there is no God. They say to my Josif, 'Maybe your Mama

A Traveler's Story

LOST INNOCENCE

Alejandro is only twelve years old. But at his tender age, he has already experienced things most of us can scarcely imagine. Before moving into a safe house with other youngsters, he had been living the nightmare now common to many children in Colombia:

Often those committed to violence approached me on the streets and tried to convince me to join them. They told me that they would give me money to buy anything I wanted, even guns. Once they came to our house and told my parents that since I was the oldest son, my parents had to hand me over to them. My father refused. They threatened him, saying that they would kill him if he did not comply. A few days later, they killed my father in front of our house . . . I saw it happen.

My mother was very worried because she knew the violent group could come for me at any time. They could "recruit" me by force. Then a friend told my mother that in a nearby town there was a pastor who could arrange a meeting with the person in charge of a Christian youth center. She wanted to get my younger brother and me out of our town as soon as possible.

My mother went to that town and met with someone who would take us to a safe house, but by the time she returned to take us to the center, members of the violent group had already kidnapped me and taken me to one of their camps. There, in the middle of the jungle, I had to march every day. They were training me to use various types of arms. They also kept me busy working in the coca fields and scraping coca leaves. They didn't feed me every day, and they treated me harshly. I felt sick and terribly lonely.

Continued

tells you differently, but we know better, don't we? You must remember that Mama has no education. We will humor her.' So? My Josif is not with me. I am being humored."

A few days later in another town, we were visiting a Christian family when I saw a little girl playing in the dust outside the house in the middle of the day.

"Why isn't she in school?" I asked Nikola.

From the mother he learned the story. Marta was accustomed to saying grace before meals at home. When it came time for the school lunch, Marta had given thanks aloud as she always did, without even thinking about it. The teacher had been angry. Who had supplied this food, God or the people through their own good government? "That was a wicked thing to say, Marta. You will fill the other children's minds with nonsense."

But the next day, so deeply was the habit ingrained, that Marta did it again, and for this she had been expelled.

It was in Macedonia, however, that we encountered the first signs of real fear on the part of churchgoers. The poorest of Yugoslavia's six states, Macedonia is also the area where the Party is strongest. Our first speaking date in this part of the country was scheduled for ten o'clock in the morning. When we reached the church, however, not a soul was there.

"I can't understand it," Nikola said, getting out the letter we had received from the pastor. "I'm sure this is the right place."

At eleven we decided it was useless to wait any longer. We went outside to where we had parked the car. Just as we were getting in, one of the villagers strolled past, paused long enough to shake my hand warmly, wish me Godspeed, and wander on. I was just turning again to open the door of the car when another villager ambled past, and the scene was repeated. For forty-five minutes that morning the entire village just happened to be out for a stroll, and as luck would have it, they all happened to pass the visiting preacher's automobile so that they could meet him and shake his hand.

Even Nikola was puzzled as to how to interpret this. A few days later we had an evening meeting scheduled in another town in Macedonia. The pastor invited us to dinner before the service at eight. At five minutes before eight I suggested to the pastor that we start for the church.

"No," he said, looking outside. "It is not yet time."

At 8:15 I brought the subject up again. "Don't you think people will be waiting?"

"No, the time is not yet." Again I noticed he looked outside before he answered.

At 8:30 the pastor finally went to the window, peered out, and nodded.

Colombia   A Traveler's Story
Continued

After three months in the camp, I went through an initiation test. They told me that in order to prove my loyalty and total obedience to them, I would have to kill a man. I was taken somewhere else and set in front of a man tied to a chair. I was told that he had been kidnapped and that he had been condemned to death because his family had not paid the ransom the group had demanded. They ordered me to kill him, adding that if I did not obey, they would kill me. The man could not talk because he was gagged, but I remember the desperation in his eyes. I had to kill him or I would die, so I shot him in the head.

I still wake up in the middle of the night because of the nightmares. I still remember his terrified eyes . . . wide open, looking at me before I shot him.

After I killed the man, the violent group told me that I was now ready to fight against the army. I had no idea why I should fight the army, and I thought about the stories kids in the camp had told me about other children like me who were sent to fight the army and never returned.

From the day the violent group kidnapped me, my mother risked her life to find me. For three months she spied out several camps until she found me. One day while I was working in a coca field, my mother ran toward me, grabbed my arm, and told me to run as fast as I could. She rescued me from the camp! The next day, I was on a truck on my way to a town where a pastor received me and reunited me with my younger brother. He took us to a city to the safe house. My mother sought refuge at a seminary.

Here at this safe house my brother and I feel happy and safe. I see my mother every other weekend. I play soccer and basketball with the other kids. We have teachers that come every day to teach us mathematics, history, social sciences, and many other things. We have Bible studies every day with the couple in charge of the center. I have various chores and responsibilities. My favorite one is opening the front gates for cars coming to the center, and I also greet visitors. I am afraid, though, that the violent group is still trying to find me, but I pray that God will not allow them to locate me.

Hundreds, possibly thousands, are living Alejandro's nightmare right now, with no way out. The Lord has saved Alejandro and given him a future and a hope. Praise the Lord for his mercy, but pray that others would be able to escape and find life in Jesus.

"Now we can go," he said. "The people won't come to church, you know, until it gets dark. It isn't that we are doing anything illegal. But—well—it pays to be cautious."

And then I saw the sight I was to become so familiar with all over Macedonia. From the darkened countryside kerosene lamps began to appear. The peasants came slowly across the fields, in twos and threes, never more, each man carrying a lamp. Then came the townspeople from the little mud houses that lined the only road, lanterns low so that their faces were in shadow.

No one seemed to mind being recognized once he was inside the church; after all, everyone there was taking the same risk.

The lamps were hung on hooks along the side of the room so that there was a warm and pleasant glow for the meeting. I spoke on Nicodemus, coming late in the night to make inquiries of Christ. He, too, I said, had felt it advisable to seek the Lord under cover of darkness. It didn't matter. Time and place would always dictate how we made our first steps toward God. More than two hundred persons had come that night to hear the foreigner speak. Eighty-five of them used the occasion to commit their lives anew to the Christian way, even when that way led for the time being through darkness.

It was in another village in Macedonia that we had our only serious encounter with the police.

I had told Nikola that I wanted to visit Christians in both the large cities and the small towns. Nosaki was a small town, all right. Just getting there was an undertaking.

We had picked up a second guide to steer us through Macedonia—which Nikola knew scarcely at all—a wonderful Christian whom everyone called "Little Uncle." Now Uncle pointed to two tracks across a field and assured us that this was the road to Nosaki. The tracks got fainter and the ruts deeper until the undercarriage of the car was scraping the soft earth, and at last we found ourselves driving across a freshly ploughed field.

"So much for your road," I said. "How much farther, Uncle?"

"But we're here!" he said, pointing to a clump of trees in the distance.

So we got out of the car and tramped across the field until we got to the little collection of mud huts called Nosaki. There was supposed to be a church here, but we saw no trace of one. Nikola made inquiries and learned that there was in fact a church in the village, but it had only one member. She was the widow Anna, who had converted her home into a church—to which no one came.

We went to visit Anna. She was amazed that a missionary had come to her little village.

"But I should not be surprised," she corrected herself. "Have I not been praying for help?"

Anna showed us her church. It was forbidden to hold religious services in a private home, so Anna had simply closed off one room and put a sign on it reading "Molitven Dom" ("Prayer House"). When she put up the sign, there were raised eyebrows among the village's few Party members, but no one really objected. After all, Anna was quite alone in this silly superstition of hers, and she was harming nobody.

Now, however, a preacher was here. Word flew from cottage to cottage. Almost no one in the village had ever laid eyes on anyone from outside Macedonia, let alone from a foreign country.

Whether this was the appeal or whether there were more religious reasons, I do not know. But that evening after dark it was as if the fields were alive with glowworms weaving and blinking their way across the fields to Anna's house. We began by teaching them a hymn, and then we told them the Gospel story, for Anna assured us that the younger generation had never heard it. We were singing a second hymn when suddenly there was a loud pounding on the door.

Everyone stopped singing.

Anna opened the door, and there stood two uniformed police. They walked to the front of the room. For a long time they simply stood there, running their eyes over the congregation. Then they went to one side of the room to get a better look at faces. Finally, they took out their notebooks and began writing down names. When they had finished, they asked a few questions about Nikola and me and then left as abruptly as they had come.

But the meeting was not the same after that. Several villagers went home at once. Those who stayed sang with no enthusiasm. When the time came for an altar call, I was surprised that anyone would raise his hand, and yet several did.

"You have seen tonight what following Christ might mean," I said. "Are you sure you want to become His men?"

And still a few insisted. So a little church was born that evening, but it never had a chance to grow. Nikola wrote me a year later that it had been stamped out by the government. For helping us, "Little Uncle" was deported from the country. He is now living in California in the United States. Anna's Molitven Dom was closed down.

As for himself, Nikola wrote, he had been summoned to court in Zagreb to account for his part in the evening. He had been reprimanded by the judge and fined the equivalent of fifty dollars but nothing worse. He believed the fact that he was a student had saved him from harsher treatment.

Why the government chose this particular isolated church to attack while it left others alone, neither Nikola nor I have ever understood.

The roads in Yugoslavia were extraordinarily hard on cars. When we weren't climbing fierce mountain trails, we were fording streams at the bottom of steep valleys.

But the worst threat to the little VW was the dust. Dust lay over the unpaved roads like a shroud; it sifted in on us even through the closed windows, and I hated to think what it was doing to the engine. Every morning in our Quiet Time, Nikola and I would include a prayer for the car. "Lord, we don't have either time or the money for repairs on the car, so will You please keep it running?"

One of the peculiarities of travel in Yugoslavia in 1957 was the friendly road-stoppings that took place. Cars, especially foreign cars, were still such a rarity that when two drivers passed each other, they almost always stopped to exchange a few words about road conditions, weather, gasoline supplies, bridges. One day we were dusting along a mountain road when up ahead we spotted a small truck coming toward us. As it pulled alongside, we also stopped.

Diary of a Smuggler

CUBA

One day on my trip to Cuba, my group went about 150 miles to visit with a Pastor Rogelio and a Pastor Maria. Wow! We really saw the Spirit of the Lord working here. When we gave a flannelgraph to the Sunday school teacher, she cried. Maria said they have not had soap since November! They also did not have meat or milk (we had brought a big supply with us). She said the Lord had told her several times in the morning that she would receive some special blessings that day—and we were it.

Pastor Rogelio shared that he is interrogated weekly by the government. He was moved by our timely visit. A member of our group wanted to give him a pair of shoes. Pastor Rogelio said he didn't need them, but that two of their workers building the church sure did. Boy was he right! I have pictures of their old shoes with their toes sticking out and the new shoes beside them. Needless to say, this was a very emotional visit, and a few tears were appropriate. Pastor Maria said she maintains a list of each person who gets shampoos, soaps, etc., too, so everyone gets something. This church needs regular visits, and attempts to reach them should be encouraged. Everyone, on both sides, will be abundantly blessed.

"Hello," said the driver. "I believe I know who you are. You're the Dutch missionary who is going to preach in Terna tonight."

"That's right."

"And this is the Miracle Car?"

"The Miracle Car?"

"I mean the car that you pray for each morning."

I had to laugh. I had mentioned the prayer in a previous meeting; the word had obviously gone on ahead. "Yes," I admitted, "this is the car."

"Mind if I take a look at her? I'm a mechanic."

"I'd appreciate it." I had put gasoline in that engine, and that was literally all since I had crossed the border. The mechanic went around to the rear and lifted the hood over the motor. For a long time he stood there, just staring.

"Brother Andrew," he said at last, "I have just become a believer. It is mechanically impossible for this engine to run. Look. The air filter. The carburetor. The sparks. No, I'm sorry. This car cannot run."

"And yet it's taken us thousands of miles."

The mechanic only shook his head. "Brother," he said, "would you permit me to clean your engine for you and give you a change of oil? It hurts me to see you abuse a miracle."

Gratefully we followed the man to his village a few miles from Terna. We pulled behind him into a little courtyard filled with pigs and geese. That night

AROUND THE GLOBE
Laos

Population: 5.3 million
Location/Size: Southeastern Asia
91,429 sq. miles
Major Religions: Buddhism
Tribal faiths
Level of Persecution: Sharp, growing

The Communist government in this Asian country provides for religious liberty in its constitution but imposes severe restrictions in practice. The government prohibits religious meetings without consent from the authorities, blocks construction of churches, and routinely imprisons believers. Buddhist monks have sought even further restrictions on Christian activity, and the government has supported attempts to force believers to renounce the Christian faith in favor of Buddhism.

The Laotian Church is growing rapidly, nearly twice as fast as the general population. But they remain a relatively small group, and there is much work to be done in evangelizing the nation.

while we preached he took the engine apart, cleaned it piece by piece, changed the oil, and by the time we were ready to leave the next morning, presented us with a grinning new automobile. God had answered our prayer.

We drove into Belgrade on the first of May, 1957. May Day, the high holy day of communism. There wasn't a bed or a seat in a restaurant to be found in the entire city.

Nikola and I would have slept in the car that night if the pastor of the church at which we were to speak had not taken us into his own home. And it was in this church that we had the experience that has shaped my ministry down to the present moment.

Nikola and I stood on the platform facing a crowded room. It was so full that we did not even have room to put up the flannelgraph with which I illustrated my stories of the Gospels. Halfway through the service someone started hammering. The next thing we knew, they had taken a door right off its hinges so that an overflow crowd in the choir room could hear. These were not the solemn-eyed country people I had come to love, but a sophisticated, fairly well-dressed city congregation.

Well, after the talk, Nikola and I gave an altar call. We asked that everyone who wanted to commit their life to Christ, or who wanted to reaffirm a previous commitment, raise their hand.

Every hand in the room went up.

Surely they hadn't understood! I explained again how serious a step this was. I made the conditions of discipleship under a hostile government painfully clear. And then I made a second appeal, this time asking the people to stand.

The entire congregation stood.

I was astonished. I had never seen such readiness. Carried away by their spirit, I launched into an enthusiastic description of the daily disciplines of prayer and Bible reading that turn newborn children in Christ into mature soldiers in His ranks.

I was outlining the plan for Bible study that we had been taught at the Missionary Training College when I noticed a change had come over the room. For the first time people in this responsive congregation were not meeting my eye. They were looking at their hands, the pew backs, anywhere but at me.

Puzzled, I turned to the pastor. He, too, seemed embarrassed as he told me through Nikola, "Prayer, yes, that we can do each day. I like what you have said about this. But Bible reading . . . Brother Andrew, most of these people do not have Bibles."

I stared at him in disbelief. I had got used to the idea in rural churches. But in educated, cosmopolitan Belgrade?

I turned to the congregation. "How many of you own Bibles?" I asked.

In the entire room seven hands, including the pastor's, went up. I was stunned. I had long ago passed out the ones I had brought with me. Now what was I to leave with these people so eager to learn, so needful of guidance in the hard walk they had chosen for themselves against the millions marching the other way?

With the pastor we worked out a system of Bible-sharing: a schedule of group study combined with individual use, so many hours on such-and-such a day for each member. But that same evening a resolve was born in me, a resolve that has burned brighter with each passing year. That night I promised God that as often as I could lay my hands on a Bible, I would bring it to these children of His behind the wall that men had built. How I would buy the Bibles, how I would get them in, I didn't know. I only knew that I would bring them—here to Yugoslavia, and to Czechoslovakia, and to every other country where God opened the door long enough for me to slip through.

Imagine This

When your atheist parents find out that you recently became a follower of Jesus, you are surprised that they are not angrier with you. They explain, however, that you are not allowed to tell anyone about your conversion. They are not going to force you to change back to your old life, but they are ashamed of your new faith. Do you obey your parents and hide your relationship with Jesus? Or do you disobey them and speak boldly about your new faith?

What Would You Do?

eleven

The Third Prayer

I eagerly expect and hope that I will in no way be ashamed, but will have sufficient courage so that now as always Christ will be exalted in my body, whether by life or by death. For to me, to live is Christ and to die is gain.

Philippians 1:20—21

Driving through the countryside of Western Europe on the way back to Holland, I tried to evaluate the trip I had just finished. I had been gone more than seven weeks. I had traveled nearly six thousand miles, held nearly a hundred meetings, established scores of contacts for future work.

Most important were the conversions, hundreds of them. New Christians, men and women and children who were actually living in the Kingdom of God while at the same time living under a government that said there was no God. What was their life going to be like now? It was hard, leaving these friends to face pressures and sacrifices that I could only guess at.

As for my determination to bring them Bibles, in the clear light of this May morning it looked a lot harder than it had in the flush of conviction that night in Belgrade. In 1957 there was not a single Communist border over which you could take books of any kind—let alone religious books! How was I to get them in? And how was I to distribute them once inside without endangering those who helped me? Which country needed them most? Which should I try first? All these questions bounced back and forth in my mind as I rolled mile after mile across Europe, ever closer to home.

No, I corrected myself. Not home. To Witte, certainly, but in one of those strange flashes of self-knowledge, I realized suddenly that Witte was no longer home to me. That was why I'd been driving so slowly, stopping so frequently to check my maps, talking crops with every farmer I met.

With a start I realized that ever since I had left Yugoslavia, I had been dawdling, stalling for time against the inevitable moment when I would be alone again in my bachelor's room. After Papa's death I had moved out of the house and into his little room above the toolshed. It had seemed such a practical idea: the room had a separate entrance, and I could come and go without disturbing the household. But the effect of the move had been to emphasize how very much alone I was.

It was a loneliness, furthermore, that I now knew was to be a permanent part of my life. At a rest stop in Germany I got out my Bible and opened it to the back cover where I had recorded God's hard answer to a prayer that I had made. I sipped my coffee and remembered the night in Yugoslavia when I had made it. I had been feeling lonely that evening too. "Lord," I had said, "in a year I'll be thirty. You made a helpmeet for man, and somehow I have not found my own. Lord, I'm going to ask You for something. I ask You tonight for a wife."

I'd noted the specific prayer request in my Bible: "April 12, 1957, Nosaki. Prayed for a wife." Beside the notation I had left a place for an answer.

And five days later the answer had come. In my Quiet Time I had suddenly known—with quite uncanny certainty—that Isaiah 54:1 was God's reply to me. I flipped excitedly through the pages of the Old Testament and read, "The children of the desolate are more than the children of the married."

Again and again I read the words, trying to apply them to myself, trying to rejoice in God's will. I might feel desolate, but He was going to give me more "children," spiritual children, than I could ever have as a flesh-and-blood father. I had written the answer beside the request.

But now as I drained my coffee cup beside a field of spring flowers, I knew that spiritual children were not at all what I had in mind. I wanted real, live, noisy, running-and-jumping children, with sticky faces and wooden shoes to mend after the fights. Above all, I wanted a wife, a living, loving human being who would make my life one fabric, instead of this patchwork quilt of places and people based nowhere, instead of this heading home to no one.

Suppose I asked Him again, right now? Suppose I just opened my Bible anywhere, just let my finger fall where it would, and took this new verse for His real answer? I had always laughed at people who looked for guidance this way. But it was a glorious spring day when anything could happen, and so I closed my eyes, opened the Bible at random, and plunged my finger down on the page. When I looked down, I could hardly believe my eyes. My finger was pointing to Isaiah 54:1. "The children of the desolate are more than the children of the married."

I told myself I must have creased the Bible open to that page from reading it so intently before. But it was no good. Thoroughly chastened, I recorded in the back of the Bible the repeated question and the reiterated answer.

"I don't like the message, Lord, but at least it's clear."

I loaded the portable stove back into the car and started up the motor. It was a long way back to Witte, back to the little room and solitary confinement.

The actual homecoming was no better than I had imagined. I sat up in the living room until late at night, telling the family about Yugoslavia. Then when I could put it off no longer, I made my way outside and up the ladder. The little room seemed damp and clammy. There was mildew on the bedsheets, my desk was white and chalky, the new wallpaper was peeling. But then, it had always been wet there on the polders. It had never bothered me before. Why should it strike me now with such distaste?

Over the next six weeks I threw myself into speaking, writing, praying for the vision of my next step behind the Iron Curtain. I visited the Whetstras to tell them about the heroic job the little VW had done. I wrote a new series of articles for *Kracht Van Omhoog*. I paid a visit to Karl de Graaf and the prayer group in Amersfoort. In general I kept busy. So busy, I kept telling myself, that I wouldn't notice how lonely I was.

In July I gave it up.

"Lord," I said one morning, sitting on the little iron fold-down bed in my room over the toolshed, "I've got to pray just one more time about this bachelor life You plan for me. Now I know about those children You promise the desolate, but Lord You also promise the desolate a home!" I quickly found the verse in Psalm 68, as though to refresh His memory: "'God gives the desolate a home to dwell in.' It isn't that I don't thank You for this room above the toolshed, Lord. Just because it's dark and dank and mildewy and— doesn't mean I'm not grateful. But, dear God, it is not a home. Not really. A home is where there's a wife and children—real ones.

"Lord, Paul prayed three times for release from the thorn in the flesh that was bothering him. And You refused him. I have prayed two times for a wife. I am going to pray once more. Perhaps You will refuse me a third time, too, Lord, and if You do, I shall never again bring up the question. I'm going to write it here in my Bible." I opened the Bible to the back cover and scribbled one last notation, "Prayed . . . for . . . wife . . . third time . . . Witte, July 7 . . . 1957." Then I closed the Bible with a snap. "Some people, Lord, are built for the lonely walk. But not me, please. Not me."

It wasn't until September that anything happened that I could interpret as an answer. And then one morning in the middle of my prayer time, a face suddenly floated in front of me. Long blonde hair. A smile that made the sun come out. Eyes never twice the same shade.

Corrie.

Corrie van Dam.

The thought of her had come to me so unexpectedly, so completely independently of what I was thinking at the moment, that I

A Traveler's Story

IMPRISONED, BEATEN, HOSPITALIZED, BAPTIZED

Akeem was first confronted with Christianity when his friend Jacob began talking to him about it. He had not liked Christians before. He didn't even want to talk to Christians and was upset that Jacob went to church. After his conversation with Jacob, he started having disturbing dreams. Once he dreamed someone was telling him, "Akeem, repent and become a Christian." He immediately got up and started praying his Muslim prayers. He thought to himself, "These are terrible dreams; please Allah, protect me from them!"

One day Jacob said to him, "Let's go and see a Fulani pastor." They walked twenty-five kilometers through the bush to visit Ezikiel, but he wasn't home. Later Jacob, accompanied by pastor Ezikiel, went to visit Akeem. When he heard the Gospel, Akeem was convicted in his heart and accepted Christ. He went back home to his parents and told them everything.

One day after church, Akeem's uncle had him arrested. He was in custody for a week, and during that time the police beat him up. The other Christians didn't know where he was. A friend, who was not a Christian at the time, went to a missionary to tell of Akeem's arrest. They bailed him out and took him to the hospital. He was hospitalized for one and a half weeks. In jail and in the hospital he thought: "Jesus, this is because of You. It is a test of my faith." These thoughts gave him the strength to carry on.

He didn't want to stay in the hospital, because his family was trying to prevent his wife from becoming a Christian. However, the Christian meetings interested her, and she gave her heart to Christ.

Despite his troubles and heartaches, he was beaming on the day of his baptism and said, "This is a happy day!"

Recently Akeem's in-laws had him arrested again and tried to take his wife away, but she refused to leave him. After three days his grandfather paid bail, and Akeem returned home to his wife and child.

wondered with a leap of my heart if the thought was God's, if He were showing me the beyond-wildest-dreams answer to my prayers.

But how could it be? Friends and teammates though we had been, I had never once considered Corrie fair game for dating. She had been a child. Still in her teens.

But that was—how many years ago—four years since I had left the factory for England and she for nursing school. Why, she was grown up. She had doubtless finished school and married by now. From being a little girl barely out of her pinafore, Corrie suddenly became for me a very adult woman who—if she was not already married—was choosing this very moment among a crowd of pushy, clamoring suitors.

Within the hour I was in Alkmaar, driving down the street where Corrie's folks lived. We had often come there after the youth weekends. And Mrs. van Dam would serve coffee and cookies, while Mr. van Dam draped the ceiling with smoke from an enormous meerschaum.

I didn't know exactly what I'd do when I got to the house. Just look at it, I guessed. Make sure it was still there. Or go to the door? "Mrs. van Dam, I wonder if you would give me Corrie's address."

But suppose it was Corrie herself who opened the door. "Hello, Corrie, are you married? If not, will you marry me?"

I reached the house before I'd settled on a plan. And right away I saw that I wouldn't need one. The shutters were closed over the windows, the garden high with weeds. A lump gnawing at my stomach, I drove on to the factory.

No, Mr. Ringers hadn't heard where the van Dams had gone. Corrie? Why, she'd taken her training at Saint Elizabeth's Hospital in Haarlem. Might still be there, for all he knew. No. If she was married he hadn't heard about it. His eyes twinkled as he answered my questions.

"It'll be a lucky man, Andy, who marries that young lady!"

It was wonderful how much urgent business I suddenly discovered in Haarlem. Bible stores to visit, church invitations I had inexcusably neglected, people to see—a wonderful city!

From a filling station just outside I telephoned Saint Elizabeth's and held my breath while the receptionist looked up Corrie's file. "Yes," the voice came back, "she's a final-year student. Miss van Dam—" my sigh of relief stopped her for a moment—"Miss van Dam is living in a private home this year away from the residence."

She gave me the address and told me that the apartment was the top floor of a private house in the nicest section of town: the owner was a wealthy elderly woman, the lady at the hospital said, who gave the apartment in return for having a nurse in the house. After a search, I found the street and quickly spotted Corrie's windows high up under the eaves. The whole house was built like a miniature castle: Corrie's room opened onto a balcony topped with a tiny peaked turret.

I parked the car down the street and gave myself up to day-dreams. She was the queen in the castle, and I was a knight in armor. She was Juliet, and when she appeared on her balcony, I would step forward . . .

But she didn't appear, either on the balcony or anywhere else. The afternoon passed. Darkness came, but no light appeared in Corrie's rooms. Abandoning all pretense at subtlety, I went up to the door and rang the bell. A maid answered. Miss van Dam? Yes, she lived there. But at the moment she was with her family in Alkmaar.

"Alkmaar?" All my studied casualness left me. "But there's no one at the house in Alkmaar! The windows are all boarded up, and the garden's been let go and—"

Attracted by the sounds of distress, a white-haired lady appeared in the hall behind the maid. Gently she told me that Corrie's father was seriously ill and that she had gone to take care of him. The family had moved from their house to an apartment in which there would be no stairs to climb. She gave me the address.

For the next few days I suffered through my appointments in the tiresome town of Haarlem. How glad I now was that I had always spent a few minutes talking with Mr. van Dam, the evenings we were in his home. What could be more natural than for me to pay him a visit?

And so a few nights later I was standing outside the van Dam apartment in Alkmaar, knocking on the door.

Corrie opened it.

The light behind her turned her hair to gold. "I've come to ask about your father," I said faintly.

The pretext would not have fooled a three-year-old child. But Corrie led me gravely back to her father's room. Mr. van Dam was very ill—I could see it even from the doorway. But he seemed delighted to have a visitor. And so for an hour I sat in a chair beside his bed and told him about my trips behind the Iron Curtain and my hopes for the future, while Corrie came and went with bottles and trays, and I tried to keep my eyes from following her. She was wearing a white nurse's uniform and seemed to me even more heavenly and unattainable than she'd been in my dreams.

And so began a curious, fumbling courtship. Twice a week I called on Mr. van Dam; twice a week Corrie and I held hushed, sickroom conversations at the front door. Oftener than that, I felt, would be intruding on this home preoccupied with its problem.

Between visits I would often try to imagine myself proposing to Corrie, and it sounded so awful that I knew ahead of time it was no use. Please marry me. I'll be gone much of the time and I won't be able to give you an address where you can write to me, and weeks will go by when I can't get letters out to you, and though we'll be in missionary work you'll never be able to talk about the places and people we're working with, and if one time I shouldn't come back you'll probably never know what happened. Add to that no foreseeable income, a room over a toolshed for a home—Corrie was just too smart, as well as too pretty, to settle for a life like that.

It was the twentieth of October, during the time I was making these semiweekly visits, that the letter came from the Hungarian consulate. My request for a visa, dated a week after the revolt, had been approved.

And suddenly I knew how I would go about asking Corrie to marry me. I would ask her then, that week, that very day, but I wouldn't let her answer until I got back from Hungary. That way—supposing she even considered the proposal—she'd have a chance to taste this brand of marriage ahead of time: the separation, the secrecy, the uncertainty. Face it, Andy, I said to myself, the plain wretchedness of it.

But now that I had a plan, my heart couldn't help leaping for hope. I jumped into the car and covered the distance to Alkmaar in record time. I pounded on the door, forgetting for a moment the sick man inside. They were taking an awfully long time answering. I was lifting my hand to knock again when the door opened. One look at Corrie's face and I knew.

"Your father—?"

She nodded. "Half an hour ago." Talking was obviously a struggle. "The doctor's here now."

And so I drove back to Witte with my proposal still burning inside me. Except at the funeral, I didn't see Corrie for three weeks. I spent the time buying or begging every Hungarian-language Bible in Holland—which wasn't many—and stowing them, along with a supply of Hungarian tracts, in the car.

At last one beautiful moonlit night I asked Corrie to come for a ride with me. We spun along a broad dike until our headlights picked out a smaller road leading off to the right. I swung down it and stopped. The moon gleamed up at us from the canal at our feet. The setting was perfect.

And I said everything wrong: "Corrie," I began, "I want you to marry me, but don't say no until I tell you how hard it will be. Hard for me and harder still for you." And then I outlined for her the work that I believed God had given me. I told her the next month would be a fair sample of the life ahead for me—and for her if she chose it. "You'd be crazy to, Corrie," I finished miserably. "But I do so want you to!"

Corrie's enormous eyes were bigger still when I had finished. She opened her mouth to speak, but I laid my hand on it. When I left her at her apartment, I had her promise that she would give me my answer when I returned from Hungary.

What a difference in the trip across Europe! I had thought this separation would teach Corrie something; I had not known how much it would teach me. The miles that had rolled away so easily beneath my tires before now tugged and called to me—every one a mile farther from her.

The border crossing, too, was harder on me than usual. Whether it was that for the first time I wanted desperately not to be caught, not to be detained, not to let anything keep me from that date in Alkmaar, or whether the stories in the refugee camps had made me particularly fearful of Hungary, I do not know.

However, once again God made "seeing eyes blind," and at last I was rolling along through the Hungarian countryside. The road I was following wound along the Danube. It was beautiful, just as the song said—although its color instead of being blue was a deep milk-chocolate brown. I began to feel hungry and decided to stop by the

Vietnam   A Traveler's Story

THE GREAT PERSECUTOR

Several years ago Tung was known as the "great persecutor" by local Christians in the central Vietnamese town where he lived. The Communist police officer had earned his infamous name because of his reputation for harassing house-church Christians.

Tung had little toleration for such people. As far as he was concerned, these "law-breakers" deserved to be punished when they continued to conduct their "illegal" religious activities by meeting in their homes.

But God had other plans for Tung. Despite his animosity toward the local Christians, several believers began to persistently pray for the police official. Some even dared to share the Gospel with him.

Gradually, as they continued to win his trust and friendship, Tung's heart began to soften. Finally it came to the point when he could no longer reject the truth of the Bible. Tung became a Christian. Like the apostle Paul, the policeman had become one of the very people he had previously persecuted.

Tung's outlook on life was transformed. Many of the villagers could not believe that this was the same man who had been so filled with enmity toward Christians.

Tung's spiritual life continued to flourish, and he soon began to move into a leadership role in his church. Some time later he attended a theological training seminar for church leaders. Tung returned to his hometown, determined that his life should be used by God to further the Gospel.

Since that time many have come to know Christ through Tung's ministry. He now oversees two house churches and is involved among the highland tribal people of central Vietnam.

river for lunch. So I pulled off the road, drove down a sandy lane, stopped in a little clearing at the water's edge, and got out the makings of my picnic. In order to get the stove out, I actually had to move several boxes of tracts that the border guards had just overlooked.

No sooner had I opened a can of peas-and-carrots than I heard a roar. I looked up. A speedboat was cutting through the water toward me at full throttle, throwing a wake higher than the boat itself. In the bow stood a soldier with a drawn machine gun. At the last possible instant the boat swerved and coasted to a neat landing at the river's edge. Now I saw that there were two other soldiers in the boat. The man in front leapt ashore, followed by another one.

"Lord," I said very softly as they approached, "help me refuse to yield to fear."

The first soldier kept the machine gun on me while the other ran to the car. I kept stirring the peas-and-carrots as I heard the door of the car open.

I began talking, speaking Dutch, which I felt sure these men would not understand.

"Well, sir," I said, stirring, "it certainly is nice to have you drop in this way."

The soldier stared stonily.

"As you can see," I went on, "I'm preparing to eat."

Behind me I heard the other door of the car open. I reached into my picnic box and drew out two extra plates. "Would you care to join me?" I raised my eyebrows and waved my hand in a gesture of invitation. The soldier shook his head brusquely as if to say he wasn't going to be bribed. "At least not for a mess of peas-and-carrots, eh?" I thought.

I could hear the other soldier poking around. Any moment now he would certainly ask about those boxes.

"Well," I said aloud. "If you don't mind, I'm going to go ahead and eat while the food is hot." I spooned the vegetables onto my plate and then faced a dilemma. Should I say grace? In the camps they had told me that Christians were particularly suspect in Hungary now, since many had taken leading roles in the revolt.

But no, here was a chance to witness to three men. In a gesture far more deliberate than normal, I bowed my head, folded my hands, and said a long and hearty thanksgiving for the food I was about to eat.

An amazing thing happened. While I prayed there was no sound from the soldier inspecting my car. Just as soon as I had finished, the door slammed and I heard the sound of boots coming rapidly toward me. I picked up my fork and took a bite of peas. For a moment both soldiers stood over me. Then abruptly they whirled. Without looking behind them, they ran down to their boat, jumped in, and roared off in a spray of white.

Budapest was the loveliest city I had yet seen in my travels: two ancient towns, Buda and Pest, built on the two shores of the

Danube. But signs of the revolt were everywhere. Buildings were pockmarked with bullet holes, trees ripped up, tram rails twisted.

I had been given the address of a Professor B, a man who held an excellent position in a famous school in Budapest. When I asked him if he would act as my interpreter, I did not appreciate the terrible significance of his answer. "Of course, Brother," he said. "We are in this together." That decision cost my friend his livelihood.

Professor B was overjoyed with the gift of Bibles. He said they were almost unattainable. He told me that there were scores of churches open and functioning as best they could. I could be just as busy as I chose, speaking and distributing the books, provided I didn't mind taking a few risks.

"A few risks?" I said.

"Well, you see, the revolt is so recent. The authorities think every church supper is hatching a plot." Those who had suffered most, he said, were the pastors. Most of those in Budapest had been in serious trouble with the regime: about a third had spent time in prison, some for as long as six years. Each preacher had to have his permit renewed every two months, and this was a regulation that kept them in constant tension.

Professor B took me to visit a friend of his, a Reformed pastor, who opened the door to us cautiously and looked up and down the hall before letting us in. His apartment was filled with lampshades! Some were completed, some just covered frames, some in the process of being rather crudely painted with street scenes from Budapest.

This man, I learned, had been summarily dismissed from his pulpit—no reason given. He was not even allowed to sit on the platform during services. Afraid that his very presence would get others into trouble, he and his wife had withdrawn from the fellowship altogether. In order to keep his family from starving, he was painting lampshades. He worked from early morning until late at night to supply their most basic needs.

After we left I asked Professor B how typical this pastor's plight was.

"Fairly typical among the churches that do not compromise," he said. "But many compromise. They 'adjust' to the regime not only in politics but in the basics of the faith, so that they become little more than arms of the government."

I asked Professor B to take me to such a church, and he told me that the pastor of one of them was officiating at a public school festival that afternoon. Sure enough, the pastor was on the reviewing stand. In a few minutes he came over to talk with us.

"Perhaps a third of that group," he said, pointing to a row of youngsters lined up on the school lawn, "belong to our church." Each child was wearing a brilliant red scarf, a symbol, he explained, of good citizenship. One of the requirements for the scarf was a "proper attitude" toward the religious superstitions of their parents.

"What superstitions?" I asked.

"Oh—miracles. And the creating story. Original sin. Fallen man. That sort of thing."

"What about the fact that Jesus was God?"

"They would put that at the top of the list."

"How do you yourself feel?"

The pastor lowered his eyes. "What can you do. . . ." he shrugged his shoulders.

The children were obviously having a wonderful time. Once again I heard that awesome clapping that I had heard both in Poland and in Czechoslovakia. As before, it started spontaneously; but within twenty seconds it picked up a group rhythm that became a single pounding, driving hammer on an unearthly anvil. Clap. Clap. Clap. All in perfect unison, all united, all one. The principal of the school let the clapping go on until it got to my very bones. I could see it was having the same effect on the pastor. I could see him lift his hands, almost shaking, as if he wanted desperately to put his fingers in his ears but dared not.

When the school ceremony was over, the pastor took us to see his church. He was talking about the improved heating plant and the new windows and the enlarged playing field out back, when suddenly he said to me, "Brother Andrew, what should I do?"

I didn't answer right away. How could I give advice when I had never stood in his shoes? It was easy to say, "Be strong." But this man knew that his license, and therefore the support of his family, depended week by week on the whim of the government.

I could not give advice, but I could tell him the stories of Christians in Poland, Czechoslovakia, Yugoslavia, facing pressures and problems similar to his own, but never failing to preach Christ's redeeming love. With this love in their hearts, it seemed to me, people could be trusted to find out for themselves the truth of these other matters of faith.

Professor B assured me that there were churches in Hungary, too, that were finding ways around their restrictions. One of the most interesting was funeral-and-wedding evangelism.

Professor B asked me one morning to take part in a Hungarian wedding.

"This will be like no wedding you've ever attended," he promised. "Now listen carefully, because I'm going to ask you to do a strange thing. You will have a chance to speak, and when you do, you are to say a quick word of congratulation to the bride and groom, and then you are to preach the hardest-hitting blood-and-thunder salvation sermon we can pray for."

I had to smile.

"Don't laugh," said Professor B. "This is the way we preach to most people these days. Folks today are afraid to enter a church except for funerals and weddings. So we preach to them then! A government official said to me last week, 'I'll bet every night you pray for your friends to die so you can get your sermon in.'"

So I preached at the wedding, and afterward I told Professor B about the other device I had discovered: that of bringing "greetings" from Holland. He was entranced at the idea. He wanted to start a campaign right away. So he got on the telephone and began making calls. That same night we held a thinly disguised revival meeting in one of the largest churches in town.

The next night we held another meeting, but in a different church. And so on, night after night. We never announced until the end of the meeting where the next meeting was going to be. Even so, people were lining up on the sidewalk to hear the visiting Dutchman talk. This was attracting too much attention, and we soon devised the technique of simply stating that there would be a meeting the following night without saying where it would

Diary of a Smuggler

PERU

(6:45 A.M.) Our sleepy-eyed team of men piled into the van with Matt and Michael accompanying us to visit their father at the prison. We traveled by van on the outskirts of Lima to a poor, impoverished area. Garbage lined the streets and lay piled next to the cement barriers in the road. Street vendors waved as we passed.

At 8:15 A.M. we arrived and began our wait to enter the prison. We saw a slight movement forward as we passed the outer walls. Here we stood in a line just inside the outer walls. The stench of urine was almost overpowering.

In front of us, we could hear a man beginning to preach the Word to those waiting in line. Dogs roamed freely in the prison yard. In the distance was a small playground.

It was 8:30 A.M. and our line began to shuffle forward. Once in the roofed area we are given paperwork to fill out. Here at the checkpoint we were given our first forearm stamp. Then we had our papers checked. It was here that I was politely relieved of two pens that I had brought in. Then to the frisking booth where I was patted down, asked for money, and relieved of an additional pen. The guards passed me on to the next line, where they checked my passport and fingerprinted me. After passing through the line, I rejoiced as I received my number, 195. We now stood in the courtyard with the high walls to the left laced with barbed wire, the mountains rising high above, creating a distinct contrast. Freedom vs. imprisonment.

Continued

be. Then all the next day people would be on the telephone, passing word along as to where we were to meet.

As we sat on the platform waiting for the service to begin, I would see the pastors searching the faces in the congregation.

"They're looking for the secret police," Professor B explained. "We know many of them by sight. After the revolt it has been dangerous to attract large crowds for any reason."

The nervousness and anxiety were contagious, so that halfway through the campaign I too began to dream at night of trouble with the police.

Diary of a Smuggler

PERU

Continued

We moved on to another checkpoint, where my number was placed on my paperwork. We passed through a gate into a building where our passports were again checked. Then ten steps forward, another passport check. Here the guard placed his fingerprint on the paper next to mine. We then exchanged our passports for a small metal disk. (This was needed for our final departure. No disk, no leave!)

After we passed through the second box, which was unmanned, we went on to another checkpoint, where they checked our metal disk against the number on our arm. From here we entered the inner court of the prison.

After a short walk to Joseph's cellblock, we had yet another checkpoint, where they took our fingerprints and names. Here, we finally met Joseph with hugs and warm greetings. He ushered us up a short flight of stairs to his cell.

Joseph shared his testimony and his hardships over the last five years. I was impressed by the uncompromising integrity he portrayed. For example, he loves Coca-Cola and for five years has been denied a Coke. Even though it is possible to obtain one in prison, his motto is "If it is forbidden, it is forbidden." This standard has set him apart from the other prisoners.

Upon exiting the prison, our hearts were heavy as we left our dear brother behind.

And then one evening the police did come.

I knew it from the look on Professor B's face.

"They're here," he whispered, and I didn't need to ask who "they" were. He signaled that I was to follow him back into the vestry. Two plainclothesmen were waiting. They asked me a lot of questions, and then they issued a summons for me to appear the following morning, along with Professor B, at headquarters.

"The last time this happened," Professor B told me when they had gone, "two men were arrested. They were in prison a long time."

After the service all of the pastors gathered in the vestry to decide what we should do. Professor B suggested that we go to his home and pray. It was the first time I had been to his house. I had forgotten what a prominent place a professor has in the society of Eastern Europe: his home was immense and luxurious. And this was the position he was risking!

Professor B introduced me to his son, Janos. I instantly liked him. He had recently married and was doing well as a young attorney, and yet he too was willing to place his career on the line by taking part in these frowned-upon meetings of Christians. There were seven of us that night, seven Christians gathered in much the same way Christians had gathered since the Church began—in secret, in trouble—praying together that through the miraculous intervention of God Himself we be spared a confrontation with the authorities.

We prayed there in the living room of Professor B, all kneeling around a low round coffee table in the center of the room. For an hour we kept up an earnest intercession, begging God to help us in our time of need. And all at once, the praying stopped. To every one of us at the same instant came the inexplicable certainty that God had heard, that our prayer was answered.

We got up from our knees, blinking at each other in surprise. I looked at my watch. It was 11:35 in the evening. At that precise hour we *knew* that tomorrow everything was going to be all right.

The next morning promptly at nine o'clock, Professor B and I were at headquarters. While we were waiting, Professor B whispered to me that he knew the staff well. The head of the department was unrelenting in his attacks on the Church; his deputy was much more likely to be lenient.

"We are scheduled," he said behind his hand, "to see the department head. Too bad."

Nine-thirty came, and then ten o'clock. Eleven. We were both used to long waits in bureaucratic countries, but this was a long delay by any standards. Finally, just before noon, a clerk appeared.

"Come this way," he said.

Professor B and I walked down a long corridor behind the clerk. We passed the department head's office and kept going. Professor B looked at me and raised both eyebrows hopefully. At last we stopped.

The head of the department, the clerk explained, had fallen ill the night before. In his stead the deputy would hear our case.

Professor B threw me a quick glance. Twenty minutes later we were walking out of the office, free men. I yearned to ask the clerk at what hour the department head had fallen ill. To this day I am certain his answer would have been: 11:35 P.M.

The encounter with the authorities ended for the time being the possibility of further meetings in Budapest. Professor B arranged a ten-day speaking tour for me in Eastern Hungary and found an interpreter to go with me.

When I returned, I went to give a report on the trip to Janos and Professor B. Right away I

AROUND THE GLOBE
Chiapas, Mexico

Population: 3.5 million
Location/Size: Southern Mexican state
28,653 sq. miles
Major Religions: Christianity
Level of Persecution: Continued, static

The Mexican Constitution guarantees every person the freedom to "profess the religious beliefs that please him or her." But evangelical Christians in Chiapas face unrelenting persecution, often with approval from elected authorities.

Homes and churches have suffered destruction at the hands of angry mobs; entire communities have found themselves expelled from their homes; evangelistic outreaches have met harassment; and Christians have been killed in individual assassinations and group massacres. Despite this extreme persecution, though, Christians in Chiapas, Mexico, have spread the Gospel effectively. Many evangelicals are optimistic about future religious freedom in the state, and outreach efforts continue to bring new members into the Church.

sensed that something was wrong. For one thing, both son and father were at home in the middle of the day. Yet neither man let on that all was not as it should be. They insisted that I return the next morning to have breakfast with them before I started for home.

The next morning I sensed again this lingering feeling of disaster. As we pushed our chairs back from the table and stood up, Janos drew a small package from his pocket. It was only later, when I learned what news they were secretly carrying, that the full impact of his words became clear.

"We have so little way of saying thank you," said Janos. "You risk much coming to our country. We want you to take this to that girl waiting back in Holland."

I had told them about Corrie. Inside the box was an antique gold pin, set with rubies. They all laughed at the expression on my face. Janos put his arm around his young wife's shoulder.

"We're praying with you, Andy, that that answer's going to be yes."

I was halfway across Austria on my way home, camping by the roadside in my little tent, when I woke up in the middle of the night with a terrifying nightmare. I was being chased by a whole squadron of police in red scarves who were all clapping, clapping, clapping. Somehow I knew that it had something to do with Professor B: I was sure that he was in some kind of danger. The next day from the very first town I came to, I sent him a letter.

In Holland I didn't go to Witte but drove straight to Haarlem. At the hospital they told me Corrie was working the three-to-eleven night shift. I was waiting for her when she came out the big front door. Under the streetlight her hair was copper instead of gold.

"I'm back, Corrie," I said. "And I love you. I love you whether the answer is yes or no."

Corrie looked tired from the hours on her feet. But when she laughed, the weariness seemed to drop away. "Oh Andy!" she said, "I love you, too! Don't you see that's just the trouble? I'm going to worry about you, and miss you, and pray for you, no matter what. So hadn't I better be a worried wife than just a cranky friend?"

Together, the following week, we went to a jeweler in Haarlem and bought two wedding rings. In Holland the custom is to wear the ring on the left hand during the engagement and transfer it to the right at the marriage ceremony. Corrie and I carried the rings up to her little sitting room in the top of the castle. There we opened the boxes and each of us placed a ring on the other's hand.

"Corrie," I began, not knowing that I was saying for the first time words that were to become a kind of motto for us. "Corrie, we don't know where the road leads, do we?"

"But Andy," she finished for me, "let's go there together."

When I got back to Witte, a letter was waiting for me from Professor B. He thanked me once again for coming to Hungary. The Church had been greatly strengthened, he said, by this tangible proof of the concern of the members for one another. He hoped I would come again, and that others would follow in my footsteps.

"But," he said, underplaying the news in a way that was typical, "I do believe I should share with you something that has happened. Do not think it is the result of your visit—it was coming anyhow. I have been forced to resign from the university. Do not feel sad: many have given up far more for their Saviour.

"Especially you must not be sidetracked from this most important work of encouragement. That is your task, Andrew, as we have ours. We pray daily for you, although you will not hear from us any more. This is being carried from the country by a friend. Our mail is censored. We pray that your ministry continue strong.

"Once again, you must not be downcast. We praise the Lord."

Imagine This

Born and raised in Colombia, you just found out that guerrilla rebels kidnapped your younger brother. They are demanding a $50,000 ransom for his return. Your family thinks they can raise the money with the help of family and friends. But the guerrillas will most likely buy drugs and weapons with your ransom payment, and you are not sure that your brother is still alive.

What Would You Do?

twelve

Counterfeit Church

Pray also for me, that whenever I open my mouth, words may be given me so that I will fearlessly make known the mystery of the gospel, for which I am an ambassador in chains.

Ephesians 6:19–20

Corrie and I were married in Alkmaar on June 27, 1958. Greetje was there and Mr. Ringers and many others from the factory, as well as a whole busload of nurses from Haarlem. Uncle Hoppy came from London with greetings from his wife, who was not strong enough for the trip. There were friends from WEC headquarters, co-workers from the refugee camps, and of course Corrie's mother and my brothers and sisters and their families. For me there were missing faces: Antonin, the medical student in Czechoslovakia. Jamil and Nikola in Yugoslavia. Janos and Professor B.

It was dark before we could tear ourselves away from so many friends and recollections. For the honeymoon we had borrowed Karl de Graaf's house trailer. We had talked romantically about driving to France. But setting out, we realized suddenly how tired we were, Corrie from her final examinations, just ended, I from the work in the refugee camps, where I had spent most of my time since our engagement. A few miles from Alkmaar we came to a restaurant in that rarity in Holland, a grove of trees. We parked beneath them and went in for coffee. And so cordial were the owner and his wife, so insistent that the trailer was no trouble, that that's as far as we got. We pulled the trailer a little deeper under the trees and spent our honeymoon right there.

The dark and dank little room above the shed wasn't dark or dank at all! How could I ever have thought so! With Corrie, sunshine and warmth came into the place and made it home.

So we didn't have a kitchen. So there was no plumbing in our home. So the roof did leak a bit here and there, and never two nights in the same place. What did it matter as long as we were together?

The only problem of any size was the clothing bundles. I had talked in churches all over Holland about the need for clothes in the refugee camps and suggested my address as a place where things might be sent. I never dreamed how much would come! It came by mail, by train, by truck, load after load deposited in the tiny front yard in Witte. Eight tons were delivered that first year, and the problem of storage was acute. Maartje was married now and living with her husband's family, but Arie and Geltje had a second child, and Cornelius and his new wife were living in the loft. There was no place for the clothes but our own room. Corrie and I had literally to scramble over bales of clothing each time we went in or out our door.

The worst of it was that so much of it came unwashed. We would scrub the dirtiest things in a tub in the backyard, and brush and spray the rest, but our room was never without fleas.

Transporting such a quantity of stuff was another problem. I packed the car as full as I could each time I left for the camps, but for all its advantages the Volkswagen made an unsatisfactory truck.

I was eager to go again, this time with Corrie at my side. I wanted her to see the camps for herself, not only so that she could meet these people for whom she was washing and packing so constantly, but because I knew what a nurse could mean in places like those. And so, that fall we piled the backseat to the roof with sweaters and coats and shoes, and set out for the camps in West Berlin.

We delivered the first load to the Fichter Bunker. This was an old circular military barracks used by the Nazis during the war and now converted into "homes" for refugees. It was Corrie's first glimpse of the squalor of the camps, and that night she could not eat.

I purposely saved the Volksmarstrasse camp for the second day, because it was even worse. This old factory building must have held five thousand people. Conditions were so desperate that a girl would sell her body for 50 pfenning—about 15 cents. As we carried our bundles of clothing to the distribution center, a group of youngsters leaned out of a window and dumped garbage over us.

"Don't be angry at them," I said to Corrie as I brushed rotting lettuce leaves off her coat. "They have literally nothing to do here but think up mischief."

But to me the saddest of all the camps was the Henry Dunant. Corrie and I went there last. This camp, named after the founder of the Red Cross, was where so many professionals—especially teachers—were sent. The camp made me sad not because it was physically any worse than the rest, but because the people in it tried harder to retain their traditions, and this made the inevitable failures more poignant.

I came out of the director's office that afternoon to find Corrie talking with a gray-haired East German lady who said her name was Henrietta. There was something in her manner that reminded me of Miss Meekle. We found a relatively uncrowded corner and sat talking for an hour. Henrietta told us that she had been a teacher of thirteen- and fourteen-year-olds in Saxony, and that this was where the trouble lay.

"If I had been teaching six- or seven-year-olds, I might have been able to close my eyes," she said. "But no, I had them right at the time of the *Jugend Weihe*."

"The *Jugend Weihe*?"

"Yes. You see," said Henrietta, "I'm a Lutheran. In our church, confirmation is a very big thing in a child's life, perhaps the biggest single day. There are gifts and speeches and congratulations and

China A Traveler's Story

A BABY, A WELL, AND A PRAYER

As I drew near the sixth village on my trip, I sensed that something was wrong. People were huddled together, talking in low tones, glancing accusingly at each other.

I introduced myself to them. "Greetings, I am the bearer of Good News, that—"

A small man interrupted me. "Well, we have only bad news here right now." With ill-concealed irritation, he explained, "A couple has just had their baby stolen."

I asked to see the couple, but the people just said to me, "Go away. We don't want you here. Stop pestering us and move on."

Tears sprang into my eyes. Should I shake the dust from my sandals and move on? Or should I strive with them a while?

"Please take me to the couple," I pleaded with the villagers. "I may be able to help."

Reluctantly, they took me to the cottage of the unfortunate couple. I stepped inside the house to find both husband and wife staring at me. Other villagers crowded at the doorway.

There was silence. The couple's grief hung in the air. I said, "I'm so sorry to hear about your plight, but I know Someone who may help. Let me pray to Him."

There was no reaction on the couple's faces, so I went into my prayer, feeling very uncomfortable indeed. Suddenly the young husband spoke. "Shut up and go away. We have prayed to our gods and nothing has happened. Why should yours be any different?" I was grabbed from behind by the other villagers and propelled out of the village.

Continued

new privileges, like long pants for the boys. It's a religious day, above all. Vows are taken, promises made."

And then Henrietta told us about the *Jugend Weihe*—the Youth Consecration. I could see right away that it was an extremely clever attack against the Church. The government substituted a ceremony of its own for the Christian confirmation.

"In the *Jugend Weihe* it is the State rather than God to whom vows are made," said Henrietta. "And the State makes a *very* big thing of the solemnity and binding quality of these promises. Teachers are expected to spend a year preparing students to take part in it."

I could see what had happened before Henrietta spoke. "And you refused," I said.

"I refused."

"That was a brave thing to do."

Henrietta laughed. "No," she said. "I certainly am not brave. I was just a schoolteacher about to retire. I'm not a martyr. But I just could not bring myself to teach these wonderful young people that the State was God."

It was expected that 100 percent of eligible students take part in the counterfeit ritual. From Henrietta's class there were 30 percent.

At first, she said, the pressure on her to conform was low-keyed. Party officials took to paying her friendly visits about once a week. Naturally it was expected that each teacher do his best to bring all of his students to the *Jugend Weihe*. Next year, they were certain, things would be different.

Well, next year, things weren't different. "And then I was really pressured," Henrietta said. "The weekly visits became nightly visits. Different people each night for a week—week after week. Round and round we went over the same old subject. Where was my loyalty? Did I realize I could be accused of holding back progress? That was a serious crime in the People's Republic."

Night after night they stayed in the apartment until late, stirring her up, frightening her until she could not sleep. Henrietta's temper grew short. Her work suffered. And in the meantime pressure was being put on the children, too, so that they began to ask why they weren't ready for the *Jugend Weihe* as everyone else was.

"And so you see," said Henrietta, and she was crying now, "I fled. I couldn't take it. I ran away. And that," she said, sweeping her arm to include the whole camp filled with teachers who, like her, had fled, "is why you must not think of me as brave. Maybe we started out to be brave, but we gave up. Every one of us."

Talking with Henrietta and other refugees, I was gradually forming a picture of the Church as a whole, as it existed under communism. In my mind I began to think of an Outer Periphery, countries where according to my own experience and the reports of others there was still some degree of religious freedom: Poland, Czechoslovakia, Yugoslavia, Hungary, and East Germany. Beyond these, according to those who had escaped, was an Inner Circle, where the attack against the Church was strong indeed: Rumania, Bulgaria,

China

A Traveler's Story
Continued

I wandered the hills in a daze of humiliation and tears. "Lord, have I prayed in vain?" I shouted. Then I began to think a little about Christmas. The Son of God had come to a world knowing He would be despised, kicked, beaten, misunderstood, and finally crucified. Yet He still came.

Kneeling there in the snow, I knew what I had to do. I had to go back to that village. This was to follow in the Master's footsteps. He had the courage. So must I.

Yet I quaked with fear. Those villagers had handled me very roughly. My arms and shoulders were still sore. With a pounding heart, I turned and began to walk slowly back toward the village. What would I say?

Suddenly, in the still afternoon air, I heard a baby's cry. I headed toward the sound. There was the cry again, coming from what appeared to be an old well shaft. I reached the shaft. Six feet down was a little baby, wrapped in a thick blanket, lying at the bottom of the dry well.

"Lord I praise you," I shouted into the well. The baby was blue in the face, and I climbed down to hug some warmth back into it.

I walked back to the village with the precious bundle of life clasped to my breast.

The villagers came running. They were amazed and overjoyed. Loving hands led me to the cottage of the poor couple, and the smile on the mother's face as I placed the baby into her lap was unforgettable.

The couple believed in Jesus that night, and I learned a great lesson.

Albania and, Russia itself. I had visited all but one of the Outer Periphery countries. Now, I knew, I had to visit East Germany.

Here in West Berlin was the obvious point of departure for such a visit. But when I proposed the trip to Corrie, she looked at me with stricken eyes.

"Oh, Andy!" she said. "How can I leave the camps? There's so much to do and no one to do it! How can I go?"

I looked at her more closely: her cheeks were flushed, her eyes had an unnatural glaze. I wondered if I had not been wrong to plunge her into such need and deprivation. It was hard enough for me to see the suffering, but for a nurse—trained to see what should be done but without facilities to do it—it must be torture indeed. She was moving from camp to camp like a woman beside herself: setting up a class for mothers here, a tank for boiled water there, at one place simply trying to get the dishes of those who did not have TB handled separately from the dishes of those who did. In the afternoons she held an impromptu clinic wherever she was, painting feverish throats, cleaning old sores, washing infected eyes, even on occasion pulling teeth.

For her own sake I began to want to get her away from this environment. But she refused. "You go," she said when the visas for East Germany came through without delay. "What good would I be there? I can't preach. I can't speak German. I can't even drive a car. But I can spot a toilet crawling with germs when I see one." She picked up the kit of disinfectant that was never far from her side in those days. "Tell me all about it when you get back," she said.

And so occurred the first separation of our married life—not because of my ministry, but Corrie's.

I crossed over from West to East Berlin at a checkpoint near the Brandenburg Tor.

The difference between the two halves of the city was observable even as I drove down the streets. I had been prepared for the slightly shabby clothes, for the shops in which large vases of flowers filled the space where suits should hang, for the lag in reconstruction after the war.

What I was not prepared for was the silence. Nobody talked in the streets. There was an eerie quality about it, as if the land were in mourning.

Or in fear. As time passed I came to feel this fear myself. There were police everywhere. They stood at the bridges, at factory entrances, at public buildings—stopping people at random, searching briefcases, shopping bags, pocketbooks. And no one complained at this arbitrary treatment. No one protested. The lack of protest was part of the dreadful silence that hung over the city like a poison-filled smog.

In sharp contrast to the silence of the people was the loud voice of the government. It was everywhere. On the radio, on loudspeakers, on billboards. Slogans were painted on walls, rooftops, telephone poles; there were posters in the kiosks, in stores, hotels, railway stations. Propaganda everywhere.

I was astonished at the baldness of the line. East Germany was just then going through a devastating food shortage. The enterprising German farmer had not taken at all kindly to the collective idea; he had quit the land in such large numbers that that fall there had been no one to harvest the crops. The government had pressed production on mechanical harvesters, accompanied by a massive propaganda campaign. There was going to be plenty of bread because socialism was superior to the enterprise of individual farmers.

There was only one trouble. To be harvested by machine, the wheat had to be dry; a couple of days more sunshine were required than for hand reaping. And of course that year it rained. It rained every day, right at the time of the harvest.

And then suddenly, all over the country, posters appeared carrying this little verse:

> *Ohne Gott und Sonnen schein*
> *Holen Wir Die Ernte ein*
> Without God and without sun
> We will get the harvest done

I could see that this slogan had really shaken the people. It was a brazen duel between the new regime and God Himself. The rains continued, and the harvest did not get in. Overnight as suddenly as they had appeared, the posters vanished—all except for the sodden few that you could still see clinging to lamp posts.

And now what did the government do? New signs appeared, along with announcements on the radio and advertisements in the newspaper. "Don't let anyone tell you there is a bread shortage. There is plenty of bread. This is another example of the victory of socialism over the forces of nature."

Only there was no bread.

I myself went into grocery stores and found none. Even restaurants didn't have any.

The saddest part of the story to me is that no one talked about the duplicity. The missing bread was never mentioned. The people were silent.

The part of East Germany I was most interested in centered around the southern tiers of Saxony, because I had heard from Henrietta and other refugees that there the Church was alive. I was not prepared for *how* alive. Germany was a land of contradictions. On the one hand, it was by far the hardest country I had yet penetrated; indoctrination and police coercion were rank. And yet, at the same time, there was more religious freedom in East Germany than I had found in any other Communist country.

The man whose name I had been given in Saxony, Wilhelm, was a full-time youth worker for the Lutheran Fellowship. The village where he and his wife, Mar, lived was in a hilly, wooded section of the state. Their front yard commanded a view to bring envy into the heart of every lowland Dutchman. A small motorbike stood outside, a bike, I was to discover, that carried Wilhelm all over East Germany in sun, snow, and rain.

Wilhelm met me at the door and without hesitation invited me in. We sat around Mar's porcelain kitchen table drinking coffee while I explained my mission behind the Curtain.

"Well, I'm glad you've come," said Wilhelm. He stopped to cough, a deep dry cough that racked his whole frame. "We need all the encouragement we can find."

"Do you need Bibles, for instance?" I asked him. "I have some German Bibles with me."

"Oh, we have plenty of Bibles."

I had heard this before, and waited for the slow admission that in fact there were very few Bibles. But Mar took me into the little study, and I could have thought I was home. There were a dozen Bibles on the shelves. I picked one up and looked at the East German imprint. "Printed in the Deutsche Demokratische Republik."

"Let me tell you about some other freedoms," said Wilhelm. "We have seminaries here that do not turn out politicians—they turn out Christians. We have evangelical campaigns that draw thousands. We have a move within the Lutheran Church that is as forceful, I would venture, as anything you can find in Holland."

"But—you said you needed encouragement."

Suddenly Wilhelm's fists clenched. I saw the knuckles go white.

"We're fighting one of the most important battles in Europe. Here in Germany the Communists are trying out a new kind of 'persuasion,' in my mind far more dangerous than outright persecution. Could you come with me to today's meeting of our synod? You'll see for yourself what I'm talking about."

I suggested that he come with me in my car, and Mar smiled at me gratefully. "It's that awful motorbike," she said. "That's what makes him cough. Thousands of kilometers in all kinds of weather. And the doctor told him two years ago to stay out of drafts!"

Wilhelm patted her hand. "Mar worries," he told me apologetically. "But if you want to reach young people all over the country, what can you do?"

In the car, he went back to his subject. "It *would* be we Germans who caught on first," Wilhelm said. "You can't use strong-arm tactics against the Church without strengthening it. It's always been that way. Under persecution a man looks at his faith to see if it's worth fighting for, and this is a scrutiny Christianity can always withstand. The real danger comes with an indirect attack, where a person is lured away from the Church before he has a chance to become strong. Keep this in mind while you listen today."

This synod meeting had been called to consider the problem that they called the counterfeit church. Pastor after pastor got up and read off statistics that at first I did not understand. "Welcoming Service, 35 percent. Youth Consecration, 55 percent. Marriage, 45 percent. Funeral, 50 percent."

But as Wilhelm whispered the explanation of these figures, the enormity of the plan began to emerge. Realizing that it was getting nowhere in its frontal attack against the Church, the regime had taken a new direction. For God and the religious instinct, it was attempting to substitute the State, and the emotion of patriotism. Using the ancient wisdom of the Church, it was offering state ceremonies in frank imitation of Christian rites.

There was, for example, an alternative to Baptism that went under the attractive name of Welcoming Service. At the time that a baby's name was officially registered, relatives and friends were invited to a celebration. The infant was brought forward by the parents to an official of the government, who received him with

Diary of a Smuggler

CHINA

I was working late in a Bible depot when suddenly there was a loud bang on the door outside. My heart thumped and I quailed inside, saying, "I'm going to jail, and I don't think I will survive it." But something warned me not to open the door, though I thought that was foolish since all the lights were on and it was obvious someone was in. So I crouched down and waited.

I could hear what sounded like three men talking. I didn't know if they were robbers or police. Then I heard one of them say he was going to climb up outside the building and videotape through the window what was inside. He clambered up the corrugated iron structure, his feet making booming sounds.

But as he neared the window, I heard him slip. He cursed, and something bounced down the side of the building and smashed. There was silence, then the men began quarrelling loudly. Apparently he had dropped the video camera, and his supervisor was furious and said the damage would come out of his wages. They got into such an argument that they forgot why they had come. They drifted off. I made a quick telephone call, and we moved the Bibles out that night.

When the police returned in the morning, there was only empty floor.

due ceremony as a new member of the state. And there was the state Marriage Service. On the continent it is customary to have two marriages, a legal one performed by a government official and a sacramental one held in a church. The new regime was taking both roles. After the legal marriage the state was offering a second service, free of charge, to which all were invited and at which there were flowers and food and a solemn ceremony welcoming the couple into the socialist society in the expectation that it would be happy and fruitful.

The same was true of the Funeral Service. The state performed a simple, dignified ceremony free of charge, and again the church service was emulated. A eulogy was said, praising this valiant soldier of the People's Democracy for his part in the war for human freedom.

And of course most blatantly competitive of all was the Youth Consecration, the *Jugend Weihe*, about which I had learned from Henrietta. This had proved especially effective because it was directed at people at an age when acceptance was supremely important. At this susceptible time in his life the youngster was told to make up his mind which to follow: his country or his church. There was intense pressure on him to follow his classmates up the aisle and receive the blessing of the state.

AROUND THE GLOBE
North Korea

Population: 24 million
Location/Size: Eastern Asia
46,540 sq. miles
Major Religions: Atheism
Ethnic faiths
Level of Persecution: Harsh, growing

Despite Christianity's long history in North Korea, less than 2 percent of the country's 24 million residents are Christians. Nearly all those who are believers are part of unregistered, underground churches.

Persecution comes in many forms in this Communist state, but all aim at the same purpose: systematic extermination of Christianity. Despite extreme pressures, however, the future of the North Korean Church is bright. The Church is growing rapidly, and Korean believers continue to work at spreading the Gospel throughout their land.

On and on the statistics went, "*Jugend Weihe*, 70 percent. Burial, 30 percent." The true significance of these figures did not hit me until Wilhelm explained that they represented church parishioners, and that this was the percent who had taken the state rites instead of, not in addition to, the religious ceremony.

"At first," Wilhelm told me, "the churches took a noncompromise line against the state services. If a child participated in the Youth Consecration, he could not receive the sacrament of confirmation."

This of course put the youngster in a terrible position, and it was precisely this tension that the regime looked for. The first year of the government's experiment there was a drop of 40 percent in confirmations. The next year the figure was 50 percent, and each year since, it had gotten worse. Bit by bit, many of the liturgical Protestant churches were easing their stand, saying that one year after participating in the *Jugend Weihe* a child could receive the Church's sacrament. The Roman Catholics, however, had not yet yielded, and for this they had the admiration of the most ardent Protestants.

"It's an open fight for allegiance," said Wilhelm, "and the churches are losing. It's hard to say no when your classmates are saying yes."

The churches' defense against this clever attack had been to retreat and withdraw, Wilhelm told me. Instead of going out on the offensive, they were pulling further and further into an attitude of private piety and isolation.

"Which is why I am so glad you have come to be with us," he said. "You can help us remember that the Church is larger than any one nation or any one political scene. We have forgotten that with God on our side we shall conquer."

He was about to leave, he said, on his semimonthly tour of youth groups. He invited me to join him. "I'd like your company. And"—with a smile—"Mar will like that automobile."

And so for nearly two weeks I traveled with him throughout southern East Germany preaching with an amazing freedom to churches that had plenty of Bibles, plenty of literature, wide open evangelical meetings—and that were demoralized beyond any churches I had yet met behind the Curtain.

Basically, during those twelve days, I preached just one sermon over and over in a hundred different versions. I urged the German Christians to become missionaries; because it has been my experience that a missionary church is an alive church.

At the first church where I made this suggestion the pastor stood up and said heatedly, "Brother Andrew, it's easy enough for you to speak about missionary work, because you can travel anywhere you want. But what about us here in East Germany? We can't even leave the country."

"Wait!" I said. "Think about what you have just said. I must take a long and costly trip to get to East Europe. But you're already here! How many Russian soldiers are there in your country now? Half a million, I believe. Think of that! How many unconverted fellow Germans are there in these hills? Don't complain to yourselves that you can't go to the mission field! Thank God for bringing the mission field to you!"

And then I told them the biblical story of a man doing precisely what I was urging them to do.

I told them about the time Paul was in prison in Rome chained between two soldiers. "Now there were two possibilities," I said. "Either he could sit there and complain that he could not get out, or he could make use of the situation. Well, Paul began to thank God that he had a captive audience. He began to preach the Gospel. After a while the guard was changed; two more soldiers came in. Paul thanked God for the two new ones and began again. And the result was that he made these men Christians. He founded a church right there in Caesar's household. And this, I feel, is the incomparable mission of Christians behind the Curtain.

Imagine This

Your family has disowned you for your faith in Christ. You have no home, no money, you are unable to get a job, and you have very few friends. Your faith in Christ is your only joy. One of your friends asks you questions about your faith, and you know if he converts, he will likely face the same loneliness and persecution. What will you tell him about Jesus?

What Would You Do?

thirteen

To the Rim of the Inner Circle

Who shall separate us from the love of Christ? Shall trouble or hardship or persecution or famine or nakedness or danger or sword? . . . No, in all these things we are more than conquerors through him who loved us.

Romans 8:35 — 37

Back in West Berlin I hurried from camp to camp, looking for Corrie. When I finally found her, conducting lice inspection on the heads of a row of five- and six-year-olds, I was appalled at the change that had come over her in less than three weeks. She had lost weight, her skin had a strange yellowish pallor, there were circles under her eyes.

I accused myself all over again for having brought her there, and above all for having left her alone. One of the things I had wanted to try, from Berlin, was to take a precious cargo of Bibles into Yugoslavia, to the church in Belgrade, among others, that had only seven among its whole membership. I knew from my previous experience that their consulate in Berlin was the place to apply for the visa, rather than The Hague.

Now, as I looked at my young wife's lined face and haunted eyes, I realized that a trip to Yugoslavia would serve a double purpose. What better place to forget the horrors of the camps than that beautiful land—loveliest I had seen. And so I took both our passports to the Yugoslav consulate and spent the rest of the day buying Bibles.

Corrie gave me an argument again. There was so much to do in the camps, she could do nothing in Yugoslavia—the same objections as before. But this time I overruled her on the grounds of her own health, and we set out for the first time together behind the Iron Curtain.

If it hadn't been for Corrie's illness, which seemed to get worse instead of better, that first week of the trip would have been perfect. This time the border guard scarcely glanced at our luggage. They spotted us for newlyweds and suggested ocean resorts to visit and scenic routes to take. For future smuggling operations I filed away this new bit of knowledge: a man and woman made a natural traveling team and aroused far less suspicion than a man traveling alone.

Jamil and Nikola greeted us with tears of joy in their eyes. When we brought the new Bibles out in church after church, the congregations could scarcely believe their eyes. And then everyone had to meet Corrie; the women kissed her, the men thumped me on the back.

For six days, things couldn't have gone better. With Nikola interpreting for me again—in spite of the fine and warning he had incurred for his earlier help—I shared with Yugoslavian churches the vision that had come to me in East Germany. A vision of Iron Curtain churches not in retreat but on the advance.

And then on the evening of the seventh day, while we were eating dinner in the house of friends in a town near Sawaweho, the police came. It happened so suddenly that for a moment I didn't realize for whom they had come. We were seated around the kitchen table eating rice and lamb—all except Corrie who didn't feel well and had gone to lie down—when there was a knock on the door, and in walked two gray-uniformed police.

Peru   A Traveler's Story

ALBERTO AÑAZCO JIMENEZ

Alberto Añazco Jimenez is a member of the Pentecostal Missionary Evangelical church, Nazareth Temple, in the district of Comas, Lima. He used to work as a bus-fare collector to support his family, as most of the working youth of Peru do. He is a hard-working, modest young man.

On December 27, 1992, when Alberto was sixteen, he was on his way home after an arduous workday and a police raid took place. A few hours earlier, some Shining Path guerrillas had been distributing subversive leaflets in the area, and Alberto, as well as other passersby, were detained by a police patrol. After throwing Alberto on the floor, hitting him, handcuffing him and covering his head with his own shirt, the police took him to the police headquarters.

Upon arrival, Alberto was forced to sign a self-incriminating form after the guards physically abused him by blindfolding him, striking him with fists, kicking him in the stomach, pulling his hair repeatedly, and smashing his head against the wall.

During his detention he was not assisted by any lawyer; despite the fact that Alberto was a minor, the Public Ministry did not object to the investigation. On the contrary, he was accused of the crime of terrorism.

At his hearing and trial, Alberto and his attorney demonstrated his innocence and discredited all the claims devised by the police. Lima's court, however, sentenced him to twenty years in prison.

He is currently serving his time at the San Jorge prison in Lima, one of the penal institutions that takes away all the rights of its inmates, even the right to appeal to the nation's Supreme Court.

"You come with us," they said to me.

"Come? Where?"

"Do not talk. Do not finish your meal. Just come."

I looked at my friends who were sitting, forks raised, mouths open in fear. Corrie appeared in the doorway, pale and disheveled.

"She is with you?"

"Yes."

"Her too."

It was soon apparent that the police knew all about my former trip to Yugoslavia. They were courteous enough, but they informed us that we would have to leave the country immediately. My visa had been canceled. There was no redress. Would I please hand over my passport then and there.

Reluctantly, because I did not want a bad stamp in my passport that other consulates would question, I turned over my papers. The officers looked at them carefully, cross-checked them with their own orders, and then took out an enormous red stamp, which they inked well and slammed down across the face of my visa. I was *persona non grata* in Yugoslavia.

Already at a low ebb physically, Corrie was shaken by the arrest. "Andy, I was scared stiff!" she kept saying as we drove across Austria toward Germany. "And those men were being nice about it!"

We intended to stop in Berlin only long enough to pick up two passengers, refugees whom we were sponsoring in Holland. My chief thought was to get Corrie home and to a doctor. Something was wrong, something more than just fatigue and strain. More and more frequently I had to stop the car and let her get out to stretch full length on the grass until the retching sickness passed.

But when we reached Berlin, there was a surprise waiting for us. Seeing that the Yugoslav consulate there was more lenient than the one in Holland, I had made the rounds of the Berlin offices of every other country I wanted to visit. And now on our return I found not one but two letters waiting at the hostel. Both Bulgaria and Rumania had considered my application and were pleased to tell me that I had only to appear at their Berlin headquarters to have my travel documents validated.

Bulgaria and Rumania! According to everything, two of the countries where persecution of the Church was most intense. At last, the Inner Circle! Surely God's hand was on the door, ready to throw it wide.

And just as surely, Corrie needed her own home and her own bed. In addition, there was the matter of that incriminating stamp in my passport. Certainly the other governments would want to know why I had been expelled from Yugoslavia.

So instead of going to the consulates, we went home to Witte. Corrie went to bed almost at once, and I called the doctor. He was with her for a long time while I sat miserably on the ladder outside.

Ethiopia   A Traveler's Story

PERSECUTION AT SCHOOL

If a pupil who attends an orthodox school becomes evangelical, he or she gets expelled. In the government schools, converts won't be expelled, but the other pupils won't talk to them, and they become very isolated. They lose their friends, and teachers won't mark their books or discuss anything with them. They also don't get the respect and support that other pupils get. Even children in elementary school are discriminated against.

Government school fees are about 500–600 Birr ($65–75) per year. One also has other expenses like books, stationery, and uniforms. If you can't afford your school fees, you have to quit school. The present government fortunately doesn't persecute Christians in schools. Many parents, however, expel their children from home when they become Christians, and they stop paying for their school fees and expenses.

The evangelical churches try to keep pupils in school, but because such a large number of converts are still at school or university, churches are unable to keep up with the financial burden. The converts, who are students, don't work, so the churches also have to provide for their everyday needs. Despite the discrimination the young Christians face and the fact that many of them have to give up their studies, they still choose to follow Jesus.

At last he emerged, lowering himself gingerly rung by rung. "Your wife is fine," he told me when he had reached solid ground. "I've given her some pills for the nausea, and she should come in to see me next month."

"But what's the matter with her?" I asked anxiously.

"Matter!" At last the man perceived that I did not understand. In a formal little gesture he swept his hat from his head and held out his hand. "Congratulations. You're going to be a father."

"But for heaven's sake," he added, putting his hat back on his head, "stop dragging that poor girl all over Europe and let her get some rest."

"And another thing," he said, pausing at the little bridge, "get rid of those stacks of clothing up there! She's going to be a mother, not a mountain climber."

It was November when we returned from Berlin and Yugoslavia, and the baby was due in June. By January, Corrie was feeling so well that I began to think seriously again about that trip into the Inner Circle—by myself, of course, under the circumstances, leaving Corrie under the watchful eye of Geltje. Allowing three or four weeks in each of the two countries, I would be back in plenty of time for the baby's birth.

But there was still that matter of the passport. What could I do about the bad page? Tear it out? That was impossible, since all the pages were numbered. Throw the whole thing away, pretend I had lost it, and file a claim for a new one? But that was not the Royal Way; the King's servants didn't have to stoop.

I went to The Hague, to the office of passport control, and showed the reviewing officer my problem. He was very understanding. "I sympathize with you," he said, "but there's nothing we can do."

"You see," I said, "I'm a missionary. I want to go to these countries to contact the Christians there."

He considered this for a moment. Then he shook his head. "We can't even give you hints about how to get a new passport quickly. Such as, for instance, doing a lot of travel to nearby countries and always insisting that they stamp your papers, so that your passport will fill up sooner. We couldn't even give you hints like that, don't you see? I'm very sorry."

Within a few weeks I had a new passport.

Corrie was reluctant to let me go. She still had not got over the shock of our arrest in Yugoslavia. But when the shipment of Bulgarian and Rumanian Bibles arrived from the British and Foreign Bible Society in London, she helped me stow them away in the car herself. "A bargain's a bargain," she said. "After all, I signed on as the wife of a missionary."

When the actual day of departure came, neither one of us was feeling very brave. We were packing the leftover space in the Volkswagen with clothes for the camps in Austria I would visit on the way. We had moved the clothing depot out of our room, per doctor's orders, and into the tiny hallway of the main house, where it was making life miserable for everyone.

"Bulgaria and Rumania," Corrie said softly. "Those aren't Yugoslavia! You get arrested in those countries, and I might never see you again. *We* want you back, Andrew, your baby and I."

And of course I tried to reassure her, but I was feeling far from cheery myself. I climbed into the heavily loaded car and started the engine.

"You've got your money?" Corrie asked.

I felt my wallet. For once I was going with more than enough. I couldn't understand why so many gifts had come from readers of *Kracht van Omhoog* lately. It cost me very little to travel, sleeping in the tent whenever I could, fixing my own meals. I had tried to leave the extra amount with Corrie, but as though with a strange foreknowledge, she had insisted that I take it with me. Yes, the money was all safe.

And so with a last kiss I was off.

It bothered me a little, as I headed from the Austrian camp toward Yugoslavia, that I was having to go back into a country from which I had so recently been expelled. But there was absolutely no other practical route into Bulgaria. The only other way to go would be a long and costly trip the length of Italy, by boat to Greece, and then the long drive up through Greek Macedonia. As I had anticipated, there had been no trouble getting a new visa: Yugoslavian paperwork was notoriously inefficient, and the fact that I was *persona non grata* had not yet been forwarded to the Western consulates. The only place where there might be trouble, I thought, was at the border itself.

Heart pounding, I pulled up to the frontier. But the guard only glanced at my passport. We chatted a while about road conditions, and within twenty minutes I was across.

By my calculations I had now four days of grace in Yugoslavia before the information about my arrival at the border was checked against the unwanted persons file in Belgrade. I stopped for a brief visit with Jamil and then pressed on south and east, fully intending to cross the border into Bulgaria on the morning of the fifth day. But as always in Yugoslavia, there was so much to do! Jamil had supplied me with enough names and churches along my route to have kept me busy for a month. There hadn't been a whisper

Diary of a Smuggler

TIBET

Our purpose in Tibet was to pray that God would turn the tide of the evil power that has been holding the people of that land captive for so long and to open their hearts to the Gospel of Jesus Christ. As "tourists" there were only so many things to see in Lhasa, most of which revolved around Buddhism and the Dalai Lama. Our first stop was the Potala Palace, where the Dalai Lama ruled for hundreds of years before the Chinese occupation. We wound our way through temple after temple, seeing the different Buddhas and Dalai Lama shrines. The rooms were lit only by huge vats of yak butter with wicks, burning sacrifices to Buddha. The smell of those vats was so strong that after we left the temples, my nostrils were burning for hours. The people all carried little vats of yak butter around the temple and put a little bit in each vat to keep the sacrifices burning. They also would lie prostrate and offer prayers to the gods.

I cannot say that I fully understood the spiritual implications of what they were doing or what in the Buddhist religion they were trying to accomplish, but I can say that my heart was deeply moved as I stood side by side with these dear people held in bondage by their false gods. Our group walked and prayed as we made our way to the top of the Palace, which overlooked the city of Lhasa. I was deeply moved by seeing with my eyes a people who have never heard the wonderful name of Jesus. They have never experienced the love of His nail-scarred hands or the freedom of His resurrection.

From the top of the Palace we stopped and joined in singing "Our God Reigns" from the rooftop. A small crowd gathered and watched. What a powerful experience to stand on top of the spiritual center for Buddhism in that country and proclaim that Christ reigns!

of trouble from the authorities. I decided to stretch my luck by twenty-four hours.

On the fifth evening I checked into a hotel after midnight, turned in my passport at the desk, and went up to my room. I had slept for perhaps five hours when there was an abrupt rap on the door. I opened it and found two men in ordinary business suits standing in the hall.

"Dress and follow us," they said in German, holding the door open. "Do not bring anything with you."

They never took their eyes from me as I struggled into pants and a shirt. We walked through the lobby, empty at that hour except for a woman scrubbing the steps. Outside, we walked a few hundred yards to a large stone building. I was shepherded down a marble corridor, echoing in its emptiness, and into an office.

The man behind the desk had my passport in his hand.

"Why are you here?" he demanded. "Why are you back in Yugoslavia?" He did not wait for me to answer but went on, voice rising as he spoke. "How did you get this passport changed? Is this what Holland does, make it easy for conspirators and lawbreakers?"

He reached into his desk, and I saw with dismay that he had taken out the enormous stamp with the red ink. He slammed it down on the Yugoslav visa three times before he seemed satisfied.

"You will leave the country within twenty-four hours," he said. "You will have no further contacts with any person in Yugoslavia. We will telephone the border guard in Trieste when to expect you."

Trieste! Surely he wouldn't insist upon that! Trieste was in the northwest corner of the country, right back where I had come from, while here we were fifty miles from the Bulgarian frontier.

"But I'm on my way to Bulgaria!" I pleaded. "Couldn't I leave the country that way? It's so much closer!"

But he was adamant. Trieste he had said, and Trieste it had to be, and as quickly as possible.

And so with a sinking heart, I headed back north to Trieste and the long round-about trip through Italy and Greece: fifteen hundred miles out of my way, when I had been almost in sight of my goal.

A depression such as I had never known before settled over me as I inched my way down the boot of Italy. The roads were maddening: an endless succession of towns strung one after another down the coast—trucks, bicycles, horsedrawn carts—I seldom got the Volkswagen out of second gear.

March 31 came; Corrie's birthday. I sent her a telegram, but instead of cheering me up, it only served to remind me how far away she was. Her first birthday since we'd been married, and there I was, not even out of Italy yet, farther away from my goal than ever, and getting farther from Corrie every minute. Suppose something happened. Suppose there was trouble with the police in Bulgaria too. Suppose I didn't get back for the birth of the baby. At least I understood now the reason for the extra money: I'd be lucky to make it there and back by this route even with all I had.

To make matters worse, there was that suspicion-arousing stamp on the Yugoslavia page again.

And then, just when I thought I'd reached my lowest point, my back began to act up. For three or four years I'd been having trouble on and off with a slipped disk. It seemed to bother me most when I'd been driving long distances. About halfway through Italy the trouble began again, worse than I'd ever known it. By the time I reached Brindisi, where the boat left for Greece, I was literally bent double, walking with a kind of strange, crouching gait on the balls of my feet.

AROUND THE GLOBE
Peru

Population: 25.6 million
Location/Size: Western South America 496,225 sq. miles
Major Religions: Christianity
Level of Persecution: Isolated, growing

Peru's current constitution guarantees religious freedom to all, but the Catholic Church predominates in the country. Of the more than 97 percent of the country's residents who profess to be Christians, 89 percent are Catholic.

Despite these high percentages, however, Peruvian churches are in crisis due to a lack of internal leadership. In the absence of solid discipleship, Christopaganism runs rampant among the people.

In recent years, national difficulties have sparked new interest in the Church, and evangelical Christians have become a recognized force for social change. Missionaries and evangelists still face harsh persecution and often find their lives at risk, particularly when in areas of greatest conflict. But the Church continues to grow and to devise successful discipleship and training programs for the future.

There was no time to stop and get treatment; I just had to let people stare. When I took the car off the boat in Greece, I was no better; after a couple of days on the Greek roads I was literally crying aloud with the pain. If the Italian roads had been choked with traffic, the Greek ones were all rocks and chuck holes. I could not read the signs with their strange Greek characters and often, after twenty spine-jarring miles, would discover I had made a wrong turn and have to give up all that hard-won distance.

And all the while, that insidious depression was working its poison in me. "Well, Andrew," the inner whispering would begin, "you got away with it that time. . . . They were easy on you. Sent you out of the country. . . . You could have gone to jail. For how many years, Andrew? Five? Ten? You'll find out in Bulgaria. They lock people up there. Sometimes they never get out. . . . Not even a letter. Corrie will never know. . . ."

And so it went, hour after hour, day after day, until every nerve was on edge. And then came the final blow. At the Greek town of Serrai I discovered that the border crossing toward which I had been heading all this time was open to diplomats only. For ordinary travelers there was no entry at all into Bulgaria from Greece. The only way was through Turkey, many miles and many days farther on.

The morning after this discovery I was grinding and bumping along a stony track toward what seemed a horizon of endless frustrations, when up ahead I saw a small blue sign. The top lettering was in Greek. But below it, in Latin characters, I read the single word:

FILIPPI

I stopped the car with a jerk. Philippi? The Philippi in the Bible? The town where Paul and Silas had been in prison—where God had sent the earthquake to open the door?

Of course! This was the very place! I got out of the car and stared through a tall link fence at a field of ruins. There were the old streets, there was what was left of a temple. A row of houses, only the walls standing now. Was Lydia's house—where Paul had stayed—one of these?

There was a gate in the fence, but it was locked and there was no one around. An immense silence brooded over the scene; the modern town of Philippi was two miles away to the north and west.

Here, there was not a sound. Only Paul shouting over the centuries: "Christian! Where is your faith!"

Paul had been in prison in this place, just as I was in prison too: a prison of pain and discouragement. Paul and Silas had been doing the same thing I was doing, preaching the Gospel where it was not allowed. God had performed a miracle to get His men out of prison then, and in that instant I knew that He was even now performing another one to get me out of mine.

The bonds of depression that had wrapped themselves around me snapped as had the chains on Paul's wrists. The spirit of heaviness lifted, and as it did I realized with a start that I was standing erect, back tall, head high. Joy welled up in me, physical joy as well as mental.

I literally ran back to the car, stopping every now and then to jump several inches off the ground. I started the engine, shoved the car into first, and with a roar set off once more for my appointment with the unknown believers of the Inner Circle.

Imagine This

Your car recently broke down, and the mechanic told you that you needed to purchase a new one. After saving a little money, you begin to feel led to use your money to purchase Bibles for people in China. You realize that it will take at least another year or two for you to make up the money you've saved, and yet you know God is asking you to give your money away. How would you respond?

What Would You Do?

fourteen

Abraham the Giant Killer

We are hard pressed on every side, but not crushed; perplexed, but not in despair; persecuted, but not abandoned; struck down, but not destroyed.

2 Corinthians 4:8—9

After all my apprehension, the border crossing from Turkey into Bulgaria turned out to be a pleasant surprise. The customs inspector scarcely glanced into the rear of the car and did not ask me to open any of my cases. He entered the date and point of entry on my Bulgarian visa but did not turn the other pages in the passport. Then he made me a little speech in English welcoming me to the country.

What was more, after the Turkish roads, which had been as appalling as the Greek, the Bulgarian highway was newly paved and well engineered. All along it I met the same welcome I had received at the border. Children shouted and ran along the edge of the road as long as they could keep the car in sight. Men and women working in the fields straightened up to smile and wave, a thing I had not seen anywhere else in Europe.

Bulgarian roads were good, that is, as long as I stuck to the main routes. That first evening I turned off on a little track up a mountainside in search of a camping site. I found a secluded spot and in the morning spent some time unpacking Bibles from the various spots where I had stowed them. Then I packed the Rumanian ones away again and drove down the mountain, slipping and sliding on the dangerous gravel road, intending to pick up the main pavement again.

Instead, I soon found myself following a track that wound through the backyards of a tiny village. The road was getting muddier every second. I splashed through a little stream and a few feet further on bogged down altogether.

There I sat, hopelessly stuck in the mud in an out-of-the-way mountain village where I had no business being. What was I going to do? I had no sooner asked the question than I seemed to hear some loud and rather brassy singing. It was coming from a building just on the edge of the village. I opened the door of the car and jumped. When the mud reached my ankles, I stopped sinking. Well, nothing for it. . . . I slogged heavily through the muck until I reached the door of the building.

It was a pub, and although it was only ten in the morning, the sounds were those of men well into their cups. I stepped inside, and instantly the singing stopped.

Twenty faces stared at me, obviously astonished at the appearance of a foreigner in their village. The air was thick with smoke, heavier and more pungent than the smoke smell of Western pubs.

"Does anyone here speak English?" I asked. No one responded. "German?" No. "Dutch?"

"Well, hello anyway," I said, smiling and touching my forehead in salute. And then while these round, brown-eyed faces stared at me, I went into a pantomime routine. I made a noise that was meant to sound like a VW getting stuck in the mud. Huumm Huumm. Splutter, splut. Stop.

No one gave a sign of recognizing my charade.

I held my hands out in what I thought looked like a man holding a steering wheel with both hands.

China   A Traveler's Story

BETRAYED

Zhemin married his sweetheart at the age of twenty, and two years later she was pregnant. He was a teacher in school but made a strong profession of faith, which made him a target of the authorities. One day he read Luke 14:26, where Jesus said, "If anyone comes to me and does not hate his father and mother, his wife and children, his brothers and sisters—yes, even his own life—he cannot be my disciple."

Zhemin recalls, "I was so frightened of this verse. I knew what God was asking me right away. He was saying I may have to give up my wife and child if I was to follow Him. But I prayed and prayed, resisting this, and pleading with God that my witness for Him would not separate me from my wife and our unborn child."

Two days before the birth of his son, Zhemin was arrested. At his trial he looked in vain for his wife and his new child, but they never came. He was sentenced to prison camp for twelve years and sent far away to the north. Then after six years he was moved to the south, quite close to home.

During this time he had no letters from his wife and assumed they were not delivered. One day, after moving back to his home province, he received a letter from her that she would make a visit. "I was delirious with happiness, and I knew I would see my son for the first time."

The day came, and his wife and child arrived. To his horror, his boy said to him, "Hello, Uncle." He turned to his beloved wife, only to see a hard set to her features, and she said, "Well, you wouldn't want me telling him he had a father in jail, would you?" When his wife rose to go, she gave him a document. "This is a copy of my divorce petition. We will be divorced in three weeks I am sure."

Zhemin recalls, "I grabbed her by the hand and asked her, 'Why?' She said to me, 'I don't love you because you put God before me. I'm in a relationship with a man who will love me and never leave me defenseless.'"

Zhemin cried all night and for days afterward. Then the paperwork came through. The divorce was finalized. He never saw her again.

"Ahh! Oh!" The man behind the high wooden bar nodded knowingly. In a moment he had run forward with two glasses of beer, shoving one in each outstretched hand.

"No, no," I said, laughing. "Automobile. Car. Huum. Huum. Brrr. Brrr. Stop." I put the glasses down and signaled with my arm. "Come!"

At last several of the men got the idea and rose from their tables, enjoying the game and shouting encouragement to their companions. I felt like the Pied Piper leading the parade. Back of the pub was the answer to what this was all about, sitting expectantly in the mud: my little blue VW.

"Ahh!" Nodding of heads, clapping of thighs. Now they understood! They were glad to help. They were wearing knee-high boots and without hesitation waded into the mud, indicating that I should get behind the wheel. I started the motor, and while these broad-shouldered men lifted, I eased the car into gear and within moments we were out on the main road in front of the pub.

I got out of the car and thanked them, a little worried at the curiosity they were showing for the car and its contents. It would never do for a story to get started about a Dutchman with a cargo of books in his car. Quickly I took one mammoth, work-hardened hand after the other, shook it soundly, and moved on.

"I really do thank you," I said. "Holland thanks you. The Lord thanks you. . . ."

And while I was speaking, one man simply did not let go of my hand. Instead he pulled me with him into the pub. Even before we reached the bar, I knew what was going to happen. They were going to buy me a beer whether I wanted one or not.

I hadn't had a drink since that stormy January night more than nine years ago when I had turned my will over to God. In my life, anyhow, alcohol had clearly always been a destructive thing.

"But what should I do now, Lord?" I asked aloud in Dutch. And suddenly I knew that I had to go ahead and drink that beer, that to turn it down would be to turn them down, that their kindness and hospitality ranked higher with God than one observance of a rule. Twenty minutes later, eyes watering from the powerful home-made brew, I once again shook twenty hands, laughed, wished them the speediest of all possible salvations, and went on my way. It took forty minutes of high-speed travel down the highway before the mud that had been trapped on the wheels of my little car stopped thumping the sides of the fenders.

My final night in Yugoslavia, the night for which I had been sent back across the border, I had met a man whose closest friend lived in Sofia.

"Petroff is one of the saints of the church," he had told me. "Will you go to see him?"

And of course I was delighted. I had memorized Petroff's address so as not to have it written down on my person in case I got into trouble with the authorities. Now as I sat on a hillside looking down over Sofia, I marveled at how God used the very last person I spoke to in one country to give me the first contact I needed in another.

Sofia was a beautiful sight, stretched out below me, the mountains rising beyond, the round domes of her Orthodox churches sparkling in the late-afternoon sun. But how in that vast metropolis was I to find the street where Petroff lived? My Yugoslav friend had warned me that it could be dangerous for him if a foreigner were to go around asking for it. So when I checked into my hotel, the first thing I did was to ask for a plan of the city.

"I'm sorry, sir, but we're all out. You might try the bookstore on the corner."

But the bookstore was out too. I went back to the hotel and asked the clerk if he was quite sure he had no maps at all. He looked at me suspiciously.

"What do you want a map so badly for?" he asked. "Foreigners shouldn't go wandering just anywhere."

"Oh," I said, "just to get my bearings. I don't want to get lost, not speaking Bulgarian."

The clerk seemed satisfied. "All we have," he said, "is this little one here." He pointed to a small hand-painted street plan under the glass on his desk. It would never be of any help to me: only the names of the biggest boulevards were shown. But I bent over the map to please him, and as I did I saw an amazing thing. The cartographer had indeed penned in the names only of major avenues, with one terribly important exception. There was a single, tiny street just a few blocks from the hotel that had a name on it. And it was the street name I was looking for! Not one other street of similar size on the entire map bore a name. I felt again the most amazing sense that this trip had been prepared long before.

Early the next morning I left the hotel and headed immediately for the street where Petroff lived. I found it with no difficulty, just where the map had indicated. Now it was only a matter of finding the number.

As I walked along the sidewalk, a man came down the street from the opposite direction. We drew abreast just as I came to the number I was looking for. It was a large double-duplex apartment house. I turned up the walkway, and so did the stranger!

As we neared the front door, I glanced for a fraction of a second into the face of the man who had arrived at the precise moment I did. And at that instant I experienced one of the common miracles of the Christian life: our spirits recognized each other.

Without a word we marched side by side up the stairs. Other families lived in the house too: if I were making a mistake, it would be very embarrassing. The stranger reached his apartment, took out his key, and threw open the door. Without invitation I walked into his house. Just as quickly, he closed the door behind him. We stood facing each other in the darkness of the single room that was his home.

"I am Andrew from Holland," I said in English.

"And I," said Petroff, "am Petroff."

Petroff and his wife lived in this single room. They were both over sixty-five, and their combined pensions from the state paid for the room, food, and an occasional purchase of clothing. The three of us spent our first few moments together on our knees, thanking God for having brought us together in this wonderful way, so that there was not a minute of time wasted, so that there was a minimum of risk involved.

Then we talked. "I've heard," I said, "that both Bulgaria and Rumania are desperately in need of Bibles. Is that so?"

In answer, Petroff took me over to his desk. On it was an ancient typewriter with a sheet of paper in it, and next to the typewriter a Bible, open to Exodus.

"Three weeks ago I was extremely lucky," said Petroff. "I managed to find this Bible." He showed me a second volume on the small dining table. "I got it for a good price too. Only a month's pension. The reason it was so cheap is that the books of Genesis, Exodus, and Revelation have been cut out and—"

"Why?" I interrupted.

"Who knows? Perhaps to sell. Or perhaps to make cigarettes with the thin paper.

"At any rate," Petroff went on, "I was lucky enough to find it and have the money to purchase it. Now all I have to do is fill in the missing parts from my own Bible—and I have another complete book! I ought to be all finished in another four weeks."

"And what will you do with the second Bible then?"

"Oh, give it away."

"To a little church in Plovtiv," said his wife, "where there's no Bible."

I wasn't sure that I understood. No Bible in the entire church?

"Certainly," said Petroff. "And there are many such churches in this country. You'll find the same in Rumania and in Russia. In the old days only the priests had them; ordinary people couldn't read. And since communism, it's been impossible to buy them. It's not often I have a piece of luck like this."

My sense of excitement mounted. I could hardly wait to show Petroff the treasure I had waiting for him in my car.

That night I drove up to the apartment, checked the street to make sure it was empty, and then took inside the first of many, many cartons of Bibles I was to deliver to this man over the years. Petroff and his wife watched me put the box on their one table, their eyes wide in frank and open curiosity.

"What's that?" Petroff asked.

I lifted the top and took out a Bible. I put it in the trembling hands of Petroff and another into the hands of his wife.

"And—and in the box?" Petroff asked.

"More. And still more outside."

Petroff closed his eyes. His mouth was working hard to control the emotion he was feeling. But two tears rolled slowly out from between his closed lids and fell on the volume in his hands.

| Vietnam | A Traveler's Story |

"WE WOULD RATHER LOSE ALL THAN FORSAKE OUR GOD"

Sister Sarah's husband was arrested and imprisoned for preaching and evangelizing. Prior to his arrest, he had won fifty new believers to the Lord. Soon after his arrest, his mother came to receive the Lord. Their family hails from the Hue tribe, and there are around three thousand Hue believers in their area alone. The couple has three small children. At present, Sister Sarah continues to experience harassment from the authorities, forcing her to sell their house and the only cow they had so they could pay the fine required for the release of her husband. Nevertheless, the couple has vowed neither to deny the Lord nor to give in to the authorities' demands.

Sister Miriam's husband was accused of evangelizing and teaching new Christians, too. Before his arrest, he and his wife had been warned to quit their involvement in Christian activities. The police had stated,

"Christianity is a religion from the West and should be avoided." But the couple stood firm and continued in their work for God.

The imprisoned believers were given a one-year sentence in prison. Sister Sarah's husband has already served nine months while Sister Miriam's has served eight. The women can only visit their husbands once a month for thirty minutes. Sometimes they were denied permission to leave their village to visit their husbands. Moreover, because of their impoverished situation, the wives cannot visit at regular intervals. A husband's absence means the wife has to assume leadership in the family, including responsibility in church. Amazingly, the situation did not stop the growth of their respective churches. Instead, the believers grew in number, and more were won to Christ.

Petroff and I set off immediately on an extended trip through Bulgaria, delivering the Bibles to churches where he knew the need was greatest. "Do you know the official reason the government gives for suppressing Bibles here?" Petroff asked me as we sped through a countryside brilliant with roses for the perfume industry. "It's because Bibles are printed in the old orthography. They hold back education, the government says. Chain people to ancient spellings and usages."

The visible Church in Bulgaria, he went on, had been purged of all elements contrary to the new regime. The Bulgarian Orthodox Church—state church of the country—was now little more than an arm of the government. The present patriarch praised the regime in all his official utterances: his speeches had as much to do with the glories of *Narodna Republika Bulgariya* as with those of the Kingdom of God.

"In effect there are two churches here now," Petroff told me, "a Puppet Church, which echoes the voice of the state, and an Underground Church. You'll see one of these underground churches tonight."

It was my first service of worship in Bulgaria. It took twelve of us more than an hour that evening to assemble for the meeting, arriving at intervals so that at no time would it appear a group was gathering.

At seven-thirty our time came. We walked past an apartment house, just happened to turn in together, just happened to stop at the third floor rear, looked around briefly, and entered the apartment without knocking. I could not help but remember Sundays in Witte, when the whole village turned out to promenade to church.

Eight men and women were gathered when we arrived, two more coming at 7:45 and 7:55. The room was very dark. Only one small lightbulb hung from the ceiling, and blankets had been draped over the window to block out prying eyes. I wondered if these people were too poor to afford shades. No one spoke. Each new worshiper took his place around the central table, bowed his head, and prayed silently for the safety of the coming meeting. Precisely at 8:00 Petroff stood up and spoke in a low voice, translating himself for me as he went.

"We are blessed tonight to have a brother visit us from Holland," Petroff whispered. "I shall ask him to share with you a message from the Lord."

Petroff sat down and I waited for the hymn, then realized that of course singing was impossible in this church underground. I spoke for perhaps twenty minutes, then nodded to Petroff. He jumped up and, with a flourish, unwrapped the package he had brought with him and held up . . . a Bible!

There were exclamations that threatened to be too loud before those assembled caught themselves and put hands to mouths.

Then there were great bear hugs from the men and warm fore-heads-on-the-shoulder from the women, before they passed the Book from one hand to another, tenderly opening it and closing it again.

One of the men at the meeting that night especially intrigued me. After we had stayed together for as long as we dared, we separated as we had come, in ones and twos, at intervals, for over an hour. The last person to get up from his knees was a mammoth grizzly bear of a man with a patriarchal beard, a square brown face, and the kindest, most guiltless blue eyes I had ever seen. This, Petroff told me, was Abraham.

Abraham had spoken little during the meeting, but there was a childlike innocence and purity about the old man that came through without words. Like Petroff, he was over the maximum age for holding a job. And so for several years the two of them had spent their time trying to locate churches that had two Bibles, so that they could beg or buy one and give it to a church that had none.

Abraham, Petroff told me, lived in a tent in the Rhodope Mountains. He had an income from the government of five dollars a week, and on this he and his wife lived. At one time he had owned land but had lost it because of his "subversive" activities.

"Some day you must try to visit him in his home," Petroff said, "because it will give you a picture of what a man will sacrifice in the name of his God." Most of the year, he said, Abraham and his wife lived on wild berries and fruit and a little bread.

Petroff called the old man Abraham the Giant-Killer, because he was always setting out to find his "Goliath"—some high-ranking Party official or army man to whom he could bring his witness. "Abraham is always seeking a new Goliath," Petroff said. "He finds him, too, and then there is a fight. Only Goliath wins, and Abraham ends up in jail. But on many occasions Abraham wins, and a new soul is added to Christ's Church."

Before he left, I went out to my car and brought Abraham the Giant-Killer the rest of the Bulgarian Bibles I had brought with me. He would know what to do with them.

Diary of a Smuggler

CUBA

I hardly know where to begin. This trip was so awesome!

I was detained for two hours at customs. I had three bags, all interspersed with Bibles, supplies, and used clothing. One suitcase was all used clothing. Interestingly they had a problem with that one and kept it. Then they decided to give me half of it back. They took forever writing up the form and asking me questions, most of which I didn't understand because they were in Spanish. But we finally got through. The good thing was that that suitcase became the distraction, and all it had in it was clothes. They ignored my other two bags, which also had clothing, supplies and, most importantly, much-needed Bibles!

The poverty of the people breaks my heart. People ask for soap as much as they ask for money. They make only 5-10 dollars a month. A bar of soap costs fifty cents. Most things we take for granted either aren't available at all (scotch tape is one) or are out of their reach. I could not turn anyone down who asked for money or things. I brought many items as well as Bibles and gave away many of my own personal belongings. We gave offerings of money, Bibles, clothing, and supplies to four desperately poor churches. The need is so great!

Abraham held the Bibles as he might have held a baby. He did not say thanks, but the words he did say have remained with me to this day. His blue eyes burned into mine as Petroff translated for him.

"The front line is long, Brother. Here we must give a little, there we may advance. This day, Andrew from Holland, we have made an advance."

The balance of that first trip to Bulgaria was spent visiting the tiny nonregistered, underground churches. "Strengthen the things that remain," became more than ever a command that haunted my sleep. How courageous they were, this remnant of the Church, how heedless of self, how utterly alone. Three ministers especially stand out in my memory from those weeks—Constantine, Arminn, and Basil.

Constantine had been in prison for eighteen months for baptizing converts who were under twenty-one years of age. He had just been released. Constantine told me that the night after his release he had taken twenty-seven teenagers out of town and baptized them secretly in a river in the country.

Arminn knew there were government observers in his congregation at Christmastime, so he was careful in no way to transgress the law against evangelizing children. Speak only to adults. Keep away from politics. But in one unguarded moment, Arminn looked down at the children who were seated beneath the church's Christmas tree and asked, "Do you know why we give each other presents at this time of the year? It is to symbolize the greatest Gift of all." For those two sentences he was brought to trial and removed from his pulpit.

Basil was notorious for working hand-in-glove with the secret police. Petroff had taken me to his service one Sunday so that I could have a chance to see the Puppet Church in action. The congregation of the church had dwindled steadily since the war. Basil was complaining about this to us before the service when suddenly, with no change in his expression, he said to me, "Would you like to hold a meeting here this afternoon?"

I could not be sure that I had heard right. Basil knew as well as I that unregistered preachers were not allowed to hold meetings. What had gotten into the man?

"I'll—I'll have to pray about that," I told him.

And pray I did, furiously, all through the service. Was this some kind of trap? Suppose he had set this up with the police to get me out of the country? And yet the answer I seemed to be getting with great clarity was a ringing "Go ahead!"

At the close of the service Basil announced to the handful of people in the congregation that the brother from Holland was going to hold a special meeting that afternoon. He invited everyone to come and to bring a friend.

We were all surprised that afternoon to see some two hundred people there. We had a wonderful meeting. At the end, when I issued the altar call, dozens came forward.

Then Basil surprised me again by suggesting that we hold another meeting that night. I was more than willing, and so was Petroff. Still, we could not understand what had happened to this man who had a reputation as a marionette.

That evening the church was packed. We all felt the presence of the Holy Spirit. That night scores of persons expressed a willingness to follow Christ, whatever the cost. And once again Basil invited everyone to come back the following evening.

On Monday night the church was so crowded, people were standing along both sides and many were sitting in the center aisle. But this time Basil spotted half a dozen of his friends from the secret police in the congregation. We went ahead with the meeting but omitted the altar call. We didn't even dare ask for a show of hands, for fear names would be taken down.

After the meeting was over, Petroff and Basil and I sat in the vestry and wondered what we should do next. Obviously we could not hold any more meetings. What about Basil himself; would he be in trouble now? It was clear to me that he was acting in a way he himself did not understand. What was going to happen now? What would the police do?

And as the days passed it became clear why Christ had chosen Basil rather than some other pastor to touch with His spirit. Because the police did nothing at all. Neither to me nor to Petroff nor to Basil. Basil was one of their most valuable collaborators, they thought. Surely what he was doing must have some orthodox motive. He was too high up in the New Outlook of the church to earn suspicion. Best, they must have concluded, to let the flame die with the departure of the Dutch evangelist.

But when I departed, the flame did not die. That little church that had had fifty-odd people attending sporadically became instead a live congregation of almost four hundred. Eventually the government did try to stop the fire. Basil went to Switzerland for a long-delayed operation that fall; when he attempted to return to his country, he was turned back at the border. A new, "safe" pastor was chosen to take his place, and within three years he had successfully quenched the flames in this one building, for the attendance was back down to its original fifty. But the three-hundred new converts left Stara Zagora, fanning out across the Balkin Peninsula, dispersed like the church in Jerusalem, to build fires wherever they landed.

None of these developments, of course, could we foresee at the time. But Petroff and I had learned one thing right at the beginning. It is never safe to call a church a puppet—no matter how dead, no matter how subservient and temporizing it may appear on the surface. It is called by God's name, it has God's eye upon it, at any moment He may sweep the surface away with the purifying wind of His Spirit.

AROUND THE GLOBE
The Philippines

Population: 75.9 million
Location/Size: Southeast Asian islands
115,831 sq. miles
Major Religions: Christianity
Islam
Level of Persecution: Isolated, growing

Filipino Christians are predominantly Catholics, and they have tremendous influence over the government. Although the state constitution officially declares a separation of Church and State, the provision is loosely interpreted and the Church enjoys complete freedom to evangelize.

Opposition to the Gospel comes predominantly from Muslims, some of whom have attacked Christians as part of an ongoing war with the government. In addition to struggles against outward hostility from Muslims, the Church faces an inward struggle against spiritism in the Catholic Church.

Revival is currently sweeping through both Protestant and Catholic churches, however, and Christians are hopeful that the Filipino Church will become a powerful base for reaching Muslims in the Asian sector of world.

Before I left Bulgaria, Petroff and I drove up into the Rhodope Mountains hoping to find Abraham. We had no idea how to locate his tent, only the name of the village nearest to it. It was just as well, for at the village the road, which had been threatening to disappear for several miles, vanished altogether, and we got out and stood, undecided, beside the town's artesian well. Above us the forest stretched away as far as we could see. Where in all that vast wilderness was the man we were looking for?

The line of people at the well were staring at us curiously as they waited to fill their jars. And then the first man in line finished drinking, straightened up, and turned around. It was Abraham himself!

His blue eyes, when he saw us, blazed like the sky at noonday. The next thing I knew I was drowning in a mammoth wet embrace, the icy water on his great beard drenching me to the skin. Abraham was even more astonished than we at this unplanned meeting, for he told us he came to the village only every fourth day, and just long enough to buy bread. He picked up half a dozen round flat loaves now from the stone wall beside the well and began leading us up the mountainside.

Again and again Petroff and I had to beg this seventy-five-year-old man to stop so we could catch our breaths. He had just returned the week before, he told us, from giving away the last of the Bibles I had brought into the country. He described in great detail how they had been received, and Petroff pantingly promised he would repeat it all for me as soon as we were sitting down.

It was two hours, including the rest stops for us, before we rounded a rocky ledge, stepped behind a screen of wind-twisted pines, and were standing in front of the goatskin tent where Abraham lived. He looked more than ever like the Biblical patriarch as he welcomed us to his home. In a moment his wife had stepped outside, as composed as though visitors were dropping into their mountain hideaway every day. She was as tiny as her husband was big, a slender, erect little woman with skin like wrinkled parchment. Only their eyes were alike, blue, childlike, trusting. I looked at this woman who had once had a house replete with rugs, cupboards, linens—servants, probably, for they had been well-to-do—and I thought that I had never seen a face more content with what life had brought.

She offered us fruit that looked like tiny blue blackberries, and wild honey. We ate little, not knowing how much they had, and we stayed only a short while because we didn't care to try the trip down the mountain after dark. The shortest of visits, no more than a glimpse—and yet in those moments was forged a friendship that is one of the bulwarks of my life.

And so the visit to Bulgaria brought encouragement and deep love. And at the same time, it ended on a note of defeat. Just as I was leaving for Rumania, a group of people who had attended the meeting in Basil's church came to ask me to hold a similar campaign in their town.

"We've been waiting for this message for years," they pleaded. "We don't care about the consequences. We care only about the will of God."

And I had to look into these loved and loving faces and say no. I was only one person. I could not go with them and at the same time move on where I felt God's spirit calling too.

"I wish I were ten people," I told them. "I wish I could split myself into a dozen parts and answer every call that comes. Someday, I'm going to find the way to do it."

Imagine This

Last summer you visited Cuba on a mission trip. During your trip, local government officials found out about your smuggling Bibles and study materials. After spending several days in prison, you were sent back home under the condition that you not return to Cuba again. The church is now asking that you come and visit. They need more Bibles and materials, and they long to see you.

What Would You Do?

fifteen

The Greenhouse in the Garden

Let us hold unswervingly to the hope we profess, for he who promised is faithful. And let us consider how we may spur one another on toward love and good deeds.

Hebrews 10:23–24

It took me four hours to get across the Rumanian border. When I pulled up to the checkpoint on the other side of the Danube, I said to myself, "Well, I'm in luck. Only half a dozen cars. This will go swiftly."

When forty minutes had passed and the first car was still being inspected, I thought, "Poor fellow, they must have something on him to take so long."

But when that car finally left and the next inspection took half an hour too, I began to worry. Literally everything that family was carrying had to be taken out and spread on the ground. Every car in the line was put through the same routine. The fourth inspection lasted for well over an hour. The guards took the driver inside and kept him there while they removed hub caps, took his engine apart, removed seats.

"Dear Lord," I said, as at last there was just one car ahead of me, "what am I going to do? Any serious inspection will show up those Rumanian Bibles right away.

"Lord," I went on, "I know that no amount of cleverness on my part can get me through this border search. Dare I ask for a miracle? Let me take some of the Bibles out and leave them in the open where they will be seen. Then, Lord, I cannot possibly be depending on my own stratagems, can I? I will be depending utterly upon You."

While the last car was going through its chilling inspection, I managed to take several Bibles from their hiding places and pile them on the seat beside me.

It was my turn. I put the little VW in low gear, inched up to the officer standing at the left side of the road, handed him my papers, and started to get out. But his knee was against the door, holding it closed. He looked at my photograph in the passport, scribbled something down, shoved the papers back under my nose, and abruptly waved me on.

Surely thirty seconds had not passed. I started the engine and inched forward. Was I supposed to pull over, out of the way, where the car could be taken apart? Was I . . . surely I wasn't . . . I coasted forward, my foot poised above the brake. Nothing happened. I looked out the rear mirror. The guard was waving the next car to a stop, indicating to the driver that he had to get out. On I drove a few more yards. The guard was having the driver behind me open the hood of his car. And then I was too far away to doubt that indeed I had made it through that incredible checkpoint in the space of thirty seconds.

My heart was racing. Not with the excitement of the crossing, but with the excitement of having caught such a spectacular glimpse of God at work.

Setting out on this trip, I had tended to lump Bulgaria and Rumania together in my mind. Now, of course, I knew that they were two very different places. Rumania was known among Iron Curtain Christians themselves as the "greenhouse of atheism." It was still Russia's laboratory in which she tried out antireligious experiments. Rigid control of the Church by the state, economic pressures against believers, sowing of suspicion among religious leaders, confiscation of property, restriction of worship services, a prohibition on evangelism. This, I was told, was what I could expect to find in Rumania.

As soon as I was over the border, I could sense a new degree of police control. At every village, it seemed, there was a police checkpoint. Officers stopped every peasant cycling into the hamlet. Where was he going? What was his business? Even I, with the relative freedom of a "hard-currency tourist," had my visa stamped with the cities I would visit and dates on which I must appear at each point along my itinerary. I found out how real this control was when I arrived in a charming little town about fifty miles from Cluj and decided, since it was already getting late, that I would like to spend the night there. The local authorities were surprised that I should even ask.

"But, sir," they said, looking at my tourist card, "you are expected for dinner in Cluj. You can barely make it now by hurrying."

Not wanting to get in trouble on such a minor point, I did as they wished. I sped into Cluj, arriving just as the hotel dining room was closing, to find my table set, the hors d'oeuvres out, and even a little Dutch flag sitting snappily in the center of the water glasses.

Inside the various cities, however, I was free to come and go as I chose. It was Sunday morning. I woke very early to a bright and cheery day, anxious to join my fellow Christians in this lovely garden of a land. The clerk in the hotel eyed me a little dubiously when I asked for a church. "We don't have many of those, you know," he said. "Besides, you couldn't understand the language."

"Didn't you know?" I said. "Christians speak a kind of universal language."

"Oh. What's that?"

"It's called 'agape.'"

"Agape? I never heard of it."

"Too bad. It's the most beautiful language in the world. But anyhow, how do I get to church?"

While the chief weapon against the Church in Bulgaria was the registration requirement, in Rumania the technique was Consolidation. Consolidate denominations, consolidate physical facilities, consolidate the hours of worship. Wherever there were churches with empty pews, the congregations were merged with others in nearby villages, and the leftover facilities confiscated by the State. In theory it sounded reasonable and even advantageous to the Church: one large united congregation in place of several small struggling ones. In practice it meant that many members of the shut-down churches simply ceased attending anywhere. Most of them were peasants, attached to their old places of worship, and travel between villages was slow and difficult.

Two church services were allowed each week, one on Saturday, another on Sunday. But Saturday was a full workday in Rumania; the Saturday night services were poorly attended, so that, in effect, worship had been consolidated into a single meeting.

But what a meeting!

I arrived at ten o'clock in the morning, and the service had already been underway for an hour. I would not have found a place to sit, except that I was recognized as a foreigner and invited to take a seat on the dais. And so, with my knees squeezed tight against the organ, I spent the next three hours with this group of Christians in the heart of communism's Inner Circle.

When it came time for the collection, I put in the plate approximately the same amount—in Rumanian currency—that I would have at home. As luck would have it, I was the first person to whom the plate was passed: there lay my bill for all to see on the bottom of the alms basin.

As the collection continued, I realized with growing embarrassment that I had put in twenty or thirty times as much as anyone else was giving. I noticed something else. Often one of the worshipers would put a coin in the basin and hold it while he made change. I had seen this in Catholic and Orthodox churches where there were pew fees, but never in a Protestant church. The entire coin was obviously more than most people could give. Probably a bill as large as

China   **A Traveler's Story**

MAKING THE SOIL SAFE FOR JESUS

Mr. and Mrs. Sun were peasants in rural Anhui province. Too poor to make their home out of bricks, they lived in a wood-and-mud shed. They farmed some thin fingers of land that stubbornly yielded millet beans and turnips, though rarely enough to feed them fully. It was a bad year, and they did not have enough food. One day Mr. Sun placed all the beans they owned into a jar and said to his wife, "We must eat only three beans a day and give seven to the boy. If God does not send us any food, we must sell him."

His wife blanched at the terrifying prospect of selling their son. She knew men combed the countryside offering vast sums of money to buy sons from poor families and give them to rich city people. But she saw how listless the child had become and simply said, "It may be the best chance we can give him. We don't want him to die with us."

One day a man visited their house. He took a look at the boy and said he would pay them 10,000 yuan for him and fix it with the authorities so that they could have another child if they wanted to. Mr. Sun haggled and eventually the man, in a bad temper, said, "All right. I will return this way in two weeks' time with 30,000 yuan. Have the boy ready." He stomped out.

The Suns felt a mixture of excitement and horror. After all, it was the answer to all their problems. On the other hand, what kind of home would their boy end up in? Eventually Mrs. Sun said, "We must pray about this. We must be sure this is what God wants."

The next day Mr. Sun was working when three of his neighbors approached him. They said, "We hear you are selling your son for 30,000 yuan. Your Jesus God can't be very good if he can't save you from the disgrace of selling your own son."

Continued

the one I had placed in the plate represented a month's free-to-spend income. I felt bad about what must have come across as the ostentation of a rich foreigner—and that made me smile, remembering how we had always been the poorest family in Witte. To make matters worse, at the end of the offertory hymn the head usher, instead of taking the plate to the altar, brought it to *me!*

He shoved the plate into my hands, repeating some words in Rumanian. Finally, I understood. I was to take my change. No one would put so large a note into the offering without expecting some back. What should I do? Accept the change in the name

China | A Traveler's Story
Continued

Mr. Sun hurried home and told his wife. At once they realized if they sold their son, their witness would be ruined. A terrible choice lay before them. They could choose to keep their son, starve, yet honor Jesus, or they could sell their son, live handsomely, but make Jesus a laughingstock.

After two weeks the man returned. He counted out the money in front of their eyes—a massive bundle of dirty notes. But Mr. Sun gave them back, saying, "We have decided not to sell our son."

The man turned away, muttering that they were crazy. As they picked out their ration of beans for the day, they wondered if they were. But the next day, two of their neighbors came to see them again. In complete silence, they handed over 200 yuan in grubby notes. Mr. and Mrs. Sun gasped. "Where did you get this, and why are you giving it to us?"

One neighbor explained, "The man who came to buy your son stayed with a local family last night. He told us what happened and when he left, we found this money. We think he left it for the host. But we have decided to give it to you." The other neighbor added, in words that made their hearts burst with joy, "You see, we respect what you did."

Mr. and Mrs. Sun were safe for the year. They had enough money to buy food for the winter and give their son a better diet. But even more importantly, both knew that the cause of Jesus Christ was safe for another year in rural Anhui.

of graciousness? Or accept the chagrin and let the church have the money I wanted them to have?

While I was debating, with every eye in the room upon me, I realized with great joy that this was not my money at all. "That was not my gift," I began in German—and fortunately a man emerged from the congregation to translate. "That was not from me." I repeated, remembering the hundreds of readers of *Kracht van Omhoog* whose anonymous gifts were represented in that bill. "It is from the believers in Holland to the believers in Rumania. It is a token of oneness in the Body of Christ."

I watched the faces in the room as the man translated, and once again I saw that incredulous question, that dawning hope: we are not alone, then? We have brothers in other places? We have friends we never knew?

When at last that long service broke, I approached the man who had spoken German and said that I would like to talk with him. It turned out that he was secretary for the entire denomination in Rumania. But it was clear that he did not welcome my suggestion of private talks. He gave evasive answers and, as soon as he could, excused himself.

Puzzled, I followed him out of the church. He was striding up the street as rapidly as he could, for he was a heavyset fellow. Perhaps it's talking to me in public that he's afraid of, I thought. And so I followed him, but at a discreet distance, until to my delight he turned in at a private house.

What a piece of luck! I thought. Now I'll have a chance to talk to him with no one to see.

I hung around for another fifteen minutes until I was sure the street was empty, then went up to the door and knocked. I could feel eyes peering out at me. Then the door was thrown open quickly, and I was pulled inside the house.

"What do you want?" said the secretary.

I tried to cover my surprise at his brusqueness with a friendly smile. I just wanted to talk with him some more, I said. To ask if there were anything I could do for him.

"Do?"

"Well, Bibles, for instance. Do you have enough Rumanian Bibles?"

The secretary looked at me sharply. "You have Rumanian Bibles with you? You brought them across the border?"

"I have Bibles, yes."

He paused a moment. Then, with decision: "We need no Bibles! And you must never again under any circumstances come to my home or to the home of any believer in this way. I hope you understand that."

Was I mistaken, or did I hear a cry for help through all this suspicion and brusqueness? "Well, could I see you in your office then? Would that be safe?"

"It isn't a matter of *safe*, I didn't *say* that." And then, "But yes, if you come to our office tomorrow, I will see to it that the president is there for a brief talk with you."

The next day I walked into the headquarters of this denomination carrying six Bibles in my briefcase. The secretary was there, looking as uncomfortable as ever. Big drops of perspiration had formed on his forehead. I could not get over the impression that he was in terror of something or someone.

I was ushered into the office of the president. "What can I do for you?" he asked in German.

I shook his hand and started to reply that perhaps I might be able to do something for him. But then I remembered that earlier conversation with the secretary: apparently to admit a need bordered on a political statement. So I simply said I was visiting his country as a Christian and wanted to bring back to my people any word of greeting he might like to extend.

The president's face relaxed. This was safe ground. A word of greeting to the exploited peoples of Holland from the people of the great Republica Populars of Romina! The secretary smiled and stopped mopping his forehead.

"Won't you sit down?" he asked, drawing up a chair. For a quarter of an hour the three of us talked, carefully avoiding any real exchange. We talked about Rumanian tomatoes, the largest I had ever seen, and about watermelon, which I had tasted for the first time in this country. We talked about the pleasant climate, kept mild, the president explained, by the Black Sea.

And while we talked I had a chance to glance around the room. I was fascinated by one observation. Every chair, every table, every picture on the wall had a number on it. I wondered if they had been inventoried by the government to keep them from being diverted to personal use.

After we had exhausted the weather and the local tomatoes, the conversation lagged. Taking a deep breath, I decided that the time had come either to be rebuffed again or else to establish a real contact with these two frightened men.

I opened my briefcase and drew out one of the Bibles. "Will you permit me—no that's not what I want to say. Will you permit the Dutch people to present the Rumanian people with these copies of the Bible?"

Right away the two men stiffened. It was amazing how quickly the secretary began to perspire again. The president took the Bible in his hand, and for the briefest moment I caught the tenderness with which he held it.

But no, he wasn't going to yield. He shoved the Bible abruptly back into my hands.

"I do not want this," he said. "We've spent too long already. I have things to do this morning. . . ."

And so I walked out of that building carrying the six Bibles I had come in with. The receptionist, I noted, crossed my name off a list as I left, almost as if she were on guard in a military establishment. Who knows; maybe she herself was a member of the secret police. How could I condemn the fear and the suspicion of the president and the secretary when I had never experienced the conditions under which they had to work?

And still, this was not the entire story in Rumania. For the following week I met Christians living under the same persecution, who had still kept alive something of divine hope and trust.

The circumstances were similar enough to make a really good comparison. In both instances I met with the stated leaders of established Protestant denominations in their official headquarters. In both instances there were two men present beside myself, an important element in the comparison, since suspicion of one's fellow Christians played such a large factor in the slow wearing down of the Church.

This time, too, I noticed the numbers. On the walls of this office were three pictures. They showed the president of the country, the secretary of the national Communist Party, and the famous old artist's conception of the Straight And Narrow Way. How, I wondered, had the government clerk described that painting?

I was worried about the president of this denomination—Gheorghe—the moment he stepped into the room. This frail little man was so winded from the effort of walking that it was several minutes before he could catch his breath.

When he did, we discovered a problem. Neither he nor Ion, secretary of the group, spoke a word of my languages, nor I of

Diary of a Smuggler

CHINA

The greatest miracle of the trip was that our total supply of Bibles (1,100 pounds) and the medicine (some 400 pounds) got through without detection. Our bags were never checked or X-rayed during the trip. God created a diversion at each checkpoint, allowing us to get by.

Following the delivery of the medicine to our contact in Ulaanbaatar, Mongolia, God showed His mercy to one of our Canadian friends. He was run down by a drunken horseman, but fortunately he only had a minor bruise in the ribcage area and minor cuts on his face from his glasses. Within the week his face cleared up to the point that you could only see minor traces of the accident.

theirs. We sat facing each other across the barren, multinumbered room, quite unable to communicate.

Then I saw something. On Gheorghe's desk was a well-worn Bible, the edges of the pages eaten back an eighth of an inch from constant turning. What would happen, I wondered, if we were to converse with each other via the Scriptures? I took my own Dutch Bible from my coat pocket and turned to 1 Cor. 16:20.

"All the brethren greet you. Greet ye one another with an holy kiss."

I held the Bible out and pointed to the name of the book, recognizable in any language, and to the chapter and verse number.

Instantly their faces lit up.

They swiftly found the place in their own Bible, read it, and beamed at me. Then Gheorghe was thumbing the pages, looking for a reference, which he held out for me.

Proverbs 25:25: "As cold waters to a thirsty soul, so is good news from a far country."

Now we were all three laughing. I turned to the epistle of Paul to Philemon.

"I thank my God always when I remember you in my prayers, because I hear of your love and of the faith which you have toward the Lord. . . ."

It was Ion's turn, and he didn't have to look very far. His eyes traveled over the next lines, and he pushed the Bible to me pointing with his finger:

"For I have derived much joy and comfort from your love, my brother, because the hearts of the saints have been refreshed through you."

Oh, we had a wonderful half hour, conversing with each other through the Bible. We laughed until the tears were in our eyes. And when at the end of the conversation I brought out my Rumanian Bibles and shoved them across the desk and insisted with gestures and remonstrances that, yes, they were supposed to keep them and that, no (to the hand in the pocket and the raised eyebrow), there was no charge, both men embraced me again and again.

Later that day, when we finally had an interpreter and our conversation became more mundane, I made arrangements with Ion to take all the Bibles I had brought with me. He would know better than I where to place them in this hard country, and he assured me that it was better to have just one contact than several.

That night, back in my hotel, the clerk called to me.

"Say," he said, "I looked up that agape in the dictionary. There's no language by that name. That's just a Greek word for love."

"That's it," I said. "I was speaking in it all afternoon."

The communications dam had been cracked at last. Over the next week and a half I traveled throughout Rumania with an excellent interpreter, following leads given my by Gheorghe and Ion.

I met every shade of attitude, from the extreme of defeat to the extreme of courage. It was easy to sympathize with the defeated ones. "What can we do?" was such a natural reaction. So many had only one ambition: to get out of Rumania altogether.

Oddly though, the more devoted a Christian, the more likely he was to stay put. In Transylvania we visited such a family. These Christians had a poultry farm that was still at least partially their own property. However, the state had given them a production quota that was beyond their capacity to meet. When they failed to reach it, they had to buy enough eggs on the open market to make up the difference. Year after year this had happened, and the economic suffering was great.

"Why do you stay then? So that you can keep your farm?" I asked.

The farmer and his wife both looked shocked. "Of course not," he said. "In fact, we certainly will lose the farm. We stay because—" he let his eyes travel across the valley—"because if we go, who will be left to pray?"

But I also met Christians who were less sure. I learned of one little church far off the beaten path that was working with gypsies. Even as we drove up, I could tell it was in trouble. The grass was

AROUND THE GLOBE

Russia

Population: 147 million
Location/Size: Eastern Europe and Northern Asia
6,592,849 sq. miles
Major Religions: Christianity
Islam
Level of Persecution: Isolated, growing

The Russian Church has experienced perhaps the most severe and sustained levels of persecution in recent history. Martyrs have been numbered in the millions, and the Church's infrastructure was largely destroyed.

Today new persecutions threaten the Church as the government struggles to stabilize itself. There is currently a window of opportunity for great Church revival, some of which is already being realized.

Peace and religious freedom are still greatly at risk in several Russian republics. Christians in these areas experience severe suffering due to local religious conflicts, civil wars, and wars for independence. It's their prayer that the Church will be able to bring healing and compassionate aid to the hurting people of these provinces.

high in the churchyard, several windows in the sanctuary were broken, the beehives out back were toppling over. My interpreter and I went around behind the church, where the pastor's living quarters were, and knocked. The pastor was not at home, but his wife greeted us, and shortly we were eating saucers-full of honey, so sweet it hurt my teeth.

The pastor's wife told us that her husband had gone to Bucharest to plead their case with the central government. The local Party chief was demanding the church building, saying it was needed for a clubhouse.

She and her husband, she said, had worked among the gypsies for almost thirty years. I had seen many of them on the road coming in, little groups, sitting by their wagons, always accompanied by a meager horse and some squawking geese. Recently, she went on, the government had at last decided to do something for them by offering them better-paying jobs. She and her husband had been delighted of course; they had been urging this for many years. But there was a condition: no gypsy who attended the church could apply for one of the new jobs.

"And so," said the pastor's wife, "we are in this crossfire. Our members are leaving us, and as our congregation dwindles, the Party has more and more of an argument for taking away our building. I don't think we will be here next year."

And all at once she began to cry, soundless, inwardly, only her shoulders betraying her. I suggested that perhaps the three of us could pray about the things she had told us. And so we bowed our heads, and I prayed for her and for her husband, for the gypsies, for the whole desperate situation in that little hamlet. When finally we raised our heads, her eyes were moist again as she said, "You know, years ago, I knew that people in the West were praying for us, but now for many years we have not heard from them. We've never been able to write letters, and it's thirteen years since we've received one. It has come to us that we are forgotten, that nobody is thinking of us, nobody knows our need, nobody prays."

I at least was able to assure her from the depth of my heart that as soon as I got back, enough people would know about them that they need never again feel that they were carrying their burden alone.

Once again the time was approaching when I should have to leave. My visa had almost expired. Most important, I knew that Corrie's time was almost here.

My last hours in Rumania were spent with Gheorghe and Ion. I arranged to leave on a Monday so I could attend the Sunday service with them. It was a meeting to remember. By now I was used to services lasting from nine to one, but this one lasted from nine in the morning until five in the afternoon, breaking then for an enormous meal.

Gheorghe was the speaker for the last sermon of the day. It was a very personal one. He talked about the shortness of breath that had plagued him for years. "But do you know," he said, "when we had that wonderful conversation with our Bibles, something happened not only to my spirit but to my body as well. I've been breathing better ever since."

And then Gheorghe opened his Bible. "I have a final scripture that I should like to share with you, Andrew," he told me through the interpreter. "Will you open your Book to Acts 20:36–38?"

I found the place.

"This," said Gheorghe, "is the passage that says goodbye the way I should like to. 'And when we had spoken thus, he knelt down and prayed with them all. And they all wept and embraced Paul and kissed him, sorrowing most of all because of the words he had spoken, that they should see his face no more. And they brought him to the ship.'"

I had to laugh at him applying words about Paul to me. "That's going from the highest to the lowest," I said.

But although we might be small in faith next to those first-century Christians, at least we could follow their example. And so after dinner I did kneel down and pray once more with them all. And then these Christians in the center of the communist world wept, and embraced me, and accompanied me to my little blue ship.

Imagine This

As a Christian parent in Sudan, you have watched your family starve to death. You have no money, and you realize that your children will die without food and water. The government offers to take care of your family on the condition that you convert to the Muslim religion. You know that your children's only hope of survival is through your conversion.

What Would You Do?

sixteen

The Work Begins to Expand

I consider my life worth nothing to me, if only I may finish the race and complete the task the Lord Jesus has given me—the task of testifying to the gospel of God's grace.

Acts 20:24

When finally I crossed the Dutch border again, I had been away from home more than two months, considerably longer than I had expected because of the lengthy detour both going and coming. I pulled into Witte late at night, exhausted, yet exhilarated. I raced up the ladder shouting, "Corrie! Corrie, I'm home!"

Corrie stumbled to the door, blinking, happy, overflowing with wonderful small talk that could hold to the subject for no longer than thirty seconds.

"Yes, everything is just fine. The leak in the roof is worse. The family is all well. Early June is what the doctor says now, but with first babies it's sometimes difficult to tell. Are you sure you don't want more coffee?"

Joppie arrived on the fourth of June, 1959. He was born at home, as I had been, and I was with Corrie the whole time, just as Papa had seen all of us into the world.

And with his arrival it was clearer than ever that Corrie and I needed a home of our own. Geltje's third child was on its way, and Cornelius and his wife were expecting their first: even by Dutch standards the little house was bursting at the seams.

The problem was where to go. Though this was 1959, the effects of the war were still being felt everywhere in Holland. Housing in our small country had never been plentiful, and since 1945 every available brick had gone to rebuilding homes bombed or flooded during the war. Although Witte's population was mushrooming, there hadn't been a new building there since the 1930s.

When I went to see the burgomaster about house-rentals, he shook his head.

"I'll have to add your name to the end of the list, Andrew," he said, "and I may as well tell you now—that list hasn't moved by a single name in almost three years."

"Well, sir, we have to start somewhere. Put us down."

"If you could find a house to buy, that would be different, of course. The waiting list applies only to rentals."

"Thank you for the compliment, sir. Where on earth would I find enough money to buy a house!"

The burgomaster nodded. "Not only that," he said. "As far as I know there are no houses for sale anyhow."

As the summer dragged on and the clothes that people continued to send again swamped the little room over the shed, we began for the first time to make a serious prayer campaign of our need. Every night for a week we laid our situation before God, trustingly and expectantly.

And on the morning of the eighth day I had an idea. I was setting out for the post office, but I had barely crossed the canal in front of our house when I remembered something. The school-teacher who was moving to Haarlem—wasn't he renting old Wim's house in town? That house was available then!

But what good did that do us; we were the last name on a long list of applicants. Still, I was impressed with the way the idea had come to me: sudden and sovereign in a manner I had come to recognize. Suppose, again, it were God's idea? Suppose Wim were willing to sell the house? He hadn't lived in it himself for many years. For the time being I wasn't even going to think about the 20,000 guilders it would cost. I'd just take a step forward and see what happened.

Forgetting all about my errand, I struck out across the polders to Wim's farm. I found him milking.

"Hello, Wim!"

"Hello, Andrew!" Wim said, twisting his head around against the cow's flank. "Hear you're traveling a good bit. Lord's work?"

"Yes, sir."

"What can I do for you?"

"Well, I hear your place in town is going to be empty. Have you ever thought of selling it?"

Old Wim's jaw literally dropped open. "However did you know!" he said. "I made up my mind to sell just last night—but I hadn't told a soul about it yet!"

I drew a deep breath and took the plunge. "Then would you consider selling it to me?"

Wim looked at me for a long time, saying nothing. "House has been in the family a good many generations," he said at last. "I'd like nothing better than for it to be used for the Lord's work, now that there are no more of us."

Only then, with heart racing, did I ask Wim the price. "Well," he said, "could you manage ten thousand?"

This time I was the surprised one. That was half what I thought he might be asking. "All right, Wim. We have an understanding. I will buy your house," said I, who still did not have a penny to my name, "for ten thousand guilders."

Before going home I telephoned Philip Whetstra. Never before in my life had I borrowed money, but it seemed to me now that this was right. Mr. Whetstra told me that if I came to his office the following day I could have the money then and there.

Ethiopia A Traveler's Story

FIFTEEN-YEAR-OLD CHOOSES CHRIST ABOVE FAMILY

Five months ago I was living with my parents in a nearby town. I was Muslim. Christians were witnessing to me, but I wasn't willing to accept Christ.

A Christian man took me to another town to see the Jesus film. I started to weep when I saw how Jesus suffered for my sins. I decided then to follow Christ as my personal Savior.

My Muslim friends came to me and said, "These believers are 666; they are a cult. You must come back to our original beliefs." I refused and said that I know what Jesus did for me. My father also said that if I wanted to follow Jesus, I would have to leave the house. I tried to explain to them that following Jesus was not a new thing. They said that these people (Christians) had come recently.

I cried because I didn't know what to do. I did not know where to go, so I went to the people who showed the film and asked them where I could go. They took me into their home, and I am still living with them; they are church leaders. They are assisting me and have sent me to school. I am in eighth grade.

So by the time I returned to our room above the shed, Corrie and I were the virtual possessors of a house. We went to look at it right away. Until that moment I don't think I ever realized what it meant to Corrie, living in borrowed space in someone else's home. She ran from room to room, touching, planning, seeing in the neglected house the home that was to be. "Joppie in here, Andy. And look, a whole room for the clothes, with the laundry tub right there! Did you see the room upstairs where your desk will just fit?" On she went, face flushed, eyes aglow, and I knew that at last she and I had come home.

The next day I went down to Amsterdam and picked up the money. Mr. Whetstra handed it to me in bills. We signed no papers, made no arrangements about paying it back. Nor did I mention the loan to anyone else. And yet over the next three years, enough money came in above and beyond the needs of the work that we were able to repay the loan in that short period of time. Immediately, mysteriously, as soon as the house was paid for, the flow of excess funds stopped—and it remained dried up until there was need for it again. In the years of living this life of faith, I have never known God's care to fail.

We have a Dutch phrase to describe the conditions of old Wim's house when Corrie and I moved in. We call such a place "lived out." The floors were sagging, the plaster peeling, the roof rotting away: all the ills native to the polder land. But Corrie and I loved it all the more. As we mended and rebuilt, the house became uniquely ours.

The only room dry enough to sleep in at first was the parlor. So there we lived while we scraped walls and painted and replaced rotten boards—and of course started a garden. We did all the work ourselves, so it was a slow process. It was five years before the home that Corrie had seen on that first visit was visible in its entirety to other eyes as well.

And meanwhile the work grew ever larger. That first year after Joppie's birth I revisited every country I could get back into—several of them more than once. And as the work grew, so did the problems. Correspondence was number one. Each time I got home, instead of reaching first for my hammer and paint brush, I would go up to my little study—Corrie had been right, the desk did just fit—and spend miserable days pecking out answers, with two fingers on an ancient portable, to a mountain of mail. I never reached the bottom of the pile before it was time to set out again.

Anonymity was becoming a problem too. If I kept using my real name when I spoke, wouldn't I jeopardize my freedom to come and go across borders? I finally reached a working solution that still is only partially satisfactory. I stopped using my full name and began instead to use the name by which I was known behind the Curtain, where last names have almost ceased to exist among Christians: "Brother Andrew." For an address, I took out a post-office box number in my brother Ben's home town that served for inquiries about the work.

It was a compromise: I knew that anyone who wanted to could learn who I was.

But of all the difficulties posed by the expanding work, the one that seemed to offer least solution was the matter of the ever-increasing time away from home. Travel was one thing for a bachelor, quite another for a married man with a child. Out of Joppie's first twelve months, I missed eight. The first tooth, the first word, the first step—I heard about them rather than saw them. Shortly after Joppie was born, Mr. Ringers reminded me of his standing offer of a job at the factory—at a salary that to us sounded kingly. Later that year I was offered the pastorate of a church in The Hague. I was truly tempted, both times.

But I was never tempted for long. Just as the pressures became strongest to stay home, a letter would arrive. It would bear no return address, it would often have been mailed weeks earlier, and sometimes show signs of having been opened. It would be from some believer in Bulgaria or Hungary or Poland or elsewhere telling me of new troubles they were facing, new needs that had developed. Whatever the message, these letters always seemed to arrive just at the time I needed them most, to make me pack my bags once again and seek a visa for travel to some land in the world of the Communists.

It was on one of these trips that year that the courageous little car engine breathed its last.

It happened in West Germany. I was on my way home from a trip to East Germany and Poland. With me in the car were two Dutch boys I had picked up in Berlin, students who had spent their Easter vacation working in the refugee camps. At five o'clock one afternoon we were spinning along, when suddenly there was a crackling sound in the rear of the car and the engine died.

We coasted to a stop and opened the little door in the rear, but nothing we could do would make it start again.

Then I straightened up and saw that beside the road, at the spot where the car's own momentum had deposited us, was an emergency telephone box. I picked up the receiver and asked for a tow truck. Within twenty minutes we were all bending over the engine with the manager of the service garage.

Philippines   A Traveler's Story

"I PREFER TO DIE IN THE CHURCH"

Pastor Severino Desagana III had received several death threats in the past, but he had consistently ignored them. He was asked to cut down the activities of his sixty-member church in Barangay Alat, Jolo. He refused. The church was burned some time in 1993. The congregation continued on. In fact, the work prospered with the leadership of Bennu, as he was fondly called by those who knew him well.

He had premonitions about his final moment. Days before the fatal shooting, Bennu confided to a friend, "If I am killed, so be it. I am ready to die for Jesus. But if I have to be killed, I would prefer to die in the church, doing the Lord's work."

In a bizarre way, Pastor Bennu got his wish on January 21 when a lone gunman approached him from behind and pumped two bullets in him. Pastor Bennu was seated on the front pew, listening to the sermon. His sister sat beside him. Suddenly two shots were heard. At first, people thought that they were the sounds of firecrackers, and nobody paid any attention. Last December, some hecklers threw firecrackers inside the church building during the service. The members apparently had gotten used to the sound.

But the members found out too late that those sounds had fatal consequences. One bullet went through Bennu's left cheek and another through his chest. He slumped on his sister with blood oozing from his wounds. The pandemonium started only after his body fell to the ground.

Continued

He inspected the various parts in silence for some minutes, then walked forward and looked at the odometer.

"Ninety-seven thousand kilometers," he read aloud. His puzzled frown had not left him. "It's a good mileage, of course, and yet unless you've been over unusually rough terrain. . . ."

Now I saw what was bothering him. A little shamefacedly I admitted that the odometer had long since reached its maximum reading of 99,999 and flipped over the zero mark again: this was the second time it had registered ninety-seven thousand.

"Then I should say," said the manager, wiping the oil from his hands, "that you've got your money's worth. That engine just hasn't any more to give."

"How long would it take to put in a new one?"

He stopped to consider. "My crew leaves in ten minutes. They could have a new engine in for you in an hour, but you'd have to pay them a good tip for staying overtime."

"How much would the whole thing cost, including the tip?"

"Five hundred marks."

Without hesitation I said, "Go ahead. I'll go get some more money changed at the train station."

It was on board the streetcar going to the station that I counted my money and realized that all I had with me would not make five hundred marks. There'd be no help from the two students back at the garage: they were riding with me in the first place because they were flat broke.

Should I go back and cancel the work order? No. I could see God's hand too clearly in all of this. Stopping precisely at the emergency telephone, having the engine wear out here in Germany where it came from, rather than in some distant and hostile spot where replacement would have been impossible and questions awkward. I was far too familiar with the way Christ looks after the practical side of the ministry to miss these signs. This was all His timing, and the question of the money was also in His hands. I was not worried, just fascinated to see how He was going to work it all out.

When I had changed every last guilder, it came—with the German money in my pocket—to 470 marks. Fifty shy of the amount I needed to pay the bill and buy gasoline on the way home.

"Well," I said to myself, "something will happen on the streetcar going back."

But nothing did. I got to the garage to find the workmen just finishing up and my two passengers nowhere to be seen. They'd gone for a walk, one of the men said, packing away his tools. The others were cleaning up too. I could delay the moment of reckoning no longer.

And at that instant, the two young Dutchmen raced through the door, one of them waving something in his hand. "Andy!" he shouted. "Craziest thing ever happened to me! We were just walking along the street when this lady came up to us and asked if we

Philippines   A Traveler's Story
Continued

Before his death, Bennu had been dialoguing with a member of the Tablig, a group of itinerant Muslim evangelists. Bennu would share the Gospel with him, and he in turn would try to convince Bennu to join the Islamic faith and be a member of the Tablig. He evidently saw potential in Bennu. There was even a time when that person would attend the young people's meetings. And this would encourage Bennu a lot.

But this harmonious relationship didn't last long. The friendship between the two began to show strain. It was at this stage that Bennu received a letter from an anonymous sender—"If you will resist from joining us, then we advise you to stop what you are doing in your church. If you refuse, then something will happen to you, and your life will be shortened."

Bennu tore the letter to pieces, keeping mum about the possible danger to his life. A few days later, he shared the contents of the letter with a sister and his girlfriend. Many suspect that the Tablig friend was the source of the letter.

Some witnesses claim that hours before his death, Bennu was seen distributing tracts among the people. A Christian leader who is an acknowledged authority in Islam believes this could have triggered the shooting.

were Dutchmen. When I said yes, she gave me this bill! She said God wanted us to have it!"

The bill was for fifty marks.

And yet in spite of this experience—and others like it occurring almost daily—I was still a novice in this whole business of God's bountiful care. I still depended on the isolated miracle, the emergency dispensation to get me out of one spot or another, instead of leaning back in the arms of a Father Who had more than enough and to spare.

Back home there were several new expenses, the biggest of which was the arrival of a second baby. Just a year after Joppie was born, Mark Peter came to join our household. We started buying a little less meat in the market, depending a little more on the vegetables from our garden.

This was no hardship, for we loved vegetables. What we did not realize, though, was that it was part of a whole mental set, an "attitude of lack," into which we had slipped.

The error came to my attention through the words of a lady I have never met.

One day we received, through our box number in Ermelo, a rather large gift, the equivalent of about forty dollars. Attached to the check was a note from the donor saying, "Dear Brother Andrew: This is to be used for your own personal needs. It is *not* to go into the work! Use it in Christ's love."

I was touched by this thought. We had received personal gifts from time to time from friends, but this was the first time a total stranger had ever made such a stipulation. Instead of putting her note at the bottom of the pile of unanswered mail—three months high it must have been at that point—I sat down and pecked out a thank-you that very day. I told her we especially appreciated the note, because this was something we were very scrupulous about: all donations went into the work unless they were specifically marked otherwise. Even our clothing, I told her, came out of the refugee bins to save money.

Well, I have wished often that I had saved the letter that this good lady shot back. She began by reminding me of the scriptural injunction that the ox grinding the corn must not be kept from enjoying the grain. Did I think God felt less about His human workers? Hadn't I better examine myself to be sure I was not nursing a Sacrificial Spirit? Wasn't I claiming to depend upon God, but living as if my needs would be met by my own scrimping? I remember her close. "God will send you what your family needs and what your work needs too. You are a mature Christian, Brother Andrew. Act like one."

I gave that letter a long and prayerful reading. Could she be right? Was I really living in an atmosphere of want that was most un-Christian?

About this time, Corrie and I were invited out to dinner. The time came to leave, and Corrie had not appeared. I went up to our room and found her still in her bathrobe.

"I have nothing to wear," she said in a very small voice.

I started to laugh: wasn't this what women always said?

And then I saw the tears in her eyes. Silently I began to look over her wardrobe myself. Warm dresses. Serviceable ones—at least with Corrie's meticulous mending they'd been made serviceable. But somehow the clothes she had salvaged from the refugee room had not managed to include anything pretty. Nothing feminine and happy. . . .

And suddenly I saw that this was part of a whole pattern of poverty into which we had fallen, a dark, brooding, pinched attitude that hardly went with the Christ of the open heart that we were preaching to others.

So we determined to change. We still live frugally, and always shall, partly because both of us were raised that way and wouldn't know how else to act. But at the same time we are learning to take joy in the physical things that God provides. Corrie bought some dresses. We went ahead with the tearing down of a wall so that she could walk directly from the house to her kitchen.

And when our third baby, Paul Denis, arrived—again just one year after the second—we actually went out and bought him some clothes. And I can't say that he turned out any the worse for having passed his first days in clothes that still had the store labels in them.

Funny how long it took us to learn the simple fact that God really is a Father, as displeased with a cramped, niggardly attitude of lack as with its opposite failing of acquisitiveness.

Fundamentally, this was a lesson in abundance. And having learned the lesson in our personal lives, I was able in time to apply it to the work.

For years I had been working alone. It meant traveling over 80,000 kilometers a year; being away from home two-thirds of the time. I was prepared to do this as long as it seemed to be what God wanted. But how many times, lately, the work itself had suffered simply because I could not be in two places at once! I had never forgotten those people in Bulgaria who had asked me to come to their town just as I was leaving the country. By the time I got back to Bulgaria, nearly a year later, much had changed. The meetings they had believed would be so life-changing were no longer possible.

But suppose—just suppose I had had a partner traveling with me! Suppose there were two of us . . . three of us . . . ten! Someone to be where another could not, to spell each other with the travel, the speaking, even the letter-writing!

The possibility began to haunt me day and night. It would have to be an unusual fellowship, an organism, really, rather than an organization. The less formally we were organized the better, for if we were arrested we would not involve each other. We would be a small band of men—women, too, why not?—captured by the same vision of bringing hope to the Church in its need. Each of us would be a pioneer, probably not even sharing procedures and techniques, because then we would fall into a pattern that would be too easily recognized and too easily controlled.

When I shared my dream with Corrie, she practically shouted with joy.

"I'll be frank, Andrew—my reaction is altogether selfish. Do you realize that the four of us would be able to *see* you once in a while?"

Immediately she was sorry she had said it. But I wasn't. Of course my long absences were hard on us all. I could actually see Joppie and Mark Peter and Paul Denis grow between the time I took off and the time I came home again. Surely if I had help, these long, long trips would not be necessary.

But how to go about finding the people? It wasn't that others hadn't offered from time to time. In fact, fairly often, at the close of a talk, I'd find three or four eager young men standing around the rostrum. "Brother Andrew, can I join you in your work behind the Iron Curtain? God has told me, too, to preach the Gospel there." Others were probably a little more honest. "It sounds so exciting!" they would say. "I'd like to come just to carry your suitcases!"

But I had never felt free to continue these conversations. It wasn't as though I had a trick or system for getting across these borders again and again, which I could pass on to others to insure their safety too. It was no cleverness or experience of mine that had prevented disaster so far, only the fact that every morning of every trip I consciously placed myself in God's hands and tried, in so far as possible, not to take a step outside His will. But these are not actions that one person can take for another. And so I would usually say, "Well, if I meet you behind the Iron Curtain, then by all means let's talk some more."

And that would be the last I would hear of them.

"Still," I said to Corrie one night, "if God wants us to expand the work, He certainly has prepared the people. How do I find them?"

"Try prayer."

I laughed. That was my Corrie. The one thing I had not yet done was to ask God for direct guidance to the right person. So we did pray, then and there. And immediately a name came to my mind.

Hans Gruber.

I had met Hans in Austria, working at a refugee camp. He was a Dutchman, a giant in size, six-feet-seven, heavy even for that height, and awkward beyond belief. He seemed to have six elbows, ten thumbs, and a dozen knees. And he spoke the most atrocious German I had ever heard.

Everything about Hans, taken individually, was wrong. But put together into one stupendous whole, he was the most totally right personality I had ever met. He could stand up in the camp recreation area and hold five hundred people spellbound hour after hour, simply with words. I had seen it begin to rain while Hans spoke, in that indescribable German, without a single one of his listeners glancing at the sky. Even in the orphaned boys' compound he was master. This group of 240 bored, restless kids was the terror of every other speaker who visited the camp. For Hans they sat like statues and then followed him around the camp afterward like pet sheep.

That very evening I wrote Hans asking him if he had ever felt led to bring this preaching ministry behind the Iron Curtain. I knew, I wrote him, where my next trip would be. Newspapers for weeks had been full of the new relaxation of travel restrictions in Russia. It was now possible for foreigners to travel in the Soviet on their own, without an Intourist guide. It was the news I had been waiting for, for so long. The time had come to make my long-dreamed-of penetration into the heartland of communism.

Diary of a Smuggler

SUDAN

Greetings! It's great to be back from Sudan and to be able to report about the trip.

Our first priority was to find much-needed medical supplies, blankets, food, transportation, camping gear, and all the logistics of a trip into the African bush, in less than a week. Only with God's help did this all come together in such a short period of time.

Our mission was to fly into Southern Sudan, where a large displacement camp was developing in the Upper Nile region. The goal was to deliver blankets, medical supplies, a vehicle for ground transportation, and food. Little did we know, but we were also going to provide a glimmer of hope to people who have suffered for so long. These were simple people who had been forced to flee from their land by the longest-running civil war this world has ever seen. A brutal civil war has engulfed this country, fueled by religious persecution, ethnic cleansing, regional strife, and now because there is valuable oil in the ground in Southern Sudan.

Continued

By return mail Hans's answer came back. He was ecstatic. My suggestion was for him the fulfillment of an old prophecy. When he was in the sixth grade—the last year of school he had attended—he had had a strange sensation every time he looked at the map of Russia. It was as though a voice kept telling him, "Someday you will work for Me in that land."

"And ever since then," he wrote, "I've studied Russian to be ready when the time came. My Russian is very good now—almost as good as my German. When do we go?"

With Hans's letter came a major new step in my ministry, the taking on of a partner, the doubling of the work Christ was doing through this channel.

There were a few rather important details to get behind us before we could get off. For one thing, we needed a new car. Even with the replacement engine, the VW no longer offered the security we needed. As for Hans folding his great bulk into that front seat—it was a clear impossibility. And so we purchased a new Opel station wagon. We could sleep in it, and we could carry a good many more Bibles.

A problem of a more baffling nature turned out to be Hans's driving.

"I'll never learn," he moaned as I showed him for the thousandth time the coordinated motion of clutch and gear shift. One of the great side benefits in having a teammate, I had thought, would be someone to share the driving. I knew Hans could not drive, but I had assumed it would be a simple matter to teach him. Six hours later I admitted to myself that it might take a little longer than I had thought.

The day of our departure came, and still he had no license. However, in most of Western Europe it is permissible for a learner to drive without one, provided he is seated next to a qualified driver and provided there is a brake between the two of them. We planned to take off on schedule. . . .

And so we stowed our gear aboard, I hugged the boys one by one, kissed Corrie again, and we were off. The Opel handled well in spite of its load. In addition to the Bibles, many more than I had ever carried before, there was all the camping and cooking equipment for two people. The extra weight did make the car weave slightly, and I thought I ought to let Hans get used to the new action before crossing the West-East border. So in Germany I turned the wheel over to him. Three miles later I took the wheel back again. Behind us was a line of cars and trucks several miles long.

"Well, that was fine, Hans. You're actually handling the car a little slowly for this highway, but never mind. The feel of it will come in time."

"I'm never going to get it. I know it."

"Nonsense. You ought to have seen me when I first started driving." And to make him feel better I told him about my experience in the army driving the Bren carrier. And so we laughed our way into Berlin.

If Hans was slow at learning mechanical skills, he was miles ahead of me in other ways. One of them was daring. The friends with whom we stayed in Berlin were enthralled at the idea of taking Bibles to the Soviet Union.

Diary of a Smuggler

SUDAN

Continued

The village had one young man who had been trained as the official Public Health Officer. He was trained to identify diseases and record them, but he had no paper or writing instruments to record his findings. He was not trained to treat the sick. We could not find any medical supplies to treat something as simple as a cut. The nearest clinic was two days' walking distance, crossing many rivers to get there. Many people were half-clothed; most of the children were completely naked. Clean drinking water did not exist; their water was drawn from a muddy river near the village. There had been no structured schooling for the children for two generations. The church, as is typical in many parts of Sudan, was under the shade of two large trees. Bibles and hymnals were in very short supply. We learned that the Bible has never been translated for several of the tribes in this area.

During the short time we were in the Upper Nile region, we are able to provide the following aid to this area: 1,500 blankets, 15 tons of sorghum, medical supplies, clothing, tools, a vehicle for ground transportation, fuel, and Bibles.

On the morning of our departure from Sudan, we were treated to a group singing "Onward Christian Soldiers." As I listened to their singing in the shade of this humble church, I thought of Matthew 16:18 where Jesus said, "On this rock I will build my church, and the gates of Hades will not overcome it." Nowhere is this statement more evident than in Sudan, where the Church continues to prevail and grow even under the intense persecution and suffering that exists.

I believe that when we left the village there was a glimmer of hope on the faces of the people we came to serve. At the very least they had come to know that they were not forgotten. The simple giving of a blanket may seem like nothing to us, but to a family in Sudan it can mean warmth on cold nights. Its emotional meaning is even greater: It means that they are not forgotten.

"Our church has some Russian Bibles, Andrew! Couldn't you take them along?"

I wasn't so sure. Already our gear was knobby to the point of looking suspicious.

"Of course we'll take them," said Hans. And then he turned to me. "If we're going to be arrested for carrying in Bibles, we might as well be arrested for carrying in a lot of them."

So we squeezed the extra books in. Then just as we were leaving, some other friends arrived with a whole carton of Ukrainian Bibles. I looked at Hans pleadingly, but I knew already that that box was going with us. This time there was simply no storage place left.

"Well," said Hans, "you told me you always leave a few Bibles in plain sight, so God can do the job and not you. I'll just carry these on my lap."

Our transit visa allowed us seventy-two hours in Poland. There were many changes in Warsaw since my first visit to that city six years earlier. We passed the school where my hotel had been and the barracks where I had talked to the Red soldiers. But the rubble heap where I had seen the little girl was cleared away, and a park was on the site.

I introduced Hans to friends both in Warsaw and other towns across the country as we made the most of our three days. And then, not thirty miles from the Russian border, I realized I had made a serious mistake in changing money, way back in Warsaw.

"Do you know what I've done!" I said to Hans. "I exchanged too many guilders into zloty!"

"Can't you change them back again at the border?"

"No, Warsaw's the only place where you can get foreign currency. And if we go back there now, our visa will run out."

We were far out in the country, and Hans was at the wheel. He had agreed to drive only if there was no other car in sight, and there were many such times in Poland, even in 1961. I sat in the passenger's seat beside him, trying to figure out just how much money we were out and how I could have been such an idiot, when suddenly up ahead I saw that we were coming to a tricky bit of driving. A bridge was out, and the bypass road plunged steeply down from the highway, crossed the stream on a flimsy temporary bridge, and rose straight up the embankment on the other side. A Polish Warszawa was even now ahead of us down in the gully, inching its way across the little bridge.

I glanced at Hans to see how he was taking the situation. Perspiration was standing out on his lip as he gripped the wheel, but there was a determination in his eyes. Good! I thought: a few tough maneuvers like this one, and he'll gain confidence.

Hans turned off the pavement and started down the slope. To my delight he seemed to have the car in perfect control. We went neither faster nor slower than before. At his perpetual fifteen miles an hour he crept down the slope and onto the bridge. Now we were across. But now also the other car was directly ahead of us, toiling up the opposite side.

AROUND THE GLOBE
Saudi Arabia

Population: 21.6 million
Location/Size: Southwestern Asia
830,000 sq. miles
Major Religions: Islam
Level of Persecution: Severe, growing steadily

Ever since Islam gained control of Saudi Arabia in the seventh century, Christian missionaries have been prohibited from ministering in the country. The Saudi Arabian government is firmly committed to maintaining Islam throughout the kingdom, and it employs surveillance, arbitrary detention, travel restrictions, and political and economic discrimination to support its bias.

Most Christians in the country are foreign expatriates who live and work on military bases or for oil companies. These believers are permitted to meet privately in home fellowship, but not publicly. And evangelism is strictly forbidden.

A small number of secret Saudi believers belong to underground churches that exist in constant fear of discovery, arrest, and execution. Their fear and suspicion of potential new converts hinder church growth; to trust the wrong person could mean death as a Saudi Christian.

Too late I realized that Hans was not going to stop. Like a movie in slow motion, he ground relentlessly into the rear of the Warszawa.

The driver came spluttering back. His broad Slavic face was red, his fists clenched.

"You pray while I try to talk with him," I said to Hans.

"Good morning, friend. Beautiful day." I said in German. Together we stepped to the rear of his car and inspected the damage. Thanks to Hans's snail's pace, it was not great: the taillight and one rear fender were damaged. Our bumper and a front fender were dented.

"Police," said the man. "Police. Police." That German word he knew well.

But that was the one thing that mustn't happen! Here we were loaded down with Bibles in a Communist country, and here was Hans with no driver's license at the wheel.

And then I remembered my wallet, stuffed with zloty. Was this why God had allowed me to make that foolish overexchange? "Well now," I said. "How much do you think it will cost?"

The Pole's face did not change. "Police, police," he said. I put a piece of glass back up against the taillight and shrugged, hoping to indicate that I didn't think the damage was too great.

"Six thousand zloty?"

The man understood that all right. His fists unclenched, but he repeated again the single word "Police."

"Eight thousand zloty? Nine thousand? Surely the repairs wouldn't cost more than nine thousand." With a dramatic gesture, I reached into my wallet and drew out one more thousand-zloty note. "Ten thousand, and that's a fair amount," I said, holding the money out.

He took it. As he raced back to his car, he shouted over his shoulder, "No police." He started up the Warszawa and left us in a ring of dust.

"Can I breathe now?" said Hans.

"You can breathe."

And there in the dusty bypass we thanked the Lord for having allowed us to make one mistake in order to get us out of another.

We made the border crossing at Brest. Hans could hardly contain his excitement as the barrier gate swung open. He insisted on using his Russian with the customs officials. I doubt if they could understand one word in ten, but they were tremendously complimented that he was making the effort.

We must have been among the very first cars to enter without an Intourist guide. The guards were interested in their novel job of inspecting our papers and effects themselves, and they were delighted when we presented them with American dollars for exchange.

"Russia and United States make insults," one of the guards said in English with a wink. "But for these, we forgive." He took the dollar bills. "One ruble for one dollar. That makes it easy."

At last came time for the inspection of the car itself. Hans and I had agreed ahead of time on the technique that we used ever afterwards whenever two people were crossing a border together. Only one of us would be talking at a time; the other would be constantly in prayer: prayer that God's will be done in each detail of the inspection, prayer for the country we were entering—beginning with these employees at the border.

In this case the guard asked us to open a couple of suitcases, but he hardly more than glanced inside. What he wanted to see was the Opel motor. He asked me some technical questions, then apparently felt embarrassed at having shown unofficial curiosity, and slammed the hood shut. He walked back with us through the little garden in front of the customs shed, stamped our papers, and wished us farewell.

We were across.

Imagine This

Living in Iran, you secretly meet with friends each week for Bible study and prayer. You are very careful not to be discovered, because if you are you will be interrogated by police and arrested. A new friend comes to you and asks if he can join your group. You don't know how he found out about your group, but you suspect that he is a spy for the police.

What Would You Do?

seventeen

Russia at First Glance

Remember those in prison as if you were their fellow prisoners, and those who are mistreated as if you yourselves were suffering.

Hebrews 13:3

It was Hans's first trip into Russia but not mine. The year Mark Peter was born I had accompanied a group of young people from Holland, Germany, and Denmark to a Youth Congress in Moscow, much like the one in Warsaw years before. We were gone only two weeks, traveling by train and of course following an official schedule. Nevertheless, as a scouting trip it had been of enormous value. Several scenes especially had impressed me.

They came back to me now as Hans and I drove across the vast Russian landscape. The drive from Brest to Moscow was 700 miles. I passed the time recalling for Hans those memories of my earlier trip.

The hotel where I had been assigned, in reality a mammoth barracks, was in a village eight miles outside of Moscow. On our first free evening I walked into the village in search of the church.

It was a Russian Orthodox onion-dome structure, which had obviously once been the heart of the village, standing in front of the town's only well. Now it was in complete decay. Weeds grew where once feet had kept the walk packed and clear. The windows were boarded up. Packing cases were stacked outside as if the building were now being used as a warehouse.

I walked around the entire structure looking for the cross, but it was gone. And then as I rounded the church for the second time, I saw the little sight that I never forgot. For here, tucked into the lock on the front door of the church was a little bouquet of fresh yellow flowers!

Stepping closer, I saw that hundreds of withered flowers lay on the ground, as if these bouquets were changed regularly. In my mind's eye I could see a peasant woman, dressed in black, slipping up to the church late at night with her act of love and remembrance.

That Sunday I had made my way to the only Protestant church in all of Moscow that was still open. From what I had read in the Dutch press I was expecting a small and demoralized congregation.

At first I wasn't sure I had the right address. Why was that long line of people waiting outside? I took my place uncertainly at the end of it, when suddenly a man came up and spoke to me in German.

"You've come to church?" he asked.

"This is a church then?"

"Of course. Come with me. There's a special balcony reserved for foreign visitors."

So we went through a small door, down a hall, up a flight of steel stairs, and out onto the balcony. And there I saw for the first time the sight with which I was to become so familiar in future years: the Moscow Protestant Church at worship. The hall was rectangular in shape, narrow and long with two sets of balconies on each side, a platform seating twelve in the front, a fine organ, and a stained glass window facing east and bearing words that my friend translated as: "God is Love." The seating capacity of the church was about one thousand, and there were closer to two thousand there that morning.

I had never in all of my travels seen so many people crowded into one building. Every seat was taken. The aisles were packed

Colombia   A Traveler's Story

CONFLICT

We, as Christians, have lived through several stages of the conflict: first from the armed groups outside of the law and later from armed groups operating within the parameters of the law.

The first group killed our pastor. Afterwards there was armed combat between the two groups, during which bullets passed over our houses. In this altercation we had to abandon our lands and houses and just go.

When they left the area we were able to return to our lands, but now we will have to leave again because the second group is forcing us to grow coca in our fields.

The second group told me they would either buy our lands, or they would cultivate them, or they would buy our lands from our widows (meaning that they would kill us first).

with standees, down the center and down both sides. The balconies were overflowing.

Then the singing began. Two thousand deep Slavic voices in perfect unison. They drowned out the organ. Rich, throaty, full, lusty, masculine. I closed my eyes, and it was easy to imagine that I was hearing heavenly choirs. On and on they sang until there were tears in my eyes.

When the time came for the collection, there was no way for the ushers to pass among so many, and so the banknotes were passed along hand-over-head to the front. As soon as the collection was taken, the sermons began. Yes, sermons. There were two of them, each standard length, one following the other.

While the sermons were being delivered, it seemed to me that some of the congregation was acting very strangely. They were making paper airplanes and sailing them forward from the rear of the church and down from the balconies over the heads of the congregation below. No one seemed a bit disturbed by this bizarre behavior. The planes were captured and passed forward until finally they were collected by one of the men on the platform.

At last my curiosity could stand it no longer, and I turned to the man who led me up the stairs.

Diary of a Smuggler

CHINA

As far as my first three weeks were concerned, from what I could count, my friends and I delivered about 1,500 to 1,700 pounds of Bibles and Christian literature. While we were doing this, I marveled at how much wisdom and creativity God continually gave to the staff people who took care of all the many emergency situations that came in from all parts of China. They were also able to continually arrange the needed training sessions for the young Chinese house-church leaders. To meet with other Christians whose lives are a living witness and testimony of dedication to Jesus' love has been humbling and awesome. More than ever before, this summer's experiences make me want to draw closer to Jesus, for I have seen how much more I need to be open for Him to work in me. This summer I learned even more about Christian unity, teamwork, and support as I worked with Christians from around the world. I also learned how to convert currency back and forth and how to bargain with Chinese hand signs for numbers. For me it was a summer of learning to walk and trust in a beginner's course that was filled with the thrills and adventures of life with Jesus.

"Those are the prayer requests," he explained. "The pastor is putting them into two groups. One is for individual petitions and the other is for visitors from all over the Union who want this congregation to pray for their home churches. You'll see when the time comes."

Sure enough, as soon as the second speaker had sat down, the pastor stood up and held the first of the piles high. Then he read off the names of the visiting churches and said, I learned through my interpreter, "Are we glad to have these visitors?"

"Amen!"

"And do we hold them up in our prayers?"

"Amen!"

"And these requests"—he read two or three of the individual notes—"Do we pray for these needs?"

"Amen!"

"Then let us pray."

And with no further preliminaries that entire congregation of two thousand began to pray aloud simultaneously. From time to time a single voice would rise above the babble of sound, clear and pleading, while the other voices faded to a background hum. Then the tide of sound would swell again, until again an individual rose to express the thoughts of all. It was an experience that stirred me to the depths of my spirit.

After the service it was announced that the pastors would be glad to greet any visitors to the Youth Congress in the vestibule downstairs and to answer their questions. Perhaps a dozen of us accepted the invitation. Questions were fired in quick succession. "Where is the next closest Protestant church?"

"Oh, there are many Protestant churches in Russia. There are others very near."

"But how near?"

"One hundred and eighty kilometers."

"Is there religious freedom in Russia?"

"We have complete religious freedom here, yes."

"How about pastors who have been jailed?"

"We know of no pastors who are in jail, except, perhaps, political subversives."

And then I asked my question. "How about Bibles—do you have enough Bibles?"

"There are plenty of Bibles, yes." In proof they passed a copy around the room. "This excellent new edition has just been printed here in Russia." That was news to me.

"How many copies?"

"Oh, lots. Many copies."

On and on it went, the questioning and the smooth answers that said nothing. The next day, on the off chance that I might be able to see one of the pastors alone, I made my way back to the church. It was Monday morning, yet even at that day and hour it was a busy place. Then I learned that the church building also served as the central office of the Baptist Union for all of the Soviets.

"I wonder if I can help you?" a voice asked. I turned and recognized the face: it was one of the men who had been on the platform the previous morning and afterward had answered questions. He introduced himself as Ivanhoff and invited me to join him in his private office. I wondered just how I was going to go about challenging his statements of the day before. Perhaps the best way would be to say right away that I had brought Bibles with me and to see what his reaction would be.

"I've brought something from the Baptists of Holland to the Baptists of Russia," I began, placing a package tied in brown paper on his table.

"What do you have there?"

"Bibles."

"Russian Bibles?"

AROUND THE GLOBE
Somalia

Population: 7.2 million
Location/Size: Eastern Africa
246,201 sq. miles
Major Religions: Islam
Level of Persecution: Severe, growing steadily

Although there are a large number of Christians in Somalia, most are Orthodox refugees from Ethiopia who have little influence on Somali society. Muslims have prompted public attacks against Christianity by accusing Christian relief organizations of spreading the Gospel. Muslim political parties have issued warnings for Somalis to stay away from Christian evangelistic programs.

There are only a small number of indigenous Somali believers, and they live under harsh persecution from all sides. Faced with opposition in every sector of society, the Church's future looks dim. Revival and replanting is necessary for the Church's survival in years to come.

"From the British and Foreign Bible Society. I have taken the liberty of tearing out the imprint page."

It seemed to me that he was maintaining his composure with difficulty as he said, "May I please see them?"

So I untied the string and showed him the pitiful little pile of three Bibles that I had been able to bring with me on the train. The problem, as with so many East European Bibles, was the size of each volume. Russian—like Serbian and Ukrainian and Macedonian—is written in Cyrillic script, which produces bulkier books than Latin script. In the same amount of space I could have brought ten or twelve Dutch or English Bibles. But what interested me was the pastor's reaction to this tiny offering. Clearly he was restraining his eagerness with great effort.

"Did you say these were a gift?"

"Yes." And then I couldn't resist teasing him a little. "But you say there is a new Soviet edition. Perhaps there is no need to have brought Bibles."

"Well . . ." the pastor remembered his talk of the day before. "As a matter of fact, that edition was largely shipped out of the country. To the Brussels Fair, and around, you know."

"I see."

Then, leaning forward, he asked another question. "Tell me, my friend, why did you really come to Russia?"

On the tightrope that he was walking it seemed to me that perhaps a scriptural answer would be most tactful. I cast about for a moment and then came up with one.

"Do you remember in the Bible when Joseph was wandering among the Shechemites? One of the Shechemites saw him and asked him a question. Do you remember what it was?"

The pastor thought. "He asked, 'Whom are you seeking?'"

"And Joseph's answer?"

"He said, 'I seek my brethren.'"

"Well that," I said, "is my answer to your question too."

Imagine This

You are a Christian living in Indonesia, and most of your friends are also Christians. One day, a group of Muslim warriors raid your town. Having lined you all up in a single file line, soldiers command each of you to deny your faith in Jesus Christ. When your best friend is pulled out of line and questioned, he refuses to renounce Jesus and the soldiers brutally kill him. You are next in line for questioning.

What Would You Do?

eighteen

For Russia With Love

I consider that our present sufferings are not worth comparing with the glory that will be revealed in us.

Romans 8:18

Hans had listened with great interest to these recollections, interrupting occasionally with questions. When I came to the end of them, he offered one of his blunt and faith-filled prayers that we be led to Ivanhoff again, since the contact was now made and a relationship begun.

"I think it's time for a break, Andy," he added. "I'd like a cup of coffee."

"So would I."

Up ahead was a break in a tall hedgerow, through which we plunged, scarcely noticing that there was already an automobile parked off the road there, its occupants enjoying a picnic lunch.

We pulled to a stop and began to get out our gear. It seemed to me that the Russians in the other car were behaving in a most unfriendly way. They kept glaring in our direction and muttering. The man threw half a cup of tea on the ground, complaining, while the two women began to pile plates, fruit, half-eaten loaves of bread, into a straw basket.

We were still wondering what this was all about when all at once there was a screeching of brakes from the other side of the hedge. Car doors slammed. And suddenly we were confronted by two uniformed police. They stood in the opening in the hedge, hands on hips, glancing quickly over both parties. Then one officer came toward us while the other went over to the Russian car.

"How do you do?" said Hans, smiling brightly at this opportunity to use his Russian.

The officer did not reply, and Hans's face fell. "He just doesn't want to be sociable," said Hans, returning pointedly to his coffee. Knowing Hans, however, I knew that he was praying hard. This man must not begin poking around inside our automobile. Even as we prayed, the officer abruptly left us and walked over to join his companion at the other car. There was an exchange of heated words, a shrug, and then the Russians began to unload their automobile.

We watched for twenty minutes while those poor people took everything that could be removed out of their car and spread it on the ground. Then the officers looked inside the motor, inside the trunk, underneath the car. We knew that somehow we were responsible for the discomfort they were being put to, but we did not know what to do about it. So we just stirred our coffee until it was cold.

After half an hour, when the officers still had not so much as glanced in our direction, we decided it was time to try leaving. So we drank the awful coffee, stowed the little stove away, and made as much noise as we could closing doors and finally starting the engine. Still the officers paid no attention to us. We crept through the hedge and nosed back onto the highway around the police car.

"What was that all about?" said Hans as we were under way.

"I don't know, unless they thought we were smugglers making an exchange there beside the road. Hans, we've got to pray for that family, that they don't get into trouble through our clumsiness. And it's something to remember when it comes time for us to get rid of our cargo."

The avenues of Moscow were enormous, wide enough to carry ten cars abreast, and they were more heavily traveled than I remembered. We passed the huge GUM store, drove through vast Red Square, passed the Mausoleum, and eventually made our way to the campsite that had been assigned to us. Right away we pitched our igloo-shaped tent and prepared to take out at least a few of our Bibles.

"Don't look now," Hans said, "but we've got prying eyes."

Without looking up, I tossed a road map on top of the two Bibles I had taken out. Then casually I glanced around and saw the man. He was wearing a green fatigue uniform and stood a few feet away from the car watching us. I got out our coffeepot, and Hans and I started preparing a rather unwanted cup of coffee. As soon as we had stopped unpacking the Bibles, the prying eyes walked away.

"What do you make of it?" I asked Hans.

"I don't like it. I wish we could get rid of this cargo."

We took just one of the Bibles, locked the car, and left the campsite. It was Thursday night: the night of the midweek service at the Baptist church that we had been heading for.

There were about twelve hundred people attending the Thursday night prayer meeting! The form of the service was much the same as the one I had attended two years earlier, but I did not see Ivanhoff either on the platform or in the part of the congregation I could see.

When the meeting was over, Hans and I walked out to the vestibule and began milling about in the crowd. The main purpose of the evening for us was to make contacts to whom we could deliver our supply of Bibles. I edged my way around the big entrance hall, glancing into face after face, asking God to give me as He had so often before, that moment of recognition that, for Christians, can do the work of many years of acquaintance and growing confidence.

And before long I saw him: a thin, balding man in his middle forties standing against a wall and staring into the crowd. I had such a clear directive to speak to him that I almost forgot about Hans. But in a real Christian partnership, one member's guidance

China   A Traveler's Story

SARAH YANG AND HER TORMENTOR

They came as she was speaking.

Public Security Bureau officials swooped in as Sarah Yang, a female house-church leader, finished expounding her text to her congregation. She was whisked out into the bitter cold. It was December 1998 in northeast China. She shivered in the freezing cell, waiting for her interrogator to come in.

Soon he swaggered in. Wu Pei Fu was the head of the Public Security Bureau in the area. For some reason he took an instant dislike to Sarah Yang, and instead of using more subtle psychological techniques, he began to beat and kick her. "Tell me who the other leaders are? Who supplies your Bibles?" He screamed questions, and when she refused to answer, he would rain blows upon her, slapping her flesh. The police station echoed the sound of his hands stinging her body.

But Christians were praying. Wu was in for a shock. He interrogated Sarah Yang for only twenty-four hours, but the hours were full of nasty surprises. First, he heard his mother was in the hospital from a bad car accident. Next, news came that his son was very sick with a stomach ailment. Finally, when he went home he had a fierce argument with his wife, who threatened to leave him.

In the morning he took his frustration out on Sarah Yang, beating her repeatedly and then sending word to her congregation: "If you don't pay 20,000 RMB for her release, I will send her to a labor camp for three years." The sum was exorbitant (nearly $2,500). The congregation could not afford to pay, since in the area the average yearly salary was less than half that amount. But they prayed, and a contact in another city agreed to raise the money. Sarah Yang was released.

Hearing that her interrogator's mother was ill, Sarah Yang went straight to the hospital to see her. She located the mother, who was lying on the bed with her other son in attendance, and began witnessing to her. She preached the Gospel to her and sent word to the other Christians. They all came and prayed at the bedside. In a matter of hours, the mother and her other son both trusted Christ. The Christians also prayed for Wu's wife and son. The son was healed.

Wu was amazed at the boldness and the effectiveness of the Christians, and when his mother started attending the house church of Sarah Yang, whom he abused so badly, he made no objection. He sent word saying, "I will not disturb your church. You are good people."

But he gave them this helpful warning: "I had to act against you because one of your group filed a report with this office. You have spies in your midst. Be very careful what you do and say, even with each other."

is always submitted to the other's for correction and confirmation. So I waited until Hans had inched his great bulk over to my side.

"I've spotted our man!" he said before I could speak. And out of the hundreds of people in that vestibule, he nodded to the man I too had chosen. Hearts high, we pushed our way to him.

"*Kak vi po zhi vayete,*" Hans began.

"*Kak vi po zhi vayete,*" the man answered, instantly alert.

As Hans launched into a description of who we were and where we were from, however, the man's face grew more and more perplexed. But when Hans came to the word "Dutch," he burst out laughing. He told us that he himself was German; he was a second-generation immigrant living in Siberia, and his family still spoke German in the home.

Immediately the three of us fell into conversation. And as we talked, Hans and I grew more and more incredulous. For this man was from a little church in Siberia, two thousand miles away, where there were 150 communicants but not a single Bible. One day he had been told in a dream to go to Moscow where he would find a Bible for his church. He resisted the idea at first, he said, for he knew as well as anyone that there were precious few Bibles in Moscow.

And that was the end of his story.

Hans and I looked at each other in disbelief. I gave Hans a nod, and it was his turn to share with our Siberian friend the good news.

"You were told to come eastward for two thousand miles to get a Bible, and we were told to go westward two thousand miles carrying Bibles to churches in Russia. And here we are tonight, recognizing each other the instant we meet."

And with this, Hans held out the big Russian Bible we had brought along with us. The Siberian was without words. He held the Bible at arm's length and stared at it, and then at the two of us, and then at the Bible again. All of a sudden the dam burst, and a flow of thank you's and bear hugs followed until we had drawn a group of onlookers. I was sorry for that: I hadn't wanted to attract attention. In a whisper I told the fellow the rest of the news, that we had more Bibles, and that if he would meet us there again at ten o'clock the next morning, we would let him have half a dozen to take home.

Southern Sudan   A Traveler's Story

GOD'S COMFORT IN PRISON

Maktu, a Moro Christian, testified about the truth of Hebrews 13:5: "Never will I leave you; never will I forsake you." He was caught by government forces in 1996 and thrown into prison. It is not clear if it was because of his Christian beliefs or simply because he was a civilian caught up in the ongoing civil war. Either way, the ordeal was a severe test of his faith.

As he lay in his cell, tied up so tightly that he could not lie down or sit properly, the pain and discomfort was intense. Then thoughts of doubt started to creep into his mind. Where was God in this time of need? Why should he continue in his faith when it only brought him problems?

He was on the verge of denying his faith when he suddenly heard a voice speaking clearly to him. The voice asked him why he had those thoughts and continued by saying that many people in the past had suffered for God's sake. He should not be surprised that this was happening to him as well. Then he saw a vision: Known and unknown Christians comforted him and praised God. There was such a joyous worshipping atmosphere that he forgot for a moment that he was still tied up in a prison cell! In fact, he desired to die so that he could join their ranks permanently.

God in His great mercy took this man through the crisis and put new strength in his faith. After he was eventually released from prison, he continued to follow God with fresh dedication and also blessed many others with his testimony.

The Siberian grew suddenly suspicious. "They are free of charge?"

"Of course," we answered. "This is simply one arm of the Church looking after the needs of another."

The next morning at nine o'clock Hans posted guard while I again tried to get the Bibles out of their hiding place in the car. I was no more than halfway through when Hans whistled the Dutch national anthem, and I knew that our friend in the green uniform was back. With a sigh I went to work making coffee.

"Coffee's ready!" I shouted to Hans.

He came over and took an ice cold cup of liquid from my hands. "He's back?" I asked.

"Just as nosey as yesterday. He's suspicious about something. How many did you get out?"

"Four."

"Well, that'll have to do. Slip them in the flight bags and let's go." Owning a Bible for your own personal use was no crime; but commerce in smuggled Bibles was illegal, and it was dangerous to look as if you might be dealing in contraband. So we put just four Bibles into our KLM bags and strolled down the lane to the bus stop. At precisely ten o'clock we walked into the church and sat down on a bench near the door. At 10:30 we were feeling anxious and very conspicuous. And then, at 10:45, a voice spoke at my elbow. "Hello, brother."

I whirled around. It was not the man from Siberia. It was Ivanhoff, the pastor I had met on my previous visit to Moscow.

"Are you waiting for someone?" asked Ivanhoff.

"I—we—yes. Someone we met here last night."

Ivanhoff was silent for a moment. Then, "Yes," he said softly. "That's what I was afraid of. Your Siberian friend cannot come."

"What do you mean, *cannot* come?"

Ivanhoff looked around. "My friends," he said, "at each service there are secret police. We count on it. They saw you and this man talking, and so he cannot come. He has been 'spoken' to. But you have brought something for him?"

I looked at Hans. Could Ivanhoff be trusted? Hans gave a shrug and then a barely perceptible nod.

"Yes," I said briefly. "Four Bibles. In these bags."

"Leave them with me; I will see that he gets them."

Again Hans and I exchanged glances. But we ended by taking the Bibles—wrapped in newspaper—out of the bags and handing them over. Then, asking God for protection, I took a plunge: There seemed to be no other way.

"Is there somewhere we can talk?" I asked.

"Talk?"

"Well, frankly, these aren't the only Bibles we have."

Ivanhoff caught his breath. "What do you mean? Just keep your voice low. How many Bibles do you have?"

"Over a hundred."

"You are joking."

"They're in our car at the camp."

Ivanhoff thought for a moment. Then without a word he led us down a long corridor. When it turned a corner he stopped suddenly, laid the Bibles on the floor, and held out his hands, palms down.

"Do you see those nails?" he said. We stared at fingernails ridged and thickened the way nails become when they have been damaged deep in their roots. "I have spent my time in prison for the faith," Ivanhoff said. And this was the man who had told the visiting youth delegation that there was no religious persecution in Russia! "I will be frank with you. I cannot go through it again. I cannot help you with those Bibles."

I felt my heart go out to this man. "I know," I said. "We do not blame you. Perhaps, though, you know of someone else who might be willing?"

"Markov," said Ivanhoff. "I will arrange with him to rent an automobile. He will meet you in front of the GUM store at precisely one o'clock." And then as an afterthought, "But be careful."

Hans pointed to the little stack of Bibles on the floor. "What about these? Don't you risk something taking these?"

Ivanhoff smiled, but his eyes remained sad as ever. "Four Bibles," he said. "That's not a very serious economic crime. They're worth four hundred rubles. How long do you go to jail for four hundred rubles? Four months at the most? But a hundred Bibles! That's worth ten thousand rubles here in Moscow, more in the provinces. Ten thousand rubles worth of pornographic literature! Why, a man could—"

"Pornography?" said both Hans and I together. "What does that have to do with us?"

"Nothing," said Ivanhoff. "Except that if you are caught, that's what they'll accuse you of selling." And then, as if receiving some sort of signal, he whirled on his heels, snatched the books from the floor, and walked rapidly away, his shoes clicking down the empty corridor as he disappeared from sight.

That afternoon at one o'clock we pulled up in front of the GUM store. A man emerged from a car parked a hundred yards away

Diary of a Smuggler

CHINA

What an incredible experience that could only have occurred because the hand of the Lord was involved in every step! I thought I knew some real Christians and that I was a pretty good one myself until I witnessed those Christians in China and the few we met in Mongolia. The Lord cleared the way for each of our three border crossings and protected us from some close calls with the PSB (Public Security Bureau). We carried in over 1,200 Bibles and New Testaments, 600 Gospels of Mark, and 400 pounds of medicines and numerous tracts without one bag ever being inspected, opened, or any of our team of 19 being questioned! We were on a mission for God, and He made sure we succeeded. The diversions at each checkpoint could only have been planned and executed by Him.

One place we visited was Huhehot (Green City) in the province of Inner Mongolia, China. Through two contacts we learned of a teacher named Amy, and three of us attempted to make contact to arrange a delivery. That was an experience of going in the night to an unknown address with a taxi driver who spoke no English, and trying to find an apartment at the Chinese Polytechnical Institute. After knocking on several doors (with pounding hearts, I might add) we found this beautiful Chinese girl named Amy. Her phone was bugged but not her apartment, so she invited us in. We explained we had a drop we wanted to make, and she said the situation there was very tight and it may not be possible. At 11:00 P.M. we received a phone call to say the situation was not good and we couldn't arrange anything. We returned to the town square, where many of our team were discreetly passing out tracts. We finally decided that we had attracted enough attention, so we left the square.

China and Mongolia need our continued prayers and Bibles! The enemy and the government are hard at work, and persecution continues.

and strolled by, looking at us cautiously through the window. Then he strolled back again.

"Brother Andrew?"

"You're Markov," I said. "Greetings in the Name of the Lord."

"We're going to do something very bold," said Markov, talking rapidly. "We're going to exchange the Bibles within two minutes of Red Square. No one will ever suspect us in such a location. It's a stroke of genius."

Clearly, this brother was more of a genius than I. I didn't like the sound of it. He led us to a street that was, sure enough, less than two minutes from Red Square. There was a large blind wall running along one side of the street, but houses lined the other. At any window there could be a pair of curious eyes.

"You'd better pray," I said to Hans as I parked behind Markov's car.

Hans did pray, aloud, as I got at the Bibles and stowed them an armload at a time into cartons and sacks. Markov opened the rear door to his car, and we made the transfer right out in the open, trip after trip on the busy sidewalk. When we were finished, Markov allowed himself time only for a quick handshake apiece before he was back in his car starting the engine.

"By next week," he said, "these Bibles will be in the hands of pastors all over Russia."

As Markov drove off, I looked at Hans. He was still praying, but he was grinning too. This part of our mission was accomplished. Except for that one carton of Ukrainian Bibles, our green-uniformed friend could peer as hard as he liked. The car was empty.

We went home by way of the Ukraine, delivering the last Bibles to churches ourselves. And it was at one of these stops that a dream caught hold of me that for the next three years would not let go. For it was there in the Ukraine—when we had just two Bibles left—that one of the parishioners brought something for us to see, a treasure of his family's: a pocket-sized Ukrainian Bible.

I held the little volume in my hand, unbelieving. Yes, the man assured me, it was a complete Bible. But it was one quarter the size of the Bibles we had brought! I turned the India-paper pages, marveling at the tiny type, so small and yet so sharp. Each word was clear and well-spaced. I bombarded the man with questions—where had this been printed, who published it, where had they bought it—but he knew the answers to none of them.

I couldn't lay the little book down. I hefted it in my hand. I slipped it into my pocket. I brought it out and held it up beside one of the standard Bibles. Why, we could bring in three and four times as many, every trip, if they were this size! And once inside, they'd be so much easier to transfer and conceal. And if it could be done for Ukrainian, Russian could be printed in this format too, and the other East European languages. . . .

Seeing how the Bible intrigued me, the owner made a suggestion. If he could have the two new ones we had brought, would we like to keep this one? The church would still be one Bible ahead.

To my delight, the minister

AROUND THE GLOBE
Sri Lanka

Population: 19 million
Location/Size: Southern Asian island
24,962 sq. miles
Major Religions: Buddhism
Hinduism
Christianity
Islam
Level of Persecution: Isolated, static

The Church in Sri Lanka enjoys limited freedom, but persecution is still a problem. Anti-Christian propaganda, accusations against the Church, pleas for new restrictions, and even church burnings have come in response to new growth in the Christian community. Buddhists and Hindus remain hostile to the Gospel, particularly in some areas of the deep south.

Although the Church is growing in numbers through births to Christian homes, defections to Buddhism have left the Church's share of the population in decline. Persistent nominalism in the Church necessitates prayers for the Church to effectively contextualize the Gospel and return to biblical theology.

and the rest of the congregation agreed, and I left that town with the dream in my pocket. I could hardly wait to show it to our Bible societies in the West.

Our last Sunday in Russia we attended a Baptist church in a Ukrainian village not far from the Hungarian border. The singing was stirring, the prayers fervent. But when it came time for the sermon, the pastor did a strange thing. He walked off the platform, borrowed a book from one of the congregation, and took it back to the pulpit. It was the Bible! We had heard that there were ministers in Russia who did not have Bibles of their own. But this was the first time we had seen it with our own eyes.

After the service the pastor invited us to join him and his elders in his study for a brief visit. The visit began, as it so often did in Russia, with an attack. We had learned that this was a safety device, since all pastors knew that their actions were observed. On this occasion the attack was against my automobile.

"Tell me," the pastor said through a German-speaking parishioner, "which industrial complex are you the head of?"

"But I'm not with any company."

Our interpreter translated, but the pastor did not let the subject drop. "I know you're not telling the truth," he said, "for you have an automobile parked just outside. Only capitalists own automobiles; laboring people walk."

What could I do? It was impossible to convince him that I was a former factory worker, the son of a village blacksmith, with a good deal less guarantee of an income than he himself had. He just could not grasp these facts and left the subject only out of politeness—or perhaps because he felt that he had safely established his antipathy for idle and monied classes!

At any rate, we got to talking about the Second Coming of Christ—by far the most popular theological topic in Russia—and the tone of our conversation immediately changed. I drew my own Dutch Bible out of my pocket to follow the references he was making and when he was through, laid it on the desk.

I noticed almost at once that he had lost interest in the conversation. His mind was taken up with the Bible! He picked it up and weighed it in his hand, unzipped it, stared at the Dutch words he could not read, zipped it up again.

Then he put it back on the desk. Not as I had put it down, but with great precision. He set it down on the corner and slowly ran his finger along the edge so that it was aligned with the desk. And then—his voice distant, talking more to himself than to us—he said, "You know, Brother, I have no Bible."

My heart broke. Here was this important man, the spiritual leader of a thousand souls, who did not own a copy of the Bible.

All of the ones we had brought with us were gone—and then I remembered. The little Ukrainian pocket Bible! "Wait!" I shouted. I jumped up from my chair. The Bible societies would just have to take my word for it. I raced outside to my car, threw open the door, got the little Bible from under the seat, and ran back to the study.

"Here." I shoved the Bible into the pastor's hand. "This is for you. To keep."

The translator repeated the words, but still the pastor did not understand.

"Whose is it?" he said.

"It's yours! To keep, to own."

When Hans and I left that day, our chests ached from the embraces of that group of elders. For now their pastor had a Bible of his very own. A Bible he did not have to return at the end of the service. A Bible to pick up whenever he wanted. A Bible to read and to love.

And as we left Russia I knew there was a task ahead of me bigger than any I had yet attempted behind the Iron Curtain. I had to talk some organization into printing Slavic-language Bibles in pocket-sized editions. And I had to bring these books into Russia not by the hundreds, but by the thousands.

Imagine This

In Colombia a group of guerrillas approach you to join their militia. Knowing the violence that they regularly commit, you are unwilling to participate. They become more threatening and aggressive, warning that they will murder your family if you do not become a part of their movement. Do you risk your family's death and not join the group? Or do you become a participant?

What Would You Do?

nineteen

Bibles to the Russian Pastors

We also rejoice in our sufferings, because
we know that suffering produces
perseverance; perseverance, character; and
character, hope.

Romans 5:3–4

The one thing on my mind now was the need for a Russian pocket Bible. It became an obsession with me. I made the rounds of the Bible societies, but even when a society agreed that such an edition was possible in theory, there were practical problems. The American Bible Society, which had been supplying me with Russian Bibles free of charge, although sympathetic, could not see their way clear to printing a special edition just for this operation. The British and Foreign Bible Society was in the same position, the Dutch Bible Society was committed to work in Africa and Indonesia and did not handle Eastern European languages.

"Why don't you print your own pocket Bible?" said Philip Whetstra one evening when I was talking over my problem with him.

"Very funny."

"I'm serious. You know exactly what it is you want. Print it yourself."

"You must be dreaming, Mr. Whetstra. That would cost at least $5,000. Wherever would I get $5,000?"

Mr. Whetstra looked at me sadly. "After all this time, you ask that?" he said.

Of course he was right. It would not be I who supplied the funds for such a project; it would be the Lord. Before I left the Whetstras' that night, I knew that I was launched onto another grand experiment—the grandest yet. This time, though, it took longer than usual for the dream to unfold. And in the meanwhile there was the usual work to be done. Having Hans as part of this work was even better than I had imagined. We formed a team, one strong where the other was weak. It was while we were in Bulgaria one hot summer night in 1962 that Hans suddenly said, "Andrew, it is time we prayed for a new team member."

I was sitting up in bed with the perspiration drying on me, trying to write a letter home. "Yup. That's right," I said absently.

"You remember when the visa finally came through to go to Czechoslovakia, only you were in East Germany and I was in Russia? If there were more of us, we wouldn't have to make these choices."

"Yup. That's right."

"You're not listening."

I put the notepaper down. It stuck to the heel of my hand. "Of course I'm listening." I tried to remember what he had said. "We have more opportunity than we can satisfy. That's true, Hans. But you know how it is if you expand too rapidly—"

Hans interrupted. "I'd hardly call one new member in seven years expanding too rapidly, let us pray."

I looked at Hans closely. He had run the "let-us-pray" onto the end of his sentence so closely, I wasn't sure I had heard correctly. But he was well into the prayer. I bowed my head too, and as Hans spoke I began to get his sense of urgency about finding another man who would give himself with us—full time, without salary, without reservation.

Almost simultaneously, Hans and I thought of the same person.

"What about Rolf?" we said together, and then laughed.

"It could be guidance," Hans said.

"It could indeed."

Rolf was a young Dutch seminary student finishing his post-graduate work in systematic theology. A brilliant theologian, Rolf was still a man of action. That same night I composed a letter asking him if he would consider joining us. And sure enough, on our return to Holland there was a reply waiting for us. He had read my letter with annoyance, Rolf wrote. Becoming a sticky-voiced, Bible-waving missionary was the last thing on earth he wanted to do. What did I think he had gone to school all these years for, if all he needed to know was "Onward Christian Soldiers"?

But since my letter had come, he went on, he hadn't had a night's sleep. God had thrust it under his nose night and day, eating or working, sitting or walking, until at last he'd given in, and when could he start?

And so, kicking and protesting, a third member came to join us. Hans took him right away on an orientation trip into Rumania. They had a fantastic time there, seeing a real break in the reserve of the Church in that beautiful land. They were spied upon by two men who hardly ever left their sight, but in spite of this managed to get rid of their Bibles and even to do some preaching in private homes.

Rolf came back open-mouthed and utterly convinced.

We shared with Rolf our longing for a small-format Russian Bible. Hardly had we finished our tale of difficulties before Rolf echoed Philip Whetstra's thought that we should print the Bibles ourselves.

"How much *would* it cost to print five thousand Bibles?" Rolf asked.

And I had to admit that I had never asked for a bid. Rolf would not let me get away with that. Together, he and I contacted printing houses in Holland, Germany, and England. The best quotation we got was from an English printer who said that with a press run of five thousand he would print the Bibles for $3 each.

"You see?" I said to Rolf, Hans, and Corrie the day we received this bid in the mail. "Why that comes to $15,000!"

A Traveler's Story

VIOLENT FORCES AND FLOODS

In the area where I live, I am president of Area Five of our denomination, which already boasts 115 communities. The work is demanding because only four churches are in the urban area, the rest being in the countryside in very dangerous, mountainous terrain.

We have had problems here because people live on what they cultivate on their land. We have had so many conflicts between those who try to impose the law and the different armed groups who are marginalized from the law. Because of this, many pastors and believers have had to abandon their homes and their little parcels of land and move into the urban areas. This generates substantial economic crises, because when they go, they leave everything. As a result, about thirteen churches have been completely closed.

We have even seen several families lodging together as refugees in the small home of one of the believers, which gives rise to unhealthy overcrowding. In one case some basic warehouses were constructed, and more than seventy displaced people live there. The Violence group had expelled them from their lands and set the houses on fire, leaving them totally destitute.

In the warehouse, they receive different kinds of support from NGOs (Non-Government Organizations), but the Violence group threatened the NGOs, so they left the area. Among the NGOs are, for example, Doctors Without Borders and the Red Cross, who were also categorized as part of the enemy. When they departed, we were left without any support. My work has been demanding because it has been my responsibility to visit the many believers to encourage them not to give up.

We lack everything . . . so there is also much disease.

We don't understand why even nature has caused such disaster. When the volcano erupted, the mud running into the San Jorge River caused the river to flood its banks, threatening the people. Others were left totally destitute when the river grew to such an extent that it swept away everything in its path, including cultivated lands and thirty houses. Twenty Christian families were left with absolutely nothing.

Rolf and Hans were amused at me. "You sit there immobilized by such a little matter as money!"

And of course again they were right. I had learned to count on the Lord for toothpaste and shaving cream. But when it came to such a staggering sum as $15,000, I had trouble believing that the same principle held.

That night I sat down at the kitchen table with a bankbook open in front of me. It was labeled "Russian Bibles." The entries, starting in 1961 just after our return from Russia, were now well into 1963. With all our hoarding, the total still came to less than $2,000.

Corrie sat down. "What are you thinking, Andy?"

I shoved the account book toward her. "In two years that's all the money we've saved." I took a deep breath, hating to say what I had to next. "How much do you think our house is worth?"

Corrie did not answer me. She just stared.

"We got it at a bargain, and with the work we've put into it, it's gone up in value many times. What do you think it's worth? Ten thousand dollars? Twelve thousand? We need that much."

"Our *house*, Andy? Right when we're expecting a new baby?"

"We need to do something to get us off dead center."

Corrie's face had gone white. "Maybe God doesn't want us to have those pocket Bibles," she said in a small voice. "Maybe the very slowness is guidance."

"I know," I said. "I know."

That was all we said that night about selling the house. But Corrie told me the next week that she had begun to pray that she could think of the house not as our own but as belonging to God.

"It should be Yours to do with as You will," we started praying together every evening. "And yet we know we really don't feel this way, Lord. If You want us to sell the house for the Bibles, You will have to work a small miracle in our hearts to make us willing."

The new baby came: the child we had been waiting for so long, a little girl. We named her Stephanie. Every cash present that came in for her went into the Bible fund. But twenty years of this kind of saving would never be enough. We stopped asking for willingness and just asked God to make us *willing* to be *willing* to sell the house.

And at last He answered our prayer. One morning Corrie and I suddenly knew that we didn't need that house or anything else on earth to make us happy.

"I don't know just where we'll live," Corrie began, and then she laughed. "Remember, Andy? 'We don't know where we're going—'"

And I supplied the end of the sentence we had spoken so often, "'—but we're going there together.'"

That very day we got an appraisal on the house and land. The total, coupled with our savings account, came to just over $15,000!

It was the confirmation we needed. We put the house on the market, and I wrote to the printer in England asking him to start making the plates as we had discussed them. That night Corrie and I slept in a happier, more positive frame of mind than we had enjoyed for months.

How faithful God is, how utterly trustworthy, how good beyond imagining! He asks for so little in order to give us so much. For although the housing shortage in Witte was still acute, not a single person came to look at our house all that week. And on Friday, Corrie called, "Telephone, Andy!"

With Hans and Rolf traveling so much of the time, we had been forced to install a phone in the house. I often resented the interruptions it caused. But not this day. For it was from the Dutch Bible Society, asking me if I could see them that same afternoon.

Within a few hours I was seated across the table from the board of directors. They were committed, they explained again, to their own work. But they had not been able to get my need out of their minds. If I could make arrangements to have the printing done somewhere else. . . .

I had? In England? Well, here was what they proposed. They would pay half the cost. If the Bibles cost $3 each to print, I could purchase them for $1.50. And although the Society would pay for the entire printing as soon as it was ready, I would need to pay for my supplies only as I used them. If this was satisfactory—

If it was satisfactory! I could scarcely believe what I had heard. I would be able to buy over six hundred Bibles—all we could carry at one time—right away out of our "Russian Bible" fund. And we wouldn't have to leave our home, and Corrie could go on sewing the pink curtains for Steffie's room, and I could set out my lettuce

Diary of a Smuggler

MEXICO

When my group stopped at our first church, we had quite a distance to walk, as the bus could not make it through the roads. As we walked we noticed the woods seemed to change colors, and soon we saw men and women coming out of the woods toward us and the church.

The women wore beautifully colored clothes and looked like bright-colored flowers coming from the woods into the fields. One of the first things I noticed was that the men and women sat on separate sides of the church. This was on a Monday, and the men who attended gave up a day's wage to meet us and pray with us. Some of the women worked too and gave up what little they earned in a day to meet and pray with us. Some of these women had husbands who had been killed, jailed unjustly, or maimed to the point they could not work. Some of the women and men had been tortured for their faith, and some had endured unspeakable acts performed on them.

Our leader told us before we went to the first meeting that we might be offered something to eat at each church, and that we must eat it if offered. We could not take away their blessing of giving to us something they really could not afford to offer. At the end of the service we were offered a blessing from the members of the church. It was bottled Cokes. We took the Cokes, knowing that each one was a price these people had sacrificed for our comfort. It was a small thing, but there was not a dry eye in the group for their sacrifice for us.

flats and—I could hardly wait to tell Corrie what God had done with the thimbleful of willingness we had offered Him.

The pocket Bibles were a reality at last. As I left the offices of the Dutch Bible Society, I knew that within six months, by early 1964, we would be able to begin supplying Russian pastors with the Bibles they so desperately needed.

Rolf was getting married.

Corrie and I had dutifully recited to him the disadvantages and separations that went with this type of work. But, as Rolf pointed out, our own happiness was the world's best argument against bachelorhood. Elena could go with him on his trips. She would be just as effective a team member as the men.

So we stood up for them at their wedding and gave them a honeymoon assignment dear to our hearts. The first print order of Bibles was ready. Rolf and Elena were to go pick them up in England.

We had a second vehicle now, a van especially built for long distance travel. It had a windowless rear section and could carry more than the Opel. Rolf and his bride ferried the van across to England and picked up our first order of pocket Bibles. What a red-letter day it was when Rolf and Elena burst into the house carrying one of the new Bibles, our own edition! I held it in my left hand, and in my right hand a standard copy. What a difference! I knew that we must be on our way as quickly as possible.

The 16th of May, 1964, was our departure date. I knew I would need all the partnership support I could get for this venture, and Hans was in Hungary; so newlywed Rolf was tapped.

It was Sunday morning in Moscow, time to go downtown to church. Rolf and I left the van with considerable uneasiness. How much was our undeclared merchandise worth? A Bible could buy a cow now in the country districts. Six hundred and fifty cows—this cargo represented a sizable smuggling operation in cash value alone. We were planning to give the Bibles away, but that would make no difference if we were caught with them in our possession. A man was on trial right now for an "economic crime" against the people's State. A man convicted of the same charge had recently been executed by firing squad. If we were caught . . . well this was not the time to think of that.

Ivanhoff was on the platform at church that morning. As he glanced at the visitors' balcony, I was sure he recognized me, although he gave no sign. A few minutes later he got up and left the sanctuary. He did not return, nor was he in the vestibule after the service. But suddenly a hearty voice behind me said, "Welcome to Russia!"

It was Markov. I introduced him to Rolf. "We brought gifts," I said.

"Wonderful!" he cried. "That's grand news!" His voice was louder than necessary, and I knew it was a defense. No one would bother to listen if we were speaking openly.

"I wonder where we might go to visit a spell."

"How about the same place as before?"

The same place! Two minutes from Red Square! Markov might have nerves of steel, but I did not.

"I'd rather see some new scenery."

For the first time Markov lowered his voice. "On the road to Smolensk there is a large blue sign saying 'Moscow.' Rendezvous there at five o'clock. I will lead you to another place. Have the gifts unpacked so we can move fast."

This sounded better, but Rolf and I were still faced with the problem of where to unpack those Bibles. It would take at least half an hour of uninterrupted privacy to do the job.

Back at camp I had an idea. "Let's go for a ride," I said. "You just keep sightseeing, and I'll crawl into the back and begin unpacking. Whatever you do, keep moving."

But I had barely begun when the van jerked to a halt. I crept forward and peered over the seats. A police officer was coming toward the car.

"Pray!" Rolf hissed, and then stuck his head out the window.

"What is it officer?" he asked in Dutch.

The policeman rattled off a long angry sentence in Russian, then produced a few words in English. "No turn! No turn! Sign say."

"Was there something wrong with that turn, officer?" said Rolf, still in Dutch. "I'm terribly sorry. I'm not used to driving in such a vast and handsome city as Moscow."

The policeman was raging in Russian again. I flattened my back against the side of the van, praying that the officer would not look inside. At the end of a lifetime I heard him say something else in Russian, more calmly. "The same to you, officer," Rolf answered in Dutch. "And I do wish you and your people the very best of God's love."

Rolf put the van into gear and moved slowly out into traffic. Not until several blocks further did I let out my breath.

"Let's not try that any more. It's too much for me!"

We spent the rest of the afternoon looking for a place to finish our work. Finally, at four o'clock we knew that, ready or not, we had to head for the rendezvous. So with hearts that did not match the sunny sky overhead, we drove out the Smolensk road.

"Why are we worried!" Rolf said suddenly. "This is God's work! He'll make a way for us." And as if to prove his conviction, he started to sing.

Oddly, as the mood inside the van brightened, the sky overhead darkened. First an overcast hid the sun, then a heavy buildup of clouds spread swiftly across the sky, dark and threatening. Lightning flashed in the distance. Thunder answered. And still Rolf and I drove on, singing.

Then the rain began.

In all my travels I had never seen a rain like this one. It was as if a celestial reservoir had burst, letting a solid sheet of water fall to earth. We had no choice but to pull to the side of the pavement. Other cars too had to abandon the road. The windows steamed up. We could hardly make out our own struggling windshield wipers. . . .

"Say—"

"I know—"

"God has made us invisible!" said Rolf.

Praising Him, we crawled back into the van, unhurriedly dislodged the rest of the Bibles, and packed them into cartons. We settled back in our seats comfortably just as the rain lifted and the skies lightened once again.

AROUND THE GLOBE
Sudan

Population: 29.4 million
Location/Size: Eastern Africa
967,500 sq. miles
Major Religions: Islam
Christianity
Tribal religions
Level of Persecution: Severe, growing steadily

In Sudan, the National Islamic Front's forced Islamization campaign continues as one of the most vicious attacks on the Church worldwide. Ongoing reports describe countless Christians sold into slavery, families torn apart, children forced to embrace Islam, churches being destroyed, and believers being tortured and killed. Despite this extreme hardship and persecution, however, the Church in Sudan continues to grow.

Warfare pervades the Sudanese countryside, and peace is unlikely until Christians grow to be a majority in the nation. Unfortunately, as the number of Christians in the country rises, so does the level of persecution from the government. Until the spiritual blindness that blankets the land is lifted, Sudanese Christians will continue to face intense struggles for their faith.

At precisely five o'clock we drove past the Moscow sign. Markov passed us, his headlights still on after the storm. He blinked them once. At ten minutes past five we stopped in front of a sort of shopping center where people all around us were unloading boxes or piling them into trucks. It took five minutes to make the exchange. After three years the first payment had been made on a promise to some pastors.

Imagine This

As a Christian student in Iran, you are required every day to recite the Muslim Creed at school. You know that if you don't say the Creed, you will likely be suspended. You notice that several of your Christian friends recite the Creed without giving it a thought. But you know that saying the Creed would mean you are participating in a Muslim practice. Do you say it but not mean it? Or do you refuse to recite the Creed, risking punishment from the school?

What Would You Do?

twenty

The Awakening Dragon

Boldly and without hindrance he preached
the kingdom of God and taught about
the Lord Jesus Christ.

Acts 28:31

Below my plane lay the great rock called Hong Kong, capital of
the British crown colony that sits like a fragile butterfly on the tail
of the not-so-sleepy dragon that is Communist China. Beyond it
was the China mainland stretching off as far as eyes could see.

For a fraction of a second I was startled not to see a high wall
running around it. That was how Red China looked in my mind:
shut off, closed, unassailable. Even when I was learning to dis-
tinguish between Outer Circle and Inner Circle countries in Communist Europe, I had never even attempted to give China a rank.
To me it was in a sealed world by itself, more inaccessible to a
Christian outreach than the most totalitarian European regime.

And then one day in Moscow I took a seat in a bus next to a
Chinese man. There were hundreds of Chinese in Moscow in those

days, but this man wore a cross in his lapel. We got to talking, in English, and he told me that he was the secretary of the Shanghai YMCA. I was astonished. The "Y" still open in Shanghai? Yes, he assured me, open and busy: he gave me his card and invited me to visit him.

And from that day on, a hope-beyond-hope began to grow within me of someday ministering to the isolated Christians of China.

But there were so many questions to answer before we could begin. How many Christians were there in China anyhow? I knew that the vast majority of the population never had been Christian. On the other hand, China had probably been the scene of more missionary effort than any other country. What had become of the devotion of so many men and women? Were the congregations they had founded still functioning? Were they suffering persecution? Were they meeting in secret? If they still existed, were they as hungry for Bibles as the churches in Eastern Europe?

These were the questions we needed answers to. And so when, in 1965, a speaking tour took me to California, I decided just to keep going: to visit Taiwan to talk with people who knew China, and then to try to get onto the mainland itself. I was counting on my Dutch passport: Dutchmen under some circumstances were still permitted to travel behind that stronger-than-iron curtain.

But now, even on the plane to Hong Kong, I discovered that I had started out all wrong. The man next to me, a Hong Kong banker, looked at me oddly when I told him I was bound for China. "Didn't you get aboard at Taiwan?" he said.

"Yes, I spent ten days there."

"Let me see your passport." He flipped through the pages looking for the Taiwan stamp but stopped short at the American visa. "United States!" he said.

"Yes. I've just come from there."

"Man, you'll never get into Red China with that passport."

Now usually I enjoy it when people tell me a missionary adventure is impossible, because this allows me to experience God's way of dealing with impossibilities. But no sooner had I checked in at the Hong Kong "Y" than I began to hear more discouraging facts.

All of Hong Kong, it seemed, was filled with missionaries who had tried and failed to get into mainland China. They included doctors and teachers with long records of service to the people. Today none of it counted: the fact that they had been accredited under the pre-Communist regime automatically barred them from the country.

When I'd heard these things for the one hundredth time, my confidence wavered. Maybe I could get a new passport with none of my earlier trips stamped in it.

I took the ferry from Kowloon, where the Hong Kong "Y" is located, across to the main part of the city on its rock island and went to the Dutch consulate. I found the consul behind a screen of thick pungent smoke, puffing at a long-stemmed clay pipe, which made me ache for Holland. When I told him I wanted to go to the China mainland, he took the pipe from his mouth and began to smile. When I went on to explain that I was a missionary, his smile broadened. When I told him frankly that I wanted to look for Christians there and explore the possibilities of getting Bibles to them, he actually began to laugh.

"May I see your passport?" he said. He ruffled through the pages, shaking his head. "Impossible," he said, stabbing the damaging visas with the stem of the pipe.

"Sir," I said, "that's why I'm here. I want a new passport."

"Impossible," he said again. The consulate in Hong Kong had no authority to issue passports. If he were to send my request to Indonesia, he'd have to show legal cause, and there was none. He sent a cloud of smoke spiraling to the ceiling. And I knew the interview was over.

At first I was disappointed with the failure of my stratagem; then suddenly I knew I was glad. Now there was no possibility of my getting into China by my own cleverness. I believed that the desire to go to China had come from God: I would leave the means to Him too. The next morning I would simply go to the Chinese consulate and apply for a visa, knowing that if God really wanted me to go, the necessary papers would be forthcoming.

First, though, I had some homework to do. I thought of Joshua preparing to invade the land of the Canaanites, and how he had sent spies ahead to scout out the land. Perhaps this is what I must

Bangladesh   A Traveler's Story

FAITH THAT CANNOT BE BOUGHT

Adil became a Christian about four years ago. One day a Christian he met told him that Jesus is the Spirit of God. Adil did not contradict what the Christian said, but as soon as he got home, he began to search the Bible he owned.

As soon as the village people learned of his conversion to Christianity, they denounced him. In their anger they broke his teeth and inflicted bodily harm on him. The local government leaders confronted him and asked, "Are you now a Christian or still a Muslim?"

He replied, "I don't know. All I know is that I follow Jesus."

The Muslim village leaders accused him of being a Christian only because of money. He was publicly humiliated when they offered him 4,000 taka [approximately $70] to renounce his faith in Jesus and return to Islam. Without fear, he responded to them, "I still will not give up my faith in Jesus."

To this day he is still hounded by the people and the Muslim leaders in the community where he lives. He is only able to move about in the dark.

do: spy out the land of Chinese officialdom. It was dark now—stores and offices were shut—but I set out in search of the Chinese "travel agency," as the tourism department of that government was called.

As I had expected, it was closed. On a large pillar outside the door, a sign announced in English: "Chinese Travel Service." On the dark sidewalk in front of the barred door, I began to pray the Prayer of Victory, binding any force that could prevent me from going where God willed, proclaiming the fact that Christ had been victorious once for all over any power opposed to the rule of God. Back and forth in front of the building I walked. I prayed for two hours there in the dark.

The next morning I was back again. This time the door was open. At the top of a flight of stairs sat a Chinese soldier. Behind him was a large room jammed with people. I chose a line, and while waiting, I prayed for the officials and clerks on the other side of the counter, praying that God was opening channels with which to reach these citizens of China.

And then it was my turn. I stepped forward, and the man in the pale blue "people's uniform" looked up at me inquiringly.

"Sir," I said in English, "I want to make application for a visa to China."

The man took his eyes off mine and began stamping papers. "Have you ever been to the United States or to Taiwan?" he asked.

"Yes, sir. I've just come from Taiwan, and before that I was in California."

"Then," he said with a smile, "you cannot possibly go to China, because these countries are our enemies."

"But," I said, smiling back at him, "they are not my enemies, for I have no enemies. Will you give me the forms?"

We held each other's eye. I do not know what the other man was doing, but I was praying. He looked at me steadily, without expression, for a long time. Then at last his gaze broke. "It will achieve nothing," he said with a shrug. But he handed me the application forms.

When I had filled them out, he told me that I could not have my answer before three days. The application, with the incriminating passport, would have to travel up to Canton.

That night I had dinner with an old China missionary. "They said I might hear after three days!" I told him jubilantly.

My host threw back his head and roared. "That just shows how little you know the oriental mind!" he said. "They always tell you 'three days.' Three days is Chinese for never."

Resolutely I closed my ears to his merriment. For those three days I fasted and prayed almost continually. I did more than this. I went to the local Bible shop and purchased supplies of Chinese Scripture to take with me behind the Bamboo Curtain. I made arrangements to store some of my clothes, since I would have so little room in a suitcase filled mostly with Bibles. And I waited.

On the third day I returned to my room at the "Y" to find a note telling me to telephone the Chinese travel agency. Instead of returning the call, I went directly to the office. I tried to read the face of the Chinese official as he looked up and saw me. But he was as inscrutable as his countrymen's reputation. At last I reached the counter. Without a word, he handed me my passport; attached to it was a piece of paper, stamped with the all-important visa for travel in his country.

At eight o'clock the next morning I was aboard a train pulling out of Tsim Sha Tsui station. To get to the border required a two-hour train trip across the British Crown Colony to the little town of Lo Wu. There, over a railroad bridge across a small stream, was the entrance to the land of the awakening dragon.

On the British side were only a small restaurant and the station-and-customs office. I grew tired of waiting and strolled outside where a British soldier was on duty at the bridge. A freight train was rattling across, bound for Hong Kong, carrying live pigs and chickens and produce for the millions in the British city. The soldier told me that the place was known locally as the Bridge of Weeping. Each day it was necessary to round up refugees who had sneaked across the stream and herd them back over the bridge. He told me how they wept and pleaded and clung to the superstructure of the bridge, not wanting to return.

"Lord," I prayed silently, "some day let there be no more bridges of weeping. Bring the day soon when all mankind will belong to the one kingdom of Your love."

My job now was to do some scouting for that kingdom. At long last the British customs officer told us we could cross the bridge. We went single file, stepping cautiously on the cross ties. There were half a dozen of us Europeans in the group; the others were mostly businessmen from England, France and Canada. At the halfway point the shade of green in which the girders were painted changed. We were in Communist China.

On this side of the border was a much larger complex of buildings, neat and dull, the monotony broken by a profusion of geraniums planted everywhere. The customs inspector was a girl, very young, very trim. With the same polite smile the official in the travel agency had given me, she said, "Will you please open your valise?"

My heart beat faster. Inside, without any effort to hide them, I had put the supply of Chinese Bibles with which I would test

Diary of a Smuggler

CUBA

Profound. This is probably the only word I can think of in my limited vocabulary to describe the experience I had as a Bible courier. In actuality, there are no words to describe it.

Cuba is a nation that frowns upon Bibles being brought into the country. We were ready to have all of our material confiscated at customs if we were stopped and searched. The key was to get in and around the customs official without being stopped by a random check. When my bags came off the plane, a Cuban "red-cap" grabbed them, and I said thank you, and he proceeded to usher me and my bags over to a customs table, which I wasn't so thankful for. The whole night before, I had been in spiritual warfare about getting stopped at customs; worst-case scenarios kept cropping up. So I was now entering my worst fear for this trip. The customs official handed me a declaration form and asked me to fill it out. I figured, this isn't so bad. After he reviewed my form, he then asked me to pick up one of my bags, pointed to the one and opened it up. As I unzipped it, Bibles began to tumble out all over the table. I heard the inspector let out a soft groan, which didn't do much to calm me down. He picked one up, thumbed through it, and called over his superior.

Continued

China's reaction to the presence of a missionary. How was this young official going to react?

I raised the lid to my suitcase, revealing the stacks of Bibles. And as I did, I had my first puzzling experience with the Chinese Communists.

The customs officer did not touch a thing in my suitcase. She looked at the Bibles for a moment, then raised her eyes: "Thank you, sir," she said, with the ever-present smile. "Are you carrying a watch? Do you have a camera?"

No reaction at all to what she had seen in the suitcase. She was twenty, perhaps twenty-five years old. Was it possible that she had never seen a Bible? That she had no idea what it was . . . ?

The train for Canton was waiting for us. The ancient passenger car was spotlessly clean, fresh flowers filled little vases between the seats, a stewardess served us hot tea. As the train started I glanced at my watch: we were on schedule to the minute. The stewardess, after searching a moment for the English words, beamed at me.

"*Our* train on time," she said.

It was my first encounter with the "our" of modern China. Everywhere I heard about "our" train, "our" revolution, "our" first Chinese-made automobile. And in the railroad station in Canton I got a glimpse of how such national sentiment is created and maintained. Everywhere were racks of reading matter, beautifully printed and illustrated and free. It was the same at the hotel where I stayed: stack upon stack of literature awaited me in the lobby, the dining room, every stair landing. Those in the hotel were in European languages—German, English, French—and obviously directed at the traveler. But elsewhere the literature was for home consumption. Every magazine, newspaper, movie, and play carried a twofold message. Be grateful for the Revolution. Hate America.

One night I went to a theater where a troupe of child acrobats was performing. The comedian was a Puck-like little boy who was always trying to light a firecracker. Each time, just as the fuse was about to ignite the powder, the hero of the play would put it out. With each episode the firecracker got larger until it had become an atomic bomb, draped with a huge American flag. Again at the last moment the hero saved the day and destroyed the bomb. At this, the audience went wild, leaping from their seats in a frenzy of glee and patriotism.

The other theme of all propaganda—enthusiasm for the revolution—was equally relentless and, in its own way, just as deadening. During my stay in Canton I visited an old people's home. By European standards it was extremely primitive, but the men and women there seemed content enough: some weaving, some cleaning up the compound, all engaged in some form of productive work.

The leader of the community, an old woman in her eighties, greeted me through an interpreter and made a little speech. The

Diary of a Smuggler

CUBA

Continued

The superior thumbed through the Bible and asked me what these were. I responded, "Gifts." He asked me who I was. I said I was a Christian. He asked if I was part of an organization. I said yes, Pentecostal. He said "No, no," did anyone send me into Cuba to distribute these materials. I said yes, the Spirit of God. I was waiting for them to start loading up a box with the Bibles and cart them off when there was a commotion over at another table that required the attention of the superior. The inspector had a Bible in his hand, and he leaned back in thought. I truly believe the Spirit of God touched this man, because he laid down the Bible into my opened suitcase and welcomed me to Cuba.

In a rather obvious state of confusion, I collected all the Bibles that had tumbled out, loaded them into the suitcase, zipped it up and headed out of the building. I then reached across the table, shook his hand and told him thank you. He gave me a huge smile, one of many I was to receive while in Cuba.

So this was the beginning of the most rewarding experience of my life. As we made our drops throughout the week, I was introduced to some of the warmest people I have ever known. The Christian pastors and families are some of the most courageous people I have ever met. When I went down there, I thought I had faith in the Lord. But in Cuba there are people who live by a faith that is in action.

theme seemed to be how happy and useful old people felt since the revolution. "Before liberation," she said, old people were left to die in the fields. "After liberation," though, things had been wonderful.

The rest of the old folks scarcely glanced up as their leader talked. Every time she spoke the words "after liberation," however, it was as if a button had been pushed. Each aged face became animated. Each pair of hands began to clap. And then as the leader continued, they settled back again to the reveries of old age.

But if the enthusiasm of the elderly seemed less than spontaneous, it was not so with young people. My youthful interpreter in Shanghai a week later clearly had an evangelist's fervor. "Before," Shanghai had been noted for its prostitution; "After," the prostitutes were taken to training camps where they had learned useful skills. "Before," China had had one of the lowest literacy rates in the world; "After," it had achieved one of the highest. On and on it went.

This kind of conversation made me all the more eager to visit a commune. After all, guides were government employees, screened and indoctrinated for their jobs. Surely the average worker was not so starry-eyed about the wonderful world of After.

In all, during my stay in China, I was able to visit six communes. The first numbered more than ten thousand people. And it was here that I had my first chance to visit informally in a Chinese home.

I chose the home myself—a small, thatch-roofed house on a side street—and was allowed to drop in unannounced. An old man answered our knock. He and his wife showed us around with crackling laughs and ever-present smiles. Pride was obvious. They pointed several times to their grain store, a cylindrical bin made of bamboo and filled with wheat. I asked through the interpreter if mice were not a problem. The old man laughed.

"We have mice," he said, "but now we do not mind because there is enough for us and them too. It wasn't like that Before."

Before. My great disadvantage, of course, was that I had no mental picture of Before. I was a rank newcomer to this complex land, with no real points of comparison. At another commune, for example, I was shown through a hospital that, had it been in Holland, would have been the last place in the country we would have shown to visitors. The operating room had neither overhead lighting nor sterilizing pan, the pharmacy was a row of empty shelves, and in some of the wards the beds not only lacked sheets but mattresses as well. And yet on a tour clearly intended to impress me, I was being shown this place, as though in their own minds it represented an advance.

Did this give me a glimpse of Before?

My chief objective in Shanghai was to find again the YMCA secretary with whom I had ridden the bus in Moscow. On inquiring at the hotel, I learned to my delight that the "Y" was still open. When I got to the building, though, my delight faded: inside I saw mostly old ladies playing board games. This center was neither for the Young, nor for Men, nor did it seem very Christian. About all that was left of this YMCA was an Association.

Through my interpreter I asked for my friend. To my surprise, no one had heard of him. "Would you mind checking?" I said. The receptionist disappeared for a while and came back with the news that no one was familiar with the name. "How can that be!" I insisted. "This man was your secretary here. Surely someone will recognize his name. Would you mind asking just once more?"

This time the receptionist stayed away for a long while. When she came back she was smiling. "I'm sorry," she said, and then she used a phrase I was to hear often in China when I was looking for a particular person. "Your friend is not here. He is out of town."

And that was all I could discover. I was left to imagine why this Christian leader had simply vanished. "Permanently" out of town was my guess. How many Christians in China today were permanently out of town?

Back in Moscow the secretary had told me that there was a Bible shop still open in Shanghai. Sure enough I found it: a small store on an out-of-the-way street, but open for business and well stocked with all sizes of Bibles. Anyone in Shanghai could buy the books—books that had to be smuggled into so much of Eastern Europe!

I was welcomed in English by the manager, who showed me around the store with pride. On the wall hung a print of Christ surrounded by little children—blond and blue-eyed, every one of them.

I picked up a Bible from a table. To my surprise, I read in English that the book had been printed in Shanghai.

"Printed here?" I said. "Not in Hong Kong?"

The manager drew himself up proudly. "In China," he said, "we make everything ourselves."

Only when I asked him how much business he did, did his face fall a little. I had been in the store an hour, and not a single other person had been in.

"Not many customer," he said sadly.

How many Bibles did he sell in a month?

"Not many."

Not many Bibles. Not many customers. The government allowed this funny little shop to sell its antiques because it represented no danger. No one cared.

I thought back over my experiences trying to hand out Bibles in China. I had offered the first one to my interpreter in Canton. She handed it back: she had no time for reading. Thinking perhaps it was dangerous to be seen accepting a Bible, I had tried next leaving several behind me "accidentally" in hotel rooms as I checked out. I never succeeded. Always before I got off the floor, the chambermaid would run after me, Bible in hand, "Please, belong you?"

In desperation I had tried giving Bibles away on the street. My guides made no objection. They seemed in fact to feel sorry for me when person after person stopped to see what I was offering, then handed the book back to me.

And now this store. "Not many customer." Strangely enough I left that wide open, well-stocked Bible shop more discouraged than at any time since I had been in China. Persecution is an enemy the Church has met and mastered many times. Indifference could prove to be a far more dangerous foe.

I still had one hope. Everywhere people assured me that theological seminaries were still open. At first this seemed unbelievably good news. But after visiting one I was not so sure.

The school I visited was just outside Nanking. I spent some time with the president and one of the professors in an ideal situation: both spoke English. Here, I thought, was a chance to visit Christians free from the critical eye of an interpreter.

However, once we were alone we sat in embarrassed silence, broken only by the noisy sipping of tea. When we had reached the bottom of our cups and still no one had spoken, I decided to begin by explaining that I was a missionary. But at the word "missionary" both men looked as shocked as if I had said a dirty word within those sacred walls.

"The missionaries we knew," said the president, "were spies."

He turned to the professor and said something to him in Chinese. The professor left the room and scurried back a minute later carrying a huge book, opened to a well-marked page of correspondence between a missionary and some government officials regarding natural resources, food supplies, popular discontent.

Over the next quarter-hour this little professor in his blue uniform hustled back and forth from the library, each time bringing a new volume always opened to an underlined passage. All the books were from well-known Western publishing houses. And it did appear, indeed, that some missionaries had regularly supplied their embassies with information. We in the West had never seen a conflict between loyalty to Christ and loyalty to homeland. Had we left a confused witness behind us for that reason?

Whatever the truth, my visit to the Nanking seminary was to be a purely political affair. The president was a member of the local parliament and deeply involved in the international Communist movement. Anti-American posters were plastered on walls—with the inevitable Chinese chasing the inevitable American who was carrying the inevitable atomic bomb.

About the Christianity taught in this seminary, I learned nothing. Whatever form it takes, one thing is sure: it is dressed in the military anti-Western garb that all education in China wears today.

How much can you learn about a country in a single superficial visit hampered by a language barrier and by interpreters who, you know, want you to see only the best? Impressions, perhaps, are all you take away. Many of the impressions were positive. The cleanliness. The absence of beggars and rickshaw pullers. The honesty. Some of the impressions were sad. The enormous fully staffed dining rooms where I would be the only customer. The empty streets where my taxi would be the only motor vehicle in sight and the traffic police would hold up pedestrians blocks ahead in preparation for the rare approach of an automobile.

And some were terrifying. I remember the morning when I was leaving Nanking on the early flight. I was dressing in my hotel room when I heard shouts from the street. I ran to the window. In the square below, hundreds of men, women, and children were executing a tight-rank military drill. At this hour, before factories and schools opened, the entire population turned out to march, to shout, to lunge, and to perform a whole series of high-precision maneuvers.

My taxi drove me through the midst of the exercises. As we reached the corner a command was given to "Freeze!"—a maneuver in which each person froze in the position he had happened to be in, legs in mid-stride, arms outstretched. All those arms seemed stretched at me, the fingers pointing, the eyes accusing.

In the airplane I tried to shake off the impression. But the eyes had followed me. Was I guilty, along with my fellows of the West, for the accusing looks? What kind of representatives of Christ had we been? If our treatment of the Chinese had made them anti-Western, that was tragic—but if it had made them anti-God, that was the everlasting loss. I kept remembering the words of a commune leader when I asked if I might see his church.

"In the communes, sir," he had said proudly, "you will find no churches. You see, religion is for the helpless. Here in China we are not helpless any more."

It was eight o'clock on a Sunday morning, and I sat on the bed in my hotel room in Peking, waiting. An hour earlier I had told the guide, "Today I would like to go to church."

"Church!" the guide said. He promised to try, but he assured me there were very few churches—especially Protestant churches—still open in Peking. Half an hour went by. If he did not come soon, the time for the morning service—nine o'clock—would have passed. But just before nine he returned, his usually solemn face aglow.

"Sir!" he said, as if he had discovered something extremely quaint and rare for me. "I have *found* your church. Come with me."

The little church was unkempt and uninviting, and it did not surprise me that my guide refused to go inside. So I walked alone through the rusted iron gate and found myself in a large bare room as dull to the eye as the outside had been. In the whole room there were only two touches of color: one woman wore a red cardigan, and beside the pulpit stood a red Chinese flag.

I sat down in the back just as a granny tottered over to a little, out-of-tune piano and started to play. The melody was a nineteenth-century English hymn, whose mood and message were in no way appropriate for China. I counted fifty-six of us in the congregation—and I believe I was the only one under the age of sixty. An ancient man with a thin beard and vague, watery eyes stood up and began to preach. Most of his congregation went to sleep.

AROUND THE GLOBE
Uzbekistan

Population: 24.3 million
Location/Size: Central Asia
172,742 sq. miles
Major Religions: Islam
Level of Persecution: Harassment, growing

There is no evidence of any formal state-sponsored persecution of Christians in Uzbekistan. Although the government allows the Church some freedoms, only registered churches are allowed to function because the government does not permit any independent forms of religion. All forms of outreach are generally forbidden, and pastors are often put under surveillance and harassed.

The Church in Uzbekistan is declining, due largely to a wave of emigration. The present decline will possibly stabilize in the year 2025, with many Christians being secret believers.

My heart went out to these poor old men and women, holding on to the slim thread of the faith that had been brought to them by missionaries so long ago. But what chance did the Gospel have when it was believed only by the old? What chance did it have when it was associated at every turn with yesterday's empires? I was glad my guide had stayed outside. I had been trying to convince him that Christianity was a great adventure. But this? As I joined him outdoors after the service, I found myself thinking that if this were a fair example of Chinese Christianity, then the government would have an easy job of snuffing it out. All it needed was one little poof.

So I left China deeply distressed. I found one ray of hope in the very disregard with which the government held the Scriptures. They apparently made no effort to prevent them from being brought into the country, sold, and even printed there. Clearly they underestimated the Bible, and this might be God's opportunity. I knew from personal experience how powerful a tool the Bible could be in the hands of the Holy Spirit. Hadn't I myself been converted simply by reading this book?

But in addition, the Holy Spirit needed men in China. Dedicated, impassioned, visionary men. And even a superficial visit had told me that these men, in the second half of the twentieth century, could not be Westerners. To minister to the Chinese today, God needed Chinese hands and voices.

And so, back in Holland, a new prayer was added to the ones that Corrie and Hans and Rolf and Elena and I said daily for our work: that from somewhere Chinese Christians would come to join us, to do in their fatherland the work of encouragement and caring that history had closed to us.

Imagine
This

After a year of hard work, you are able to purchase your first guitar. You decide to bring it with you on your summer mission trip to Chiapas. After teaching several church members to play and igniting a fire in their church through music, it is time for you to return home. A church leader asks you to give him your guitar, so he can continue to lead music in the church.

What Would You Do?

twenty-one

Twelve Apostles of Hope

Therefore we do not lose heart. Though outwardly we are wasting away, yet inwardly we are being renewed day by day. For our light and momentary troubles are achieving for us an eternal glory that far outweighs them all.

2 Corinthians 4:16—17

Not only for China but also for everywhere it was clear that we needed more team members. It would do little good to appear in a country with protestations of love and concern and never be heard from again. It was our aim to revisit each Communist land at least once a year and ideally far more often. Ideally, too, we would go in pairs, having found that this was so much better than a single ministry. But where were we to find enough partners to make this schedule possible?

It wasn't that we couldn't find volunteers—almost every time one of us spoke someone offered himself for our work. The problem was to know whether or not these were the people God was sending us. In an effort to weed out the novelty-seekers and the merely curious I often said, "As soon as your own ministry of encouragement is started behind the Curtain, get in touch with us and let's see if we can work together."

And once this actually happened. One day I received a letter from a young Dutchman named Marcus. "I wonder if you remember the speech you gave to Swansea Bible College in Wales," he wrote. "You said, 'When you start working behind the Iron Curtain, we can talk about working together.' Well here I am. So let's have that talk." The letter was postmarked Yugoslavia.

"Look at this!" I said to Corrie. She read the letter too. Could it be that this man was supposed to join us? If he got in touch with us again, we decided, we should take his suggestion seriously.

And several months later we did hear from Marcus again. He was back in Yugoslavia on a second trip. When he wrote a third time from Yugoslavia, he said that he had fulfilled the conditions. Now he wanted to see us.

One day Joppie ran into the study where I was struggling with the perpetual problem of correspondence.

"Marcus is here, Papa."

I leaped up from my desk and ran downstairs. I liked Marcus the moment I saw him. Over coffee, he told us about his experiences in Yugoslavia. He had gone in with a supply of literature, which he had put on store counters or on park benches. Then he stood nearby while people came up and helped themselves. It was pretty tame evangelism, he admitted, but he was learning.

"I think I'll let you take a trip with Rolf," I said. "He'll introduce you to some pastors and church members. Get them to talking, Marcus. Then come back and tell me whether you still want to work with us."

For three weeks Rolf and Marcus traveled around Yugoslavia and Bulgaria. When they returned, I did not need to ask Marcus whether or not he wanted to be part of this ministry. I could see the answer in his face.

"I had no idea," was all he said.

And so Marcus joined our little band.

But with his arrival it seemed as though the work almost exploded, so fast was it expanding, and soon all of us were traveling more than ever.

Two months after Marcus joined us, Hans and I left Europe to visit the only Communist country in the New World. We were working in Czechoslovakia when the visas for Cuba came through, and we flew directly from there. It was Hans's first trip to America, and except for the brief speaking tour of the United States, mine too. What a contrast to cold gray Prague! In Havana the warm sun shone from white buildings and sparkled on the waves below the Malecon. The people were happy and well dressed. On the bus trip from the airport total strangers were singing together after half a dozen blocks.

Hans went directly to Oriente Province in the east of the island while I stayed in and around the capital. My hotel was the Havana Libre, the former Hilton. I was not surprised when the usual order came to report to police headquarters. Nor was I surprised at the long wait in an outer office: bureaucratic countries are the same in the sun and out of it.

The police officer who finally saw me fairly bristled with suspicion. "How are you here?" he asked in very halting English.

"I've come to preach the Gospel," I said. He was holding my passport showing my visits to Russia, the United States, and other nations. Clearly he suspected a more complicated motive. He asked me a lot more questions, took many notes, and finally let me return to the hotel. There were four other days of interrogation, but meanwhile, as I had told him, I began to preach. The church where I held my meetings was a relatively large one, an attractive building with an organ, a pastor, and exactly two members in its official congregation. Once it had had a large membership, but that was before the antireligious campaign began: the mobs outside, the shouting and blaring of loudspeakers during services, the tearing up of the street pavement, the infiltrating police.

Yet, thirty-five Cubans came to the church to hear me the first night. On the second night, the thirty-five returned; on the third and fourth nights sixty came, and then over a hundred. Undoubtedly some of these "believers" were policemen, but I was glad to have them hear me. I was careful to concentrate on the Gospel and stay away from politics. But within these limits, which are the same for any police state, I was struck with the freedoms—of assembly, of travel, of self-expression—that exist in Cuba as compared with the older Communist countries.

During the following weeks I traveled in the area immediately surrounding Havana, speaking in various churches many times a day to ever increasing numbers of people—sometimes as many as six hundred together. I spoke in English, for which I never had trouble finding an interpreter. Hans and I kept in touch regularly by telephone; he reported that police control was tighter, people more fearful in Oriente, where the United States military base is, than in Havana.

Both Hans and I learned to announce first thing that we were Dutch. This made a difference. The hate-U.S. campaign is a total offensive in Cuba, and emotions, even in the churches, are confused. The government has made much of the fact that most Protestant churches in Cuba were originally U.S. missions.

However, all churches, Catholic as well as Protestant, have suffered alike under the new regime, and the group that has suffered most is the clergy. Priests and ministers are classed as nonproductive members of society. They are given no food or clothing coupons and are frequently forced into labor battalions made up of men deemed unsuitable for service in the army. Drug addicts, homosexuals, convicts, and clerics are all lumped together and sent into the fields to cut sugar cane.

And yet most of these brave men stay on at their posts. The churches remain open; spiritual hunger is enormous. Wherever Hans or I spoke, word would circulate and people would gather, often poking their heads in at windows and doors to listen, at first, from outside. Sometimes it seemed wise not to use a church building at all. I remember sitting one afternoon on a cliff high over an ocean bay talking with a group of about fifty university students, while a jeep filled with armed soldiers drove back and forth on the road behind us.

Wherever we went, people asked questions about arrests and imprisonment in the Communist countries we had visited. They asked questions, too, that amazed us because of the knowledge they showed of the current world of religion: What about Dave Wilkerson's Teen Center in New York? Where was Billy Graham now? What was this madness about the "death of God"? That was how we learned that religious publications—even from the United States—were still coming into the country through normal postal channels.

Several months before our arrival, Castro announced his plan to permit people to leave the country. Hundreds of thousands of people put their names on the list. However, only two planes flew out of Cuba each day. It would take ten years before even the 900,000 people on the original list could be flown out. Meanwhile, those who waited lost their jobs, their houses, and property. Yet 190 a day did leave, and others believed firmly that their turn would soon be coming. It was among these people who wanted to leave Cuba that we felt our trip had the greatest effect.

As we had in Eastern Europe, we urged our listeners to reconsider the role of a Christian when his country is in trouble. Is it to run, or is it to stand? Life in Cuba in 1965 was not easy. But perhaps God had had His reasons for putting them in this place at this time. Perhaps they were to be His arms and legs and His healing hands in this situation, without whom He would have no representative in this land.

One evening when I had said something like this, a stout, well-dressed man with a heavy black moustache stood up in the congregation. "I am a Methodist minister," he told the group. "For the last two years I have worked as a barber. But God has spoken to me this evening. I am going to return to the ministry. I am a shepherd who has left his sheep, but I am going back to them."

There was pandemonium. Everyone in the church had to shake his hand. I heard shouts of joy, cries of *"Gracias, Pastor!"*

We saw many such decisions. One couple had their long-awaited airline tickets for two weeks from the night we met them. They decided to turn them back. "From now on," they told us, "Cuba is our mission field."

And as we boarded our return plane in Havana, Hans and I knew that Cuba was ours as well. Here was a country wide open to Bibles,

Bangladesh   A Traveler's Story

NEHRU

When Nehru came to know the Lord and discovered a fresh beginning for his life, he thought that his wife would be happy with him and share this joy of a new-found faith. He was wrong. His wife quickly shared the "bad" news with his parents and brothers, all of whom lived with them under one roof. One day, after worshipping in a nearby church, Nehru arrived home only to find out that his brothers were all waiting for him. They severely beat him. He was warned that he must renounce his faith, or else he would receive the same heavy beating again. He refused. He decided to leave home, and he took shelter in a church. After a few days his family fetched him and convinced him to return home on certain conditions: no church, no Bible, no prayer. He decided to practice his faith secretly. He would read his Bible at night when everyone was asleep. He prayed when everyone had closed their eyes. In secret, he praised his God. But one night, his wife, with whom he shared the room, woke up and saw him praying. She immediately called her brother-in-law to complain that her husband had broken his promise. She even said that he was disturbing her sleep when he prayed. His brother became incensed and beat him severely again. Nehru realized that it would never work to be a Christian in secret. "I would rather leave my family and die, rather than live and deny my faith," Nehru said. The next morning, he left home for good.

to religious books, and to literature of all kinds, and to visitors from all but a few countries. A country where the least spark of encouragement dropped into the generous and emotional Latin heart lit bonfires of love and consecration and self-sacrifice in response.

It was as well the Cuban trip came when it did, for the following year we entered at last the most tightly controlled Communist country of them all. It was so difficult to get into, and to achieve anything once in, that we needed every bit of optimism we could muster not to give it up altogether. I'm speaking of course of tiny Albania.

I was far away in Siberia when our group at last got its chance to enter this country. A French tourist agency scored a history-making first by arranging a two-week Albanian tour. Rolf and Marcus joined the tour as "teachers" from Holland.

They carried no Bibles with them, for we had discovered years before that no Albanian Bible existed. Worse, there was no Albanian language in which to print a Bible. In this little country of one and one-half million souls, at least three mutually incomprehensible dialects were spoken: Skchip, Gheg, and Tosk. The only Bibles in the country were in Latin, in Roman Catholic churches, and in Greek, in Orthodox churches. The rest of the country was Muslim.

The American Bible Society wrote that they had a New Testament in Skchip, translated in 1824, in their library, but that no other copy seemed to exist. It was only since the revolution that any progress had been made toward developing a unified Albanian language, and we could hardly hope this included a new Bible.

However, Rolf and Marcus did carry tracts and portions of Scripture with them in all three Albanian languages. And when the customs officials at the airport did not even open their suitcases, they felt that they had been extremely lucky. There was a strict law in Albania forbidding the importation of any printed matter whatsoever, no matter how brief and how nonpolitical, on the grounds that it constituted "propaganda." Marcus and Rolf had packed their literature out of habit as much as anything, fully expecting to see it confiscated at the border. And so when they checked into their hotel in Tirana with all of it untouched, they felt very encouraged.

They had reckoned without the well-trained and obedient Albanians. For the entire two-week trip they tried to give away those portions of Scriptures. The universal reaction of the people was to clasp both hands behind their backs. Not only would they not accept the tracts, they wouldn't even touch them. Even a Catholic bishop, to whom Rolf tried to give a St. John's gospel in Gheg, turned and stalked away down the aisle of his cathedral as though he'd been offered poison.

At last in desperation they left a pile of tracts on a window sill in a street of offices, thinking perhaps passersby would pick them up when no one was looking. To their horror, a full day later and ninety kilometers further along on their tour, two policemen arrived where the group was having lunch and demanded to know who had left those tracts on that street. The detective work did not seem quite so uncanny when they realized that theirs was the only group of foreigners anywhere in the country. To prevent the whole tour's being expelled, Marcus and Rolf had to confess what they had done and swear to stop all such "political" activity. Not one of the tracts they had left on the street had been taken.

And so, from the standpoint of any future literature work in Albania, the trip was extremely discouraging. As to other aspects of the country, the two came back with a mixture of emotions. The Albanians themselves were among the warmest, most affectionate people they had ever observed—as far as their relationships with one another went. The same affection was lavished on the country's leader, Enver Hodscha. For Hodscha was accomplishing things, there was no doubt about that. This small nation, from time immemorial the battleground of other countries' quarrels, dominated now by Turkey, now by Italy, had—probably for the first time in its history—a government concerned with Albania's own interests.

But if the language of the land had been Chinese, Rolf and Marcus could not have felt more frustrated in their attempt to establish any kind of real contact with the people. Marcus spoke a little Italian and had hoped, occasionally, to have a chat with an Italian-speaking Albanian, free of the ever-present filter of the government translator. But even when the situation appeared to be ideal, there was an almost total freeze-out of communication. It was a land where nobody knew anybody, nobody had any facts, nobody remembered.

"Say, friend!" Marcus would greet a factory worker in a deserted corridor. "You been working here long?"

A smile and a shrug. "It's hard to say, signore."

"What kind of hours do you work?"

"Ah! It varies! Different every day."

"Well, ah—how many people work at the factory here?"

The smile broadens, the shrug is enormous. "Who can say? Who has counted?"

Marcus and Rolf felt there was a kind of voluntary obtuseness about it, a sort of censorship by mutual consent of all that concerned Albania against all inquisitiveness by foreigners.

The only time when the barrier went down a little was in con-versation with a few clergymen. And even here communication was a matter of delicate wording, when what was not said became more important than what was. One young Catholic priest in particular, they felt, was genuinely glad to see them, eager to hear about the West and to tell them about his own situation. His church had been Roman Catholic until the Mao hard-line forced it to break all ties outside the country. Now it called itself the National Catholic Church.

"And within the country?" Marcus asked. "Does the govern-ment leave you pretty much alone?"

"The government does not officially interfere with religion."

"You have religious freedom then?"

"By law, we do."

"Can you say what you like from your pulpit, for example?"

"The proper answer is yes."

And so it went, the long, tedious circumlocution that appar-ently said nothing and in fact told everything. It was from this young priest that they had heard news they could scarcely believe: in one of the Greek Orthodox churches there was said to be a Bible in the new Albanian language!

Marcus and Rolf immediately requested a visit to this church. The Orthodox priest greeted them and their guide graciously. Yes, there was a brand new translation of the Gospels on the high altar of the church. They would like to see it? But of course!

He led the way down the nave of the ancient basilica. Even from a distance they could see the Book on the altar, an enor-mous volume studded with jewels. Then all at once, four yards from the altar, the priest stopped—so abruptly that Rolf bumped against him. For several moments the four stood in silence, gazing at the treasure before them. When the priest turned to go, Rolf burst out, "But—I want to go closer! Can't I look at it? I mean, open it. See the pages."

As the guide translated, the priest's eyes widened in horror. Closer! But no unordained person ever stood closer than four yards to the Holy Scriptures!

Then, faltered Rolf, what was the sense of the new translation? Since the priests read Greek, what was this Bible used for?

China   A Traveler's Story

YOUNG CHRISTIAN DIES FROM POLICE BEATING

Twenty-one-year-old Li Choi from Henan province in central China died as the result of severe police beatings. Although the immediate cause of his death was a kidney ailment that flared up after police mistreatment and a harsh imprisonment, there is no question his death was the result of his witness for Christ, which makes him a martyr for the faith.

The story of Li's death illustrates how common police brutality is for many hundreds of Christians each year. As a house-church leader in Loyang shared, "At any one moment, there are probably well over a hundred Christians detained for their faith and that receive severe beatings from sadistic policemen. Many of them have permanent injuries as a result." The callous disregard among officials for Li's worsening condition, even to the point of refusing to arrange transport from prison to a hospital when he was about to die, almost defies belief.

Privately, a government source in Beijing described the death of Li as "a bad mistake." He said, "The government does not wish to create martyrs, because they make religion uncontrollable. Better to squeeze the Church than smash it—history has taught us that much at least."

Why, to be carried in solemn procession. To receive the homage and adulation of the people. What else would a Bible be used for? And think what solace the faithful must gain from knowing that God Himself had spoken in the new language of the great people of Albania.

And so Marcus and Rolf returned home having seen only the outside of a book, with the feeling indeed that they had seen only the outside of a people and a nation.

Meanwhile our work in the rest of Europe was gaining momentum: each month we were making more trips than the month before. With the new frequency, of course, the danger of being recognized also increased. We tried never to send the same two partners to the same country on consecutive trips. If two men had gone the first time, the next trip we tried to send a man and a woman.

And it was Rolf and Elena, on a trip to Russia in 1966, who had our closest call yet. With increased travel into Russia, smuggling of all sorts was also on the increase, and the guard at the border had been trebled. The papers were full of stories of arrests, fines, imprisonments. This time Rolf and Elena were carrying a particularly large cargo of Bibles in the Opel station wagon. Corrie and I prayed with them all night long before they left.

"Remember," I said, "that these people getting caught are depending on their own cleverness. Their motives are probably another disadvantage. Hatred and greed are heavy loads. Your motive, on the other hand, is love. And instead of priding yourselves on your cunning, you recognize how weak you are . . . so weak that you must depend totally upon the Spirit of God. . . ."

As Rolf recounted it to us later, our premonitions of trouble were correct. As they neared the border they saw not one but six security officers waiting for them. He told Elena to start praying that God would confuse these men's thinking. "And don't stop until they're through, Elena."

They pulled up to the stop line. *"Dah zvi dahnya!"* said Rolf heartily. He jumped out of the car and went around to hold the door for Elena.

In his hand one of the officers held a piece of paper. Rolf and Elena were chatting casually about what an unusual honeymoon they were having, visiting a number of East European countries.

"This is not the first time either," said the officer holding the paper. And then he read off one by one the cities Rolf and I had visited on our last trip to Russia.

This really shook Rolf.

The inspection seemed to last for hours. Two officers poked into every corner of the station wagon on the inside, while three others spent their time on the outside . . . the motor, the tires, the hubcaps. They rolled windows up and down to see if they stuck halfway. They thumped the paneling.

"Confuse their thinking. . . ."

And all the while, one officer took no part in the inspection but spent his entire time scrutinizing the faces of Rolf and Elena. It was a masterful game of psychological war. The officer was depending on that too-casual laugh, that darting glance, that bead of perspiration, to tell him what he needed to know.

"Let me give you a hand," said Rolf to one of the men as he was struggling to take the camping tent out of the wagon. He volunteered to open glove compartments, take out spare tires, lift the tops off air and oil filters. And all the while Elena was praying.

At the end of an interminable time the inspection stopped for lack of anywhere else to look. The man who had held the piece of paper walked up to Rolf. "You were in Russia just a few weeks ago. Tell me, why is it that you take these frequent trips into our country?"

Rolf was leaning into the rear of the wagon, folding up the tent. He gave the canvas a resounding slap. "Well," he said, "my friend and I had such a wonderful time in your country that I decided to bring my bride here too. But there's another reason. We have a love for the Russian people. A special Love."

The officer stared at Rolf as though he would like to climb inside his mind. But they had found nothing in the car. So he gave Rolf back his papers and with obvious reluctance signaled the barrier bar open.

Rolf and Elena could hardly believe what had happened. As they drove away from the border, they were laughing and crying both at once. For safe and secure in their wagon were hundreds of Bibles. The officers had been within millimeters of them. Certainly they were hidden no better than even an amateur adventurer could contrive. What was the difference?

Rolf and Elena knew.

One year after he joined us, Marcus too got married. So now we were seven: Corrie and I, Rolf and Elena, Marcus and Paula, and bachelor Hans. Then Klaas and Eduard and their wives came to be part of our work.

Klaas and Eduard were teachers in a public school in the south of Holland; Klaas taught French, and Eduard mathematics. They came with their wives to the house, one day, after hearing a talk about the work, and asked many questions. They did not tell us that they wanted to join us. They kept their motive a secret, wanting to give the Lord a chance to open the door for them in an unmistakable way.

And at precisely the same time I was going through the same thought pattern. Just as soon as I met these four, I "knew" that they belonged with us. Yet how could I ask them to leave their good positions to take up work that had no salary, that was dangerous, that meant long separations, unless I was absolutely certain the Lord Himself had caused our paths to cross? So I too mentioned my hope to no one but Corrie.

There we all were, then, praying for exactly the same thing yet not sharing our desires lest one influence the other.

God's answer came, several months later, in such an unexpected way that at first we almost missed the guidance. One day Klaas and Eduard each discovered a registered letter in his mail at school. The directors of the school informed them that unless they stopped using their French and Math classes for evangelization of students, and unless they agreed to stop holding prayer meetings for students in their homes in the evenings, they would be asked to leave at the end of the current term.

At first Klaas and Eduard were upset, and so was nearly every parent in the community, for their reputation was excellent among pupils and parents alike. When they wrote us the news I was upset too and was wondering how Christians might fight such a decision: their "evangelization" during school hours had consisted only of mentioning the evening meetings to be held away from school property. And then suddenly, I got it!

"Corrie!" I called, "Corrie, look at this great piece of news!"

Corrie came running from the kitchen. "What is it?"

"Klaas and Ed may lose their jobs!"

Corrie looked at me as if I were joking. And then she got it too. Of course! Couldn't this be God's way of saying that Klaas and Ed were intended to join us? That same week we drove down to the school and shared with the two couples our long prayers that they might be part of our team.

Klaas and Ed looked at each other and began to laugh. Then they told us that for months they had been asking God to show them whether or not they were intended to leave school to join our teams. Then, for me, came the best news of all.

"There is just one thing I would like to ask you," said Eduard.

"What's that, Ed?"

"What I should like most to do is help with the correspondence and administration." And then, talking rapidly as if to persuade me: "I am precise and accurate, and it's the kind of work I love to do. Do you think there is any chance that I might be able to help you in the office?"

I looked at Corrie. She was having a hard time keeping a straight face. The letters even at that moment were stacked so high that one of her coffee cups had been missing beneath them for weeks. And here, handed to us without our even asking for it, was God's solution.

"Why, Eduard," I said, "I think perhaps that could be arranged."

The twelfth member of our team is a strange fellow: he is made up of many different segments. As we gave talks to various groups in Europe and America, we were constantly being asked, "Could I go with you for just one trip?"

We began to pray about these requests. Was there some way, we wondered, to incorporate part-timers into our teams?

As an experiment we began occasionally to say yes and discovered one of the most dynamic and far-reaching applications of our work so far. The system gives us a chance to spend concentrated time with one individual, teaching him what we have learned about the life of faith. It gives us a new prayer partner, after the actual physical connection is broken. But the greatest and most unexpected benefit has been the spawning of groups similar to our own in other countries.

We believe that our particular group has grown as large as it ought to. We have stopped short of being an organization; we are an organism instead, a living and spontaneous association of individuals who know one another intimately, care for each other deeply, and feel the kind of respect one for another that makes rules and bylaws unnecessary. A group is the right size, I would guess, when each member can pray every day for every other member, individually and by name, interceding for his personal needs as well as for the success of a particular mission. But what is to prevent twenty, fifty, one hundred such groups from springing up wherever the call is heard—each obedient to its own particular genius, each working in its different way for the coming of the one Kingdom.

And this is a role the part-timers play. After an indoctrination trip the part-timers go home convinced that such work is possible. "I talked of nothing else for two months after I got back to school," one student from the Bible Training Institute founded by Dwight L. Moody up in Scotland wrote us after a trip with us behind the Iron Curtain. "Three other students are interested, and we're planning a trip to Yugoslavia this summer."

This is the teaching aspect of our work, the training of other missionaries. We insist on only two things from the men and women we accept as part-timers. We insist that each have a personal experience with Christ and learn to work in the full power of His Spirit. And we stress the importance of a positive ministry among the Communists. If a man seems to be harboring personal resentments against a certain government, or if he has more to say about the evils of communism than the goodness of God, then we suspect that he is a soldier poorly armed for the battle before us.

And so the work moves on, always changing, always new.

Today Bibles may be brought into Yugoslavia legally. We no longer smuggle them into that country, because the Bible Shop is open again and doing a thriving business. Instead, last year we gave Jamil a thousand dollars with which to purchase these legal Bibles for churches that have no money. It's hard to believe that I've known Jamil for ten years.

In Bulgaria, Abraham is still seeking his Goliath. Only now he has rocks for his sling: pocket Bibles that we are bringing in by the hundreds. Our goal in the next two years is a pocket-sized edition of the Bible for every country we enter—including one in the new Albanian language. Once we have the Bible, we believe God will show us how to get it into the hands He is choosing.

In East Germany we are now able to hold mass evangelical meetings almost without hindrance. I myself have preached to as many as four thousand people at one time there: two thousand seated in a large conference hall, with two thousand more either standing at the rear or listening to loudspeakers outside.

With the arrival of Klaas and Eduard and their wives, we are achieving our goal of visiting each country at least once every year. I made a return trip to Cuba this spring, and with God's help will be in two new countries before the end of 1967: North Korea and North Vietnam. Some countries of course we can visit more frequently, a few as often as a dozen times within a single year. Whenever one team becomes too well known, another takes its place.

As God makes it possible to us, we are starting to meet a new need behind the Curtain: automobiles for the local clergy. A car is a set of wings to a clergyman, taking him to villages and towns where there may not have been a religious service in years, helping him knit together Christian communities that didn't even know about one another.

The first such car went to Wilhelm and Mar, in southern East Germany. When I came back from visiting Wilhelm and mentioned in a talk that this man with the racking cough was traveling thousands of miles each year on a motorbike, several Dutchmen got together and presented me with a large check—the largest I had yet received at one time.

"Andy," they said, "this money is for a very specific purpose. We believe that Wilhelm should have an automobile. Will you purchase one for him, and give it to him from us?"

Wilhelm could hardly believe it when I drove up to his house in the lovely Saxony hills and handed him the keys to his new automobile. Mar writes us now that the cough has almost entirely disappeared. Wilhelm has used up his first automobile and has been given a second by the same Dutch friends. With it he began a team missionary work of his own, traveling into Poland and Czechoslovakia to hold youth meetings with members of his East German groups.

And this, to me, is the most exciting new development of all: the emergence of a ministry to the Christians of one Iron Curtain country by the Christians of another. Surely this is what God has had in mind all along, that the brave remnant of His Church scattered through many lands gain strength through coming together and lose their own fears in reaching out to help one another. These

Diary of a Smuggler

SUDAN

The many unfamiliar noises around me kept me awake. A squeaking wheelbarrow passed by my hut. Our host was on his way to fetch water from the village well. In the hut next to mine, two pastors talked deep into the night. The whole village must have been able to listen in to their conversation.

Rats roamed above my head. It was hours before I finally drifted off to sleep.

I found myself in southern Sudan. For years I had wanted to accompany some of our colleagues who minister there on a regular basis. I had wanted to feel what they feel and experience what it is like to work in this troubled area of the world.

We flew in an old Antonov airplane stacked with Bibles and relief goods. I wondered on several occasions if the pilot would be able to gain enough altitude to cross over the mountain range. It was boiling hot in the plane. When we finally arrived, my handkerchief was soaked.

The highlight of our short visit was a graduation service for twelve students who had attended a three-year training program. Sadly, four of them could not be present. It was too dangerous for them to travel.

A makeshift meeting hall had been made from some sticks covered by plastic. Dignitaries sat on plastic chairs, the local community on tree trunks. The students received two certificates, one for their academic results and one for the character they had shown. All of them were also presented with a Bible and a special shawl.

During the ceremony, a local official's words touched me deeply: "Use what you have learned. Be willing to die for it."

I was very impressed and deeply thankful for the spiritual quality and maturity of our African co-workers. Unwittingly, they challenged me to search myself to see if I have my priorities right. For these Christians in southern Sudan, to live is Christ and to die is gain. I am challenged by their example.

behind-the-Curtain missionaries lack money for travel, and this we can help to supply, but the rest of their task—freedom of travel within the Communist bloc and freedom to hold meetings and exchange letters—is infinitely easier than for us coming in from outside. One church with which we have worked, in Czechoslovakia, has sent missionaries as far as Brazil and Korea, where they are working side by side with missionaries from the West!

And so the tide of change moves on. Not all of the change is good. Where there is a loosening of restrictions here, there is usually a tightening there. At about the same time that the Bible Shop was opening again in Belgrade, there was a fresh campaign of repression against Christians in Hungary. During the last few months in China, hundreds of thousands of Bibles and hymnbooks have been burned amid great rejoicing by the Red Guard. Whether this marks the end of the period of rather contemptuous laissez-faire by the Chinese government and the start of a new time of persecution for Chinese Christians remains to be seen.

But God is never defeated. Though He may be opposed, attacked, resisted, still the ultimate outcome can never be in doubt. Every day we see fresh proof that indeed all things—even evil ones—work together for those who are called by His name.

There is a Roman Catholic priest in Rumania whom we have been helping to buy Bibles and other supplies for years. On his last trip home from Vienna, his car loaded with Bibles, he was stopped at his own border and his cargo discovered.

The priest was in anguish. He had already been in jail once on a trumped-up charge of hoarding, but here was a truly serious economic crime, and he was really guilty. A Bible costs a month's wages in Rumania, and he was carrying nearly two hundred.

Just at this moment another car pulled up to the border. Out stepped a businessman who was well known at the station; he walked breezily into the inspection shed greeting each of the guards by name. At the sight of the counter ten-deep in Bibles he stopped short. "Bibles?" he said. "I don't suppose you would be willing to sell them to me? They are confiscated, right?"

"Yes, they are confiscated, but we could not possibly sell them to you."

The businessman winked. "Not even," he said, "for . . ." and he leaned over and whispered a figure into the ear of the customs man. The official's eyes grew large.

"Are they really worth that much?"

"More. I shall make a profit."

The official thought for a moment. "Let me talk with my comrades." The three guards huddled together, and when they emerged from their little ring, they had apparently decided that the price was high enough to be worth the sacrifice of principle. So the businessman paid them in cash, got the priest's help in loading his car with his own Bibles, and drove on to Rumania.

In the shed there was an awkward silence. "Am I still charged with smuggling Bibles?" the priest asked at last.

"Bibles?" said the customs official. "What Bibles? There are no Bibles here. You'd better move along while the gate's open."

And as for the Bibles, although they went on the black market, at least they too reached Rumania safely, where somehow believers will find enough money to buy them for their own.

AROUND THE GLOBE
Vietnam

Population: 79.8 million
Location/Size: Southeastern Asia
127,428 sq. miles
Major Religions: Buddhism
Level of Persecution: Sharp, but sporadic improvement

In principle there is religious freedom in Vietnam. The government has permitted Christian ministries to work in the country, especially in the area of community development and compassionate relief programs. But at the district and national levels, the Church encounters restrictions and difficulties. It is perhaps the tribal Christians who face the severest persecution in Vietnam. Government officials can arbitrarily sentence pastors to short terms of hard labor in the fields, put them under house arrest, or confiscate their equipment.

The trend appears to be one of gradual improvement in the relations between the Church and the government. Despite current restrictions, the Church is presently growing at a faster rate than the population and will likely triple its size by 2050.

But of all the signs of these times, to us the most encouraging is the ever-increasing freedom of travel into most Communist countries. Thousands more visitors from the West every year—and of these thousands, what if only a few hundred come consciously as Christians seeking their brothers? Even people who have never dreamed of being missionaries could play a role here larger than anything that has yet been done. Just in the matter of Bibles: smuggling in a carload is risky business, but most border checks would say nothing to a single copy in the local language (obtainable from the Bible societies) among a traveler's personal effects. China and Albania are the only two countries I know where a Bible left on a table or forgotten in a drawer would not find its way soon into eager hands.

A thousand tourists, a thousand ambassadors of God. Tourists who would not only visit the museums and the factories, but who would find the places—often small and out-of-the way—where Christians meet to worship. Who would stand up in these services and speak just six healing words: "Greetings from your brothers in Holland . . . in England . . . in America. . . ."

"Where would it end?" I asked Corrie. "Where could such a flood of caring be stopped?"

"I don't know," she said—and then she laughed. "We don't know what lies ahead. Remember? We don't know where we're going but—"

"But we're glad we're going there together."

Together, the two of us. The twelve of us. The thousands of us. None of us knows where the road will lead. We only know it is the most exciting journey of them all.

Imagine This

It is two weeks after the infamous Tiananmen Square Massacre. In your room is a suitcase of Chinese Bibles that you have smuggled into the country. The Communists are cracking down on people who do not toe the current party line. And faith in Jesus is definitely not within the party line. There is a loud knock at your door. A sick feeling fills the air . . .

What Would You Do?

THE SCOOP

What Can You Do?

As you have read in these pages, religious persecution is on the rise, endangering the Church as never before. The life and testimony of Brother Andrew and the brothers and sisters committed to strengthening the Body of Christ around the globe serve to remind us that one person can make a difference.

The only power able to redeem the suffering Church comes from the Lord. It is His power that enables us, as His instruments on this earth, to "will and to act according to his good purpose" (Phil. 2:13). Today, perhaps you should evaluate the commitment you wish to make to the Body of Christ, His Church. Here are ten suggestions for how you can become an intercessor for the persecuted, as well as for those who persecute.

1. Pray. Pray for those who suffer for their faith, and pray for those who cause the suffering.
2. Educate yourself. Learn about the people, the countries, and the cultures that face persecution every day.
3. Organize efforts in your church or small group to make others aware of the importance of supporting your brothers and sisters in Christ.
4. Give of your financial resources. Your money will help supply the persecuted Church with Bibles, literacy training, biblical training, and much more. For more information, visit www.open doorsusa.org (USA) or www.opendoorsca.org (Canada).
5. Encourage prisoners and workers on the frontline of persecution. Spend considerable time in prayer, write a letter, send a gift, and help educate others . . . remind Christians on the frontline that they are not suffering alone.
6. Become an advocate for the suffering Church. Write a letter to the editor of your local newspaper or to your lawmaker. E-mail your congressman. Tell your friends about

Christians in other countries and the persecution they face, and the importance of uniting together to further the Gospel.

7. Go to the frontline of your faith. Become a Bible courier or minister to others through a short-term mission trip.

8. Start a "Partners in Prayer" group in your neighborhood, and meet regularly together to pray for the persecuted Church.

9. Support the women of the persecuted Church by establishing a "Women of the Way" chapter in your community.

10. Commit to joining the cause of strengthening the suffering Church. Whether through the Internet, mail, or the telephone, become a devoted brother or sister to other Christians around the world. For information on how to become involved, contact Open Doors at 888-5-BIBLE-5 (888-524-2535).

For More Information
on Open Doors

For updated prayer points, or to learn about additional resources and involvement opportunities with the persecuted Church, please contact your national Open Doors office.

Open Doors
PO Box 53
Seaforth
New South Wales 2092
AUSTRALIA

Missao Portas Abertas
CP 45371
Vila Mariana
CEP 04010-970
Sao Paulo
BRAZIL

Open Doors
PO Box 597
Streetsville, ON
L5M 2C1
CANADA

Portes Ouvertes
BP 139
67833 TANNERIES
cedex (Strasbourg)
FRANCE

Porte Asperte
CP45
37063 Isola Della Scala,
   VR
ITALY

Open Doors
Hyerim Presbyterian
   Church
Street No. 403
Sungne 3-dong
Kandong-gu #134-033
Seoul
KOREA

Open Door
PO Box 47
3850 AA Ermelo
THE NETHERLANDS

Open Door
PO Box 27-630
Mt Roskill
Auckland 1030
NEW ZEALAND

Apne Dorer
Boks4698 Grim
N-4673 Kristiansand
NORWAY

Open Doors
PO Box 1573-1155
QCCPO Main
1100 Quezon City
PHILIPPINES

Open Doors
Raffles City Post Office
PO Box 150
SINGAPORE 911705

Open Doors
Box 990099
Kibler Park 2053
Johannesburg
SOUTH AFRICA

Portes Ouvertes
Case Postale 267
CH-1008 Prilly
Lausanne
SWITZERLAND

Open Doors
PO Box 6
Witney
Oxon 0X8 7SP
UNITED KINGDOM

Open Doors
PO Box 27001
Santa Ana, CA 92799
USA

About Brother Andrew–

In 1955, God spoke to the heart of a young Dutch missionary with the words, "Strengthen what remains and is about to die" (Revelation 3:2). From that day, Brother Andrew believed that no doors could be closed. No borders, no barriers, no armies could withstand the power of prayer . . . and no power on earth could ever chain God's Word. Committed to strengthening and encouraging brothers and sisters in the persecuted Church, Brother Andrew and the nonprofit organization he founded, Open Doors, deliver Bibles and other study materials, provide literacy training and pastoral training, and help establish schools and seminaries. Open Doors currently works in over forty-five countries, with over twenty-five international offices.

In the last several years, Brother Andrew has focused his attention more and more on the Islamic World. Still traveling extensively, mostly to the Middle East, he feels passionately that the rapid spread of Islam could be, by far, the greatest challenge that he and Open Doors have yet faced. When confronting this challenge, Andrew feels the best way to help the Islamic world to see Jesus is to "be there." Referring to Mathew 25, he says, "you cannot give a person something to eat unless you are *there*: You cannot provide drink or clothes, or visit the sick and imprisoned, unless you are *there*." He goes on to say that "being there" doesn't necessarily mean traveling great distances: "In our backyards there are plenty of opportunities for presence evangelism."

Brother Andrew's desire is that the Free World will learn many precious lessons from the suffering Church. The brothers and sisters in Christ, who for years have gone through persecution, have a lot to teach us about faith, perseverance, and character. Despite all they have endured, they still remain as shining stars in areas of the world where Jesus is not known. They stand strong for their Lord and Savior, no matter the cost.

In 1997, Brother Andrew was the recipient of the World Evangelical Fellowship's Religious Liberty Award, recognizing his lifetime of service to the persecuted Church. Currently in his seventies, Brother Andrew and his wife, Corrie, live in Holland and have five children and four grandchildren.

About Jars of Clay–

When Jars of Clay came together as an unassuming "dormitory acoustic group" while attending Greenville College in Illinois during the mid-1990s, they had no idea that just a few years later their melodic, thought-provoking music would bring them millions of fans, numerous awards, huge record sales, and opportunities to share the stage with artists such as Sting and MatchBox 20. The multiplatinum success of Jars of Clay has transported the group, once affectionately known as "Jars Boys," to a world of enormous venues, frenzied fans, and critical acclaim.

Jars of Clay is perhaps best known for the hugely successful radio single, "Flood," from their 1995 self-titled and RIAA certified double-platinum debut. The band won their second Grammy Award this year for their critically acclaimed and RIAA certified Gold recording, *If I Left the Zoo.* In addition to their two Grammy Awards and nominations, Jars of Clay has amassed an impressive twenty-two career Gospel Music Association Dove nominations and three Nashville Music Awards, received a 1995 Billboard Music Video Award, and earned thirteen No. 1 songs in just five years.

Jars of Clay compositions have been featured in such major studio film release soundtracks as *The Long Kiss Goodnight, Hard Rain, Jack Frost* and *The Prince of Egypt.* The group's music has further appeared in several television series, including *Providence* (NBC) and *One Life To Live* (ABC). The band currently has career sales of over five million units.

Last June Grammy-award winning, multiplatinum band Jars of Clay traveled to Vietnam and China with Prayer for the Persecuted Church. Travelling in coordination with Open Doors and The Voice of the Martyrs, band members met with indigenous underground churches and church leaders in both countries. Upon their return, the band dedicated their song "This Road," from the Dove-award-winning project *City on a Hill—Songs of Worship and Praise,* to the persecuted Church.

Also Available

wherever great music is sold:

jars of clay

the new release

Coming Spring 2002

www.jarsofclay.com

www.essentialrecords.com